Assisted Suicide in Canada

Assisted Suicide in Canada

Moral, Legal, and Policy Considerations

Travis Dumsday

1971–2021

30 29 28 27 26 25 24 23 22 21   5 4 3 2 1

Printed in Canada on FSC-certified ancient-forest-free paper (100% post-consumer recycled) that is processed chlorine- and acid-free.

Library and Archives Canada Cataloguing in Publication

Title: Assisted suicide in Canada : moral, legal, and policy considerations / Travis Dumsday.
Names: Dumsday, Travis, author.
Description: Includes bibliographical references and index.
Identifiers: Canadiana (print) 20210169990 | Canadiana (ebook) 2021017000X | ISBN 9780774866019 (hardcover) | ISBN 9780774866026 (softcover) | ISBN 9780774866033 (PDF) | ISBN 9780774866040 (EPUB)
Subjects: LCSH: Assisted suicide – Law and legislation – Canada. | LCSH: Euthanasia – Law and legislation – Canada. | LCSH: Right to die – Law and legislation – Canada. | LCSH: Assisted suicide – Moral and ethical aspects – Canada. | LCSH: Euthanasia – Moral and ethical aspects – Canada. | LCSH: Right to die – Moral and ethical aspects – Canada.
Classification: LCC KE3663.E94 D85 2021 | LCC KF3827.E87 D85 2021 | DDC 344.7104/197 – dc23

Canadä

UBC Press gratefully acknowledges the financial support for our publishing program of the Government of Canada (through the Canada Book Fund), the Canada Council for the Arts, and the British Columbia Arts Council.

This book has been published with the help of a grant from the Canadian Federation for the Humanities and Social Sciences, through the Awards to Scholarly Publications Program, using funds provided by the Social Sciences and Humanities Research Council of Canada.

Printed and bound in Canada
Set in Warnock Pro and Segoe by Apex CoVantage, LLC
Copy editor: Dallas Harrison
Proofreader: Judith Earnshaw
Cover designer: David Drummond

UBC Press
The University of British Columbia
2029 West Mall
Vancouver, BC V6T 1Z2
www.ubcpress.ca

For my father, Gayle Dumsday (1941–2020)
Memory Eternal

Contents

Acknowledgments

The bulk of this book was written during my stint as Canada Research Chair (CRC) in Theology and the Philosophy of Science at Concordia University of Edmonton. I am grateful to the government and taxpayers of Canada for the funding associated with the CRC and to Concordia's senior administration (in particular President Tim Loreman and Vice-President Valerie Henitiuk) for their support and extension of my teaching release. That generous assistance was instrumental in the completion of the project. I should also note that this book has been published with the help of a grant from the Federation for the Humanities and Social Sciences, through the Awards to Scholarly Publications Program, using funds provided by the Social Sciences and Humanities Research Council of Canada (SSHRC).

I wish to extend my thanks to all those who provided comments on this work while it was still incubating. My good friends Gary Colwell, Matthew Murphy, and Jonathan Strand provided feedback on the entire manuscript, and substantial portions were read by Ishtiyaque Haji, Ana Iltis, John Keown, Howard Nye, and Helen Watt. I am sincerely grateful for their many incisive comments and criticisms, which resulted in significant improvements. Thanks are likewise due to three exceedingly helpful anonymous referees for UBC Press and to my editor, Randy Schmidt, who provided excellent advice and shepherded the project through to its end. I am also grateful to Dallas Harrison for his copy-editing work, which resulted in many improvements to the book's prose style. Naturally, any remaining problems in the book are a consequence of either my own stubbornness in the face of so much good counsel or my inability to implement it adequately.

I am obliged to Sharon Kirkey of the *National Post,* who replied promptly and helpfully to my inquiry concerning media coverage of medical assistance in dying (or MAID) in Canada. I have enjoyed many productive conversations on this topic with friends and colleagues too numerous to name, though I should mention in particular some beneficial discussions with Jorge L.A. Garcia during his visit from Boston College to Concordia University of Edmonton in the winter of 2017, a visit funded by a generous lecture grant awarded by the Society of Christian Philosophers.

The book is dedicated with much love to my late father, Gayle, who always encouraged my work in philosophy. Memory Eternal.

Assisted Suicide in Canada

Introduction

In recent years, legislatures around the world have wrestled with the issues of assisted suicide and voluntary active euthanasia. Proposals to legalize some such activities were defeated by the Australian state of Tasmania in 2013 and in separate acts by both the British and the Scottish Parliaments in 2015. Other proposals succeeded in various regions of the United States, such as California in 2015. Parallel with debates in regional and national legislatures have been judicial contests: the High Court of Ireland upheld its country's ban on assisted suicide in a 2013 ruling, as did the United Kingdom Supreme Court in a 2014 ruling and the New Zealand High Court in 2015. The South African High Court ruled its nation's ban on assisted suicide unconstitutional but was overruled in 2016 by the South African Supreme Court of Appeal. In contrast, the Constitutional Court of Colombia mandated the permission of voluntary active euthanasia in 2015, and Germany's highest court did the same for assisted suicide in 2020.[1]

The Supreme Court of Canada effectively decriminalized forms of both assisted suicide and voluntary active euthanasia in its February 2015 ruling in *Carter v Canada*. A key portion of that decision reads as follows:

Section 241 *(b)* and s. 14 of the *Criminal Code* unjustifiably infringe s. 7 of the Charter and are of no force or effect to the extent that they prohibit physician assisted death for a competent adult person who 1) clearly consents to the termination of life and 2) has a grievous and irremediable medical condition (including an illness, disease or disability) that causes enduring suffering that is intolerable to the individual in the circumstances of his or her condition.[2]

The ruling thus allows physicians both to prescribe appropriate narcotics (later self-administered by patients) and to perform the act themselves (e.g., by injecting a lethal narcotic).[3] The court gave the federal government a twelve-month grace period before the invalidity of the existing law would take effect in order to allow the government to draft new legislation incorporating the ruling.

In April 2016, the federal government put forward Bill C-14 for first reading in Parliament. That bill expanded the range of legal indemnity, specifying that not only physicians but also nurse practitioners and pharmacists would be permitted to participate in these procedures. The bill also sought to clarify certain matters arguably left ambiguous by the court ruling, for instance the meaning of "grievous and irremediable," which the federal government understood to mean that "natural death has become reasonably foreseeable, taking into account all of their medical circumstances, without a prognosis necessarily having been made as to the specific length of time that they have remaining."[4] As stated, this appeared to come close to restricting medical assistance in dying to the terminally ill and thereby constituted a substantial circumscription of the acceptable conditions laid out in *Carter v Canada*. Bill C-14 received royal assent on June 17, 2016.

Since then, aspects of the bill have been subjected to multiple legal challenges seeking to expand eligibility criteria in one form or another. So far, the most important challenges have focused on the criterion of "reasonably foreseeable death." One such challenge in Quebec was successful – in September 2019, a Quebec Superior Court judge ruled that this aspect of Bill C-14 was unconstitutional and thus to be considered struck from the law. This ruling became an issue in the federal election campaign the following month, with Prime Minister Justin Trudeau vowing not to appeal the decision, thereby allowing expanded eligibility beyond the terminally ill. Opposition leader Andrew Scheer, in contrast, vowed that if his party formed the government it would appeal the ruling and seek to uphold Bill C-14 in its then current form. Trudeau's party won the election (though with a minority government), so it was to be expected that this decision regarding expanded eligibility would stand. On February 24, 2020, the justice minister introduced a draft bill to that effect, Bill C-7, before Parliament. Shortly thereafter, the global COVID-19 pandemic hit Canada, and the parliamentary agenda on this matter, as on so many others, stalled. Then Parliament was prorogued in August 2020, resulting in Bill C-7 dying on the order paper. The assumption is that a new iteration of the same bill will be reintroduced when the pandemic has subsided and Parliament can focus again on other matters.

If that bill is approved, then it would render Canada one of the most permissive countries in the world with respect to eligibility for assisted suicide and voluntary active euthanasia. Moreover, it remains to be seen whether *further* expansions would take place in the years ahead – perhaps the expansion of eligibility to include mature minors, legally incompetent adults suffering from dementia (via an advance directive written while still competent), or those suffering from no physical ailments at all (i.e., the legally competent mentally ill).[5] As we shall see, prominent Canadian politicians, ethicists, journalists, and legal scholars have been advocating for precisely these additional expansions.[6]

Assuming that it is neither negated by use of the notwithstanding clause nor overturned in future rulings by the Supreme Court itself, *Carter v Canada* and its legal aftermath will affect the lives, deaths, and attitudes of Canadians for generations to come and alter the common understanding and practice of medicine. A profession previously defined by the goals of enhancing and preserving human life will now be understood to include, as an equally legitimate feature, the deliberate termination of human life. Whether one approves or disapproves of this development, its profound import can hardly be denied. As Chan and Somerville (2016, p. 144) put it, *Carter v Canada* "is likely to go down as one of the most significant decisions ever issued by the Supreme Court of Canada."

My aim in this book is to provide a concise and accessible introduction to some of the key moral, legal, and policy issues surrounding this decision. At the time of writing, no up-to-date single work of this sort has covered all three topic areas for a specifically Canadian audience.[7] This is regrettable, especially since the issue remains a matter of active public debate in this country. My hope is that this book will not only enable interested lay readers to gain a clear idea of exactly what this new legal situation consists of and how it came about but also provide some assistance in reflecting on its normative implications. It also includes a number of original contributions of particular interest to scholars working in the area. For specialists who pick up the book simply wanting to key in on the original scholarship, those contributions are mainly in some of my evaluative remarks on the legal and moral reasoning in *Carter v Canada,* as seen in Chapters 1 and 4; in the discussion of the notwithstanding clause in Chapter 5; in the disjunctive argument against public funding, developed in Chapter 6; and in my brief discussion of a heretofore unappreciated legal risk facing Canadian health-care professionals who participate in assisted death, provided at the beginning of Chapter 8.

Although I intend to offer an accurate and fair presentation of the range of competing legal and moral arguments on offer, I have nonetheless written this introduction from a definite standpoint. I make no apology for that; in my opinion, an introductory work on a controversial topic usually functions best when the author drops the pretense of neutrality and is simply open about the framework within which she or he is operating. All else being equal, doing so tends to result in a more interesting work, providing readers with a thesis into which they can sink their teeth along the way. With that in mind, my stance is basically as follows: I will argue that the Supreme Court of Canada made errors, both legal and moral, in *Carter v Canada* and that assisted suicide and active euthanasia are morally impermissible acts that ought to be recriminalized. Perhaps many (most?) readers will disagree with that assessment. Ideally, I would like to change some minds on this count; however, I will also be content with the more modest aim of supplying readers with a clear idea of why some people remain opposed to these practices in the wake of their legalization and in the face of widespread public support for that legalization.

In the remainder of this introduction, I will say a bit about the heavily contested role of religion in the moral side of this debate, cover some key terminology, and conclude with a bird's-eye preview of the book's contents.

First, concerning religion, it is incontrovertibly true that, in both recent scholarly literature and public debates concerning assisted suicide and euthanasia, religion has played an important role, whether *directly* (by way of prominent interlocutors explicitly invoking religious doctrines) or *indirectly* (by way of those doctrines – or their rejection – informing discussants' background moral intuitions). In working through the moral issues, I will attempt to use arguments that presuppose no religious beliefs; moreover, in the hope of sidestepping contentious debates regarding the proper role of religion in public policy disputes, in the few instances when I do discuss theologically grounded arguments (specifically in Chapter 4), I formulate them in terms not of any specific type of theism but agnosticism. That is, I argue that anyone who merely allows the realistic possibility that there could be a God will have to consider seriously certain well-known arguments against the moral permissibility of these actions.

That said, in the interests of transparency, I will note that my own moral beliefs on this matter are a product of both my assessment of the relevant ethical arguments and my religious faith. Regarding the latter, I am a member of the Eastern Orthodox Church, which has always taught that suicide is gravely immoral. It is sometimes argued that one should not allow personal religious beliefs to play a role in debates on law or public policy, at least not in a modern pluralistic democracy such as Canada. Rather only arguments whose basic premises can be accepted by people of any religious faith (or none) ought to be employed. Typically underlying this claim is a broader set of commitments pertaining to the proper role of religion in public life. I am rather inclined toward the idea that a diverse range of religiously informed moral commitments ought to have a place at the table: morally relevant teachings from Buddhism, Islam, Judaism, Indigenous spiritualities, Sikhism, and so on should all receive a respectful hearing in the public domain. That diversity of views should be present whether or not these teachings are ultimately accepted by those members of the public who do not share their interlocutors' beliefs. To suggest that a range of diverse voices should be ignored or otherwise excluded from the debate in the name of religious neutrality (itself a disputed notion – can de facto atheism be considered genuinely neutral?) is problematic for a number of reasons, not least of which is the risk of missing out on helpful insights arising from these traditions. So, even though I do not ground this book in any particular faith, I look forward to productive dialogue both with secular scholars and with colleagues from a broad range of faith traditions.[8]

Second, regarding terminology, before I dive into these issues, some terminological clarification is required. I have already been using the terms "assisted suicide" and "voluntary active euthanasia": What exactly do they mean, and how do they relate to the use in Canada of the relatively new term "medical assistance in dying" (MAID)?

"Assisted suicide" is fairly straightforward. This term encompasses those cases in which one person intentionally kills himself or herself with the aid of another person, which can be indirect (e.g., providing advice on how to commit suicide) or direct (e.g., giving the individual a lethal prescription to take later). In both cases, the final act itself is carried out by the individual, not by the assisting party. "Physician-assisted suicide" means that the assistance is provided by a medical doctor.

"Euthanasia" in the original Greek means literally "good death." As the term is employed in contemporary ethics, a distinction is often made between *passive* euthanasia and *active* euthanasia. In the former, medical treatment is stopped, and the patient's death proceeds as a result of natural causes (i.e., the underlying terminal medical condition). Consider, for example, a situation in which a patient in the final stages of terminal lung cancer is being kept alive by the use of an artificial respirator. If the respirator is unplugged and the patient is allowed to die of the underlying condition then that will count as a case of passive euthanasia (PE). If the attendant physician is guided by a directive of the patient (i.e., the patient has asked to be unplugged), then this instance can be considered voluntary passive euthanasia (VPE). If for some reason the patient cannot be consulted (e.g., he has fallen into a coma), and there is no guidance from an advance directive (e.g., a living will or other indication of the patient's wishes in this situation), and the attendant physician takes it upon herself to unplug the patient, then that is an example of non-voluntary passive euthanasia (NVPE). If there is an advance directive available specifying that the patient wishes to be kept alive on artificial life support in such a situation, and the attendant physician acts *against* that wish and unplugs him, then that act can be considered involuntary passive euthanasia (IVPE).

Active euthanasia is rather different. Here, instead of a patient dying of natural causes as a result of the cessation of treatment, they die as a result of an active step taken by another person to cause death. Consider the following scenario in which a patient is in the final stages of terminal cancer. If they ask a physician to end their life (say by having the physician deliberately inject a lethal dose of barbiturates), and the physician accedes to the request, then this is an instance of active euthanasia (AE). Because that patient consented to the procedure, it is known more specifically as voluntary active euthanasia (VAE). If for some reason a patient cannot be consulted (e.g., they have fallen into a coma) and there is no advance directive (e.g., a living will or other statement of a patient's wishes in this situation), and the attendant physician decides to give the patient a lethal injection, then that would count as an example of non-voluntary active euthanasia (NVAE). If there is an advance directive available specifying that the patient wishes to be kept alive on artificial life support in such a situation, and the attendant physician acts against the patient's wishes and administers a lethal injection, then that could be considered involuntary active euthanasia (IVAE).[9]

To sum up, we are left with the following notions:

- assisted suicide
- passive euthanasia (voluntary, non-voluntary, and involuntary)
- active euthanasia (voluntary, non-voluntary, and involuntary).

VPE has long been permitted legally in Canada – any legally competent adult has the right to refuse medical treatment, even life-preserving medical treatment. VPE is also comparatively morally uncontroversial, at least in cases of irremediable terminal conditions.[10] Moral qualms, conversely, may be raised about declining treatment for a thoroughly remediable condition, such as a young and otherwise healthy person refusing to get rabies shots after being bitten by a rabid animal. However, those sorts of situations are not typically discussed in debates on the ethics of euthanasia.

The status of NVPE is more controversial both legally and morally. As interesting and important as these issues are, they are not the focus of *Carter v Canada* and its surrounding controversies, so I will not take them up here.[11] In Canada, IVPE is not legally permitted (it is generally understood that advance directives are to be respected outside extreme or unique circumstances), and most people would agree that it is morally impermissible.

With respect to active euthanasia, both NVAE and IVAE have always been and remain illegal in Canada, even after *Carter* and Bill C-14. As we shall see, NVAE has a number of prominent advocates in the ethics literature, whereas IVAE does not. (In some cases, though, advocates of NVAE seem to drift toward IVAE.) Still, these practices are outside the scope of my discussion here. In this book, I examine the novel legal situation imposed by *Carter* and Bill C-14: specifically, the legalization of assisted suicide and voluntary active euthanasia.

Bill C-14 uses "medical assistance in dying" as a blanket term covering both assisted suicide and VAE. There is precedent for this terminology in the existing ethics literature (e.g., Young, 2007), and its use has become common in Canadian media coverage of the issue.[12] However, it remains controversial among some opponents of the practice, who argue that it is misleadingly anodyne[13] or ambiguous. I am less concerned about that first aspect of the terminology – I find the term "voluntary active euthanasia" to be equally anodyne, though it is commonly employed by both proponents and opponents of the practice. I do remain worried about the potential ambiguity of MAID insofar as someone might confuse it, for instance, with standard palliative care, which, in a sense, is also a form of "medical assistance in dying."

By way of an imperfect terminological compromise, in the title of the book I have stuck to the term "assisted suicide," both for the sake of clarity – even in Canada not everyone is yet familiar with the acronym MAID – and to make the book more accessible to a non-Canadian audience for whom that acronym is unknown.[14] (Although this book is intended chiefly for my fellow Canadians, parts of it could be of use in other jurisdictions where legalization is being debated [the chapter on ethics] or has passed [the chapter on public funding].) However, with some reluctance, I use MAID as a convenient shorthand for the comparatively cumbersome "assisted suicide and VAE."

Third, concerning the contents, in Chapter 1, I provide an overview of the four crucial legal rulings that led to the circumstances permitting MAID in Canada. My goal is mostly to provide an accurate summary of the legal reasoning employed in these cases, though I include some evaluative remarks toward the end of the chapter. Chapter 2 consists of a review of developments since *Carter v Canada,* looking at reactions from the Harper government, the Trudeau government (in particular the passage of Bill C-14), as well as some responses from the provinces. Then I begin the discussion of the ethics of MAID. Insofar as some important arguments for and against the practice are grounded in divergent background ethical theories, a proper understanding of those arguments will be aided by an initial overview of some of these theories, which I take up in Chapter 3. This overview is intended for a general audience, and ethicists working their way through the book will already be familiar with this material. In Chapter 4, I move on to a discussion of some of the more prominent arguments for and against the moral permissibility of MAID. Chapter 5 briefly deals with the further normative question of what the policy response to *Carter v Canada* ought to be, given the moral impermissibility of MAID. Specifically, I argue that a future federal government ought to repeal Bill C-14 and employ the notwithstanding clause to negate *Carter.* In Chapter 6, I argue further that, should this not occur and MAID remains legal, the provinces are nevertheless obligated to refrain from funding it. I develop a four-part disjunctive argument for this conclusion, according to which public funding turns out to be immoral irrespective of the actual moral status of MAID (i.e., whether the provision of MAID is impermissible, permissible, obligatory, or its moral status is inscrutable, it should not be publicly funded). Chapter 7 briefly takes up the contentious issue of rights of conscience for health-care providers, specifically the issue of whether physicians, nurse practitioners, and·pharmacists who object to MAID should nevertheless be required to provide referrals for it. In Chapter 8, I offer a short treatment of three additional legal and policy issues: first, the overlooked question of whether Canadian health-care providers who participate in MAID are at risk of prosecution in other nations where MAID remains illegal; second, best practices for record-keeping and information sharing; and third, the legal prospects for future court rulings overturning *Carter v Canada.* Finally, in the conclusion, I provide a short recap and some final remarks.

1

An Overview of *Carter v Canada*

Before we begin exploring the moral, legal, and policy issues arising from the Supreme Court of Canada's ruling in *Carter v Canada,* we should review the ruling itself. Insofar as much of the argumentation within that ruling is bound up with prior legal precedents, to understand it thoroughly we should first examine the key rulings that led up to it. Hence, in the next section, I review the Supreme Court of Canada's ruling in the 1993 *Rodriguez v British Columbia* case; then the 2012 *Carter v Canada* ruling by the Supreme Court of British Columbia, which functionally overturned *Rodriguez;* then the 2013 *Carter v Canada* ruling by the BC Court of Appeal, which reversed the Supreme Court of British Columbia's ruling and upheld *Rodriguez;* and then the Supreme Court of Canada's ruling in *Carter v Canada.* I cannot provide an exhaustive overview of the legal reasoning employed in each case, but hopefully what follows will succeed in conveying the principal lines of argument. Since my chief purpose in this chapter is to provide an accurate and concise overview of these rulings, I will mostly delay until its final pages my own brief remarks concerning the cogency of the arguments employed in them.

To assist readers in legal scorekeeping as the chapter progresses, I provide the following summary table:

Table 1 Key court rulings on MAID

Year	Case	Result of ruling
1993	Supreme Court of Canada: *Rodriguez v British Columbia*	Maintained the existing criminal prohibition on assisted death
2012	Supreme Court of British Columbia: *Carter v Canada*	Overturned the Supreme Court of Canada's ruling in *Rodriguez*
2013	BC Court of Appeal: *Carter v Canada*	Overturned the Supreme Court of British Columbia's ruling, upholding *Rodriguez* and the original criminal prohibition on assisted death
2015	Supreme Court of Canada: *Carter v Canada*	Overturned the BC Court of Appeal's ruling and *Rodriguez*, decriminalizing assisted death by striking down section 241(b) and section 14 of the *Criminal Code of Canada*

The Supreme Court of Canada's Ruling in the 1993 *Rodriguez* Case

In the English legal tradition of which the Canadian criminal law is a part, suicide historically was viewed as a form of homicide, such that the act of attempted suicide was a criminal act subject to criminal penalties. In Canada, this changed in 1972 when attempted suicide was decriminalized. Here Canada was following the lead of the United Kingdom, which decriminalized attempted suicide in 1961. In both cases, decriminalization was prompted by benevolence and the thought that criminal prohibition failed as a deterrent. Yet in neither case could this be seen as a state sanction of suicide, especially considering that the act of assisting another to commit suicide was still classified as a form of homicide punishable by lengthy imprisonment. Moreover, the state retained the ability to commit the suicidal to protective state care in order to prevent self-harm. Although such forcible committal was carried out only under strict guidelines, the central legal ground for doing so remained the likelihood that such individuals were a danger to themselves (or others). Gorsuch (2006, pp. 46–47), for instance, writes that "the abandonment of criminal penalties for suicide betokened less any social or legal endorsement of the practice than a growing consensus that suicide is essentially a medical problem. This interpretation is confirmed by the advent of a legal privilege to detain those who attempt suicide." That attempted suicide was not subject to criminal penalty in Canada after

1972 did not imply that the state had no interest or obligation in preventing suicide, and the decriminalization of attempted suicide was not taken at the time to entail that we possess a right (whether negative or positive) to suicide.[1]

Prior decriminalization of attempted suicide played a key role in some of the argumentation made in *Rodriguez v British Columbia.* The plaintiff in this famous case, Sue Rodriguez, was dying from amyotrophic lateral sclerosis (ALS), a degenerative disease of the central nervous system. She sought permission to have a physician assist her in terminating her life, arguing that the criminal prohibition on assisted suicide (contained in section 241(b) of the *Criminal Code of Canada*)[2] violated her rights under sections 7, 12, and 15 of the *Canadian Charter of Rights and Freedoms.*[3] More precisely, with respect to section 7, her argument was that the criminal prohibition deprived her of both liberty and security of the person, interfering with her ability to control what happened to her body and infringing on her right to non-interference in personal decisions concerning the final stages of her life. With respect to section 12, the argument was that the state, by prohibiting physicians from assisting Rodriguez in committing suicide, was subjecting her to cruel treatment, forcing her to suffer through the final stages of a terrible disease when she could have ended that suffering. With respect to section 15, her argument was that, on entering into the final stages of her progressive neuronal disease, she would be unable physically to commit suicide. Since suicide itself was not a criminal act (attempted suicide having been decriminalized in 1972), the state could not properly prevent others from helping Rodriguez to engage in a non-criminal act – in fact, doing so violated her right to equal treatment under the law, for it meant that the state would be blocking her as a disabled person from carrying out an act available to the able-bodied. These arguments were first made to the lower courts in British Columbia, and after rejection by the BC Court of Appeal they were taken to the Supreme Court of Canada, which agreed to hear the case – hence its title, *Rodriguez v British Columbia.*[4]

In a narrow 5–4 majority, the Supreme Court of Canada rejected the appeal and upheld the criminal prohibition. Writing on behalf of the majority, Justice John Sopinka granted that the law engaged the plaintiff's section 7 rights:

The effect of the prohibition in s. 241 *(b)* is to prevent the appellant from having assistance to commit suicide when she is no longer able to do so on her own. She fears that she will be required to live until the deterioration from her disease is such that she will die as a result of choking, suffocation or pneumonia caused by aspiration of food or secretions. She will be totally dependent on machines to perform her bodily functions and completely dependent on others. Throughout this time, she will remain mentally competent and able to appreciate all that is happening to her. Although palliative care may be available to ease the pain and other physical discomfort which she will experience, the appellant fears the sedating effects of such drugs and argues, in any event, that they will not prevent the psychological and emotional distress which will result from being in a situation of utter dependence and loss of dignity. That there is a right to choose how one's body will be dealt with, even in the context of beneficial medical treatment, has long been recognized by the common law. To impose medical treatment on one who refuses it constitutes battery, and our common law has recognized the right to demand that medical treatment which would extend life be withheld or withdrawn. In my view, these considerations lead to the conclusion that the prohibition in s. 241 *(b)* deprives the appellant of autonomy over her person and causes her physical pain and psychological stress in a manner which impinges on the security of her person. The appellant's security interest (considered in the context of the life and liberty interest) is therefore engaged, and it is necessary to determine whether there has been any deprivation thereof that is not in accordance with the principles of fundamental justice.[5]

The majority of the court here conceded a crucial claim: namely, that the criminal prohibition on assisted suicide did in fact impinge on Rodriguez's section 7 right to security of the person. However, that did not automatically invalidate the relevant section of the *Criminal Code of Canada*, insofar as section 7 of the Charter itself allows that deprivations of the right to life, liberty, or security of the person can be permitted legally *when done in accordance with the principles of fundamental justice.*[6] So the question taken up in the remainder of the majority's ruling was whether the relevant deprivation involved was in fact in accordance with the principles of fundamental justice.

As part of his answer, Justice Sopinka first went on to observe that one purpose of the criminal prohibition on assisted suicide was

the protection of the vulnerable who might be induced in moments of weakness to commit suicide. This purpose is grounded in the state interest in protecting life and reflects the policy of the state that human life should not be depreciated by allowing life to be taken ... This is not only a policy of the state, however, but is part of our fundamental conception of the sanctity of human life.[7]

The reasonable nature of this prohibition was supported by reference to the prevailing international legal context of the time. Sopinka pointed out that, as of the court's ruling in 1993, assisted suicide had not been explicitly legalized in any Western democracy (pp. 601–602), one reason being the widely recognized risk of abuse and correlative potential for the failure of suggested legal safeguards (e.g., guidelines to ensure genuine consent/non-coercion). Moreover, public referendums in both Washington State in 1991 and California in 1992 opted against the legalization of assisted suicide.

Justice Sopinka then took note of the common objection that the distinction between voluntary passive euthanasia and assisted suicide amounted to a "legal fiction": "The criticism is based on the fact that the withdrawal of life supportive measures is done with the knowledge that death will ensue, just as in assisting suicide, and that death does in fact ensue as a result of the action taken" (p. 606). Moreover, the line between the two might seem to be even more blurred in cases in which the administration of pain medication or other methods of palliative care, intended to ease suffering, might have the side effect of hastening death. Sopinka replied that such arguments erred by ignoring the vital role of intent: "In my view, distinctions based upon intent are important, and in fact form the basis of our criminal law. While factually the distinction may, at times, be difficult to draw, legally it is clear" (p. 607). A physician who administers pain medication to a terminally ill patient, medication that has the foreseen but not-intended side effect of hastening death, is engaged, from both a moral perspective and a legal perspective, in an act very different from that of a physician who administers a drug with the active intent of terminating the life of that patient. The law rightly enshrines a recognition of this distinction by criminalizing the latter but not the former.

Justice Sopinka further noted that there exists a broad societal consensus that intentionally taking the life of another human being is inherently wrong and that the legal system ought to recognize that fact. This principle finds expression in other areas of the criminal law, notably in that Canada now prohibits capital punishment:

This prohibition is supported, in part, on the basis that allowing the state to kill will cheapen the value of human life and thus the state will serve in a sense as a role model for individuals in society. The prohibition against assisted suicide serves a similar purpose ... To permit a physician to lawfully participate in taking life would send a signal that there are circumstances in which the state approves of suicide.[8]

Sopinka stated that various major medical associations, including the Canadian Medical Association, British Medical Association, and World Medical Association, were all (c. 1993) in favour of the continued criminalization of assisted suicide. Taking all of this into account, he drew the conclusion that "it can not be said that the blanket prohibition on assisted suicide is arbitrary or unfair, or that it is not reflective of fundamental values at play in our society. I am thus unable to find that any principle of fundamental justice is violated by s. 241 *(b)*" (p. 608). So the plaintiff's argument that section 241(b) was unconstitutional was ultimately rejected, not because Rodriguez erred in thinking that the prohibition engaged her section 7 Charter right to security of her person but because she erred in thinking that the associated deprivation was not in accordance with the principles of fundamental justice.

Justice Sopinka then proceeded to consider the plaintiff's second argument: namely, that the law infringed her section 12 rights against cruel and unusual treatment or punishment. Sopinka swiftly disregarded any idea that the state was engaged in any form of *punishment* here; the question of whether the law resulted in cruel and unusual treatment was regarded as less clear, but ultimately he argued that the mere prohibition of a certain action could not, in this context, properly count as the active imposition of a form of "treatment" by the state:

> In the present case, the appellant is simply subject to the edicts of the *Criminal Code*, as are all other individuals in society. The fact that, because of the personal situation in which she finds herself, a particular prohibition impacts upon her in a manner which causes her suffering does not subject her to "treatment" at the hands of the state. The starving person who is prohibited by threat of criminal sanction from "stealing a mouthful of bread" is likewise not subjected to "treatment" within the meaning of s. 12 by reason of the theft provision of the *Code*, nor is the heroin addict who is prohibited from possessing heroin by the provisions of the *Narcotic Control Act*, R.S.C., 1985, c. N-1. There must be some more active state process in operation, involving an exercise of state control over the individual, in order for the state action in question, whether it be positive action, inaction or prohibition, to constitute "treatment" under s. 12.[9]

Thus, the plaintiff's second argument was likewise rejected.

Justice Sopinka declined to consider whether the plaintiff's equality rights under section 15 of the Charter were infringed, on the ground that even if they were such an infringement would ipso facto be in accordance with the principles of fundamental justice (given his earlier assessment of the section 7 challenge) and by extension would be allowable under section 1 of the Charter.[10]

Finally, Justice Sopinka made the point that the prohibition on assisted suicide was proportionate to its aim of protecting life, in particular protecting those vulnerable members of society most at risk of being coerced into considering suicide. To the objection that other legal means short of outright prohibition might suffice (e.g., allowing assisted suicide under certain narrow conditions and with assorted regulatory safeguards in place), Sopinka replied that "a prohibition without exception on the giving of assistance to commit suicide is the best approach. Attempts to fine tune this approach by creating exceptions have been unsatisfactory and have tended to support the theory of the 'slippery slope'" (p. 613). Moreover, the suggestion that access to assisted suicide could successfully be restricted to the terminally ill is problematic on a more foundational level, insofar as part of the intention behind the law was precisely "to discourage the terminally ill from choosing death over life" (p. 614). As such, the verdict of the majority of the court was to uphold the criminal prohibition on assisted suicide.

Before proceeding to the next two cases leading up to the Supreme Court of Canada's 2015 ruling in *Carter v Canada,* I will review briefly certain arguments put forward by the dissenting justices in *Rodriguez v British Columbia.* Justice Beverley McLachlin wrote that she agreed with the majority that section 241(b) infringed the plaintiff's section 7 Charter right, but she disagreed that this infringement accorded with the principles of fundamental justice: "In my view, the denial to Sue Rodriguez of a choice available to others cannot be justified. The potential for abuse is amply guarded against by existing provisions in the *Criminal Code,* as supplemented by the condition of judicial authorization, and ultimately, it is hoped, revised legislation" (p. 617). To deny Rodriguez the opportunity to obtain assistance in committing suicide on account of a desire to safeguard others from abuse was unreasonable: "Thus, Sue Rodriguez is asked to bear the burden of the chance that other people in other situations may act criminally to kill others or improperly sway them to suicide. She is asked to serve as a scapegoat" (p. 621). To Justice Sopinka's claim that the prohibition reflected a societal consensus on the sanctity of life and the inherent immorality of intentionally killing another person, McLachlin replied that the law does not in fact consider all cases of intentional killing to be immoral or properly subject to criminal penalty, with killing in self-defence being an obvious example:

> The law has long recognized that if there is a valid justification for bringing about someone's death, the person who does so will not be held criminally responsible. In the case of Sue Rodriguez, there is arguably such a justification – the justification of giving her the capacity to end her life which able-bodied people have as a matter of course, and the justification of her clear consent and desire to end her life at a time when, in her view, it makes no sense to continue living it.[11]

In his own dissent, Justice Peter Cory made a point that would be taken up and developed in detail in later rulings: namely, that section 241(b) could be thought to violate not just the security of the person but also the right to life, on a suitably broad understanding of "life":

> The life of an individual must include dying. Dying is the final act in the drama of life. If as I believe, dying is an integral part of living, then as a part of life it is entitled to the constitutional protection provided by s. 7. It follows that the right to die with dignity should be as well protected as is any other aspect of the right to life. State prohibitions that would force a dreadful, painful death on a rational but incapacitated terminally ill patient are an affront to human dignity.[12]

Chief Justice Antonio Lamer's dissent focused on the infringement of Rodriguez's equality rights, developing the point that a total prohibition was an unreasonably broad method of trying to fulfill the legitimate goal of protecting the vulnerable. Moreover, the *speculative* risk of a "slippery slope" toward abuse, to which Sopinka referred, had to be weighed against the *certainty* of the harm prompted by the criminal prohibition on assisted suicide:

> The truth is that we simply do not and cannot know the range of implications that allowing some form of assisted suicide will have for persons with physical disabilities. What we do know and cannot ignore is the anguish of those in the position of Ms. Rodriguez. Respecting the consent of those in her position may necessarily imply running the risk that the consent will

have been obtained improperly. The proper role of the legal system in these circumstances is to provide safeguards to ensure that the consent in question is as independent and informed as is reasonably possible.[13]

The dissenting justices notwithstanding, the vindication of section 241(b) provided by the Supreme Court of Canada in *Rodriguez v British Columbia* would prove to be long lasting and resilient in the face of periodic challenges (especially in the form of parliamentarians attempting to use private members' bills or motions to reopen the debate and liberalize the Criminal Code provisions on euthanasia).[14] However, a more significant challenge arose in the 2012 ruling by the Supreme Court of British Columbia in *Carter v Canada*.

The Supreme Court of British Columbia's Ruling in the 2012 *Carter v Canada* Case

Providing an adequate summary of this ruling is challenging because of its imposing size – at 398 pages, it is by far the longest of the four rulings under consideration here. Still, its central conclusions, and some of its principal arguments, can be summarized concisely.[15]

There were five plaintiffs in this case. Gloria Taylor suffered from ALS and argued that section 241(b) of the *Criminal Code of Canada* infringed not only her section 7 Charter rights to liberty and security of the person (as had been claimed by Rodriguez) but also her right to life, insofar as section 241(b) would force her to commit suicide prematurely: that is, it would force her to take her own life while she was still physically able to do so instead of waiting longer, delaying doing so until utter physical incapacity had taken hold, at which time a physician could terminate her life for her. Decriminalizing assisted dying (specifically, physician-assisted suicide and physician-facilitated active euthanasia, jointly referenced by the phrase "physician-assisted dying") would allow Taylor to delay suicide and thus prolong her life. In effect, the criminal prohibition on assisted suicide violated her right to life by driving her to kill herself earlier than she otherwise would in a more permissive legal context. Taylor also argued that section 241(b) of the Criminal Code infringed unjustifiably her equality rights under section 15 of the Charter (i.e., infringed them in a way not in accordance with principles of fundamental justice, contra the reasoning of the majority court in *Rodriguez v British Columbia*).

Two other plaintiffs, Lee Carter and Hollis Johnson, likewise argued that section 241(b) infringed their section 7 Charter rights, though on very different grounds: it violated their right to liberty by raising the prospect of imprisonment for their participation in helping a loved one (Kay Carter, mother of Lee Carter and mother-in-law of Hollis Johnson) to obtain assisted suicide in Switzerland, where it was legal. In other words, they feared being subject to extraterritorial prosecution – criminally charged for engaging in an action overseas involving a Canadian citizen that, though legal in the nation where the act was committed, is nevertheless regarded as homicide in Canada. The court viewed this as a legitimate fear, insofar as homicide tends to be treated as an exception to the general rule against engaging in extraterritorial prosecution. For instance, if, prior to the legalization of marijuana in Canada, a Canadian citizen bought and consumed marijuana while in the Netherlands (where its purchase and consumption were legal), that citizen had no fear of prosecution on returning to Canada. An action overseas that was legal in that nation but not legal in Canada would not result in prosecution on the citizen's return to Canada. In other words, in such a case, the Canadian citizen had no reason to fear being subject to extraterritorial prosecution. However, homicide historically has been treated as an exception to that general rule. For example, if a Canadian citizen travelled to a nation where "honour" killings were legal and participated in such a killing of a Canadian citizen, and then returned to Canada, the killer could be criminally charged. With that possibility in mind, Carter and Johnson had a legitimate fear of prosecution in Canada for what they had done to a Canadian citizen while in Switzerland (even though it had been legal there), and thus they maintained that they had legitimate standing to participate with Taylor in this legal action.[16]

There were two further plaintiffs in the case, physician William Shoichet and the BC Civil Liberties Association. Together the plaintiffs sought the decriminalization of physician-assisted dying for consenting patients who are grievously and irremediably ill, which is defined in *Carter v Canada* as:

> 1. A person is "grievously and irremediably ill" when he or she has a serious medical condition that has been diagnosed as such by a medical practitioner and which (a) is without remedy, as determined by reference to treatment options acceptable to the person; and (b) causes the person enduring physical, psychological or psychosocial suffering that: (i) is intolerable to that person; and (ii) cannot be alleviated by any medical treatment acceptable to that person. 2. A "medical condition" means an illness, disease or disability, and includes a disability arising from traumatic injury.[17]

Thus, the scope of legal permission sought by the plaintiffs was substantially broader than that envisioned by the plaintiff in *Rodriguez v British Columbia*, encompassing a far wider range of potential cases, including non-terminal illnesses, non-physical (i.e., psychological) illnesses, and curable illnesses (provided that the cure is unacceptable to the patient for any reason). It would also allow those who are physically capable of committing suicide to receive assistance in doing so or to receive active euthanasia. Moreover, the plaintiffs sought to invalidate not only section 241(b) of the Criminal Code but also other sections relevant to physician-assisted dying (understood as encompassing both assisted suicide and active euthanasia), notably including section 241(a) and section 14.[18]

Before getting into the legal arguments put forward by the plaintiffs and the attorney general of Canada and their evaluation by the Supreme Court of British Columbia, I will discuss briefly some of the specifically ethical arguments raised. The author of the verdict in *Carter v Canada*, Justice Lynn Smith, noted that "ethical principles have shaped both the law and medical practice. Ethical principles, similarly, enter into constitutional analysis (for example, Justice Sopinka referred to the positions of medical associations regarding the ethics of assisted suicide and euthanasia in his Reasons in Rodriguez (at 608))" (p. 54). Consequently, the court viewed moral argumentation as legally relevant (though not by itself legally determinative), and the court heard submissions on the matter both from the direct parties to the case and from external intervenors. Briefly, the plaintiffs argued that there is a societal consensus that individuals have the moral right to autonomy over their own bodies. However, they argued, there is no such consensus on the absolute sanctity of life. The Canadian government, for its part, questioned the legal relevance of the ethical debate, but it added that Canadian society (irrespective of religious and cultural differences) regards human life as of fundamental value and that this high degree of respect for human life is reflected in the criminal law. The BC government similarly argued that there is a broad consensus in Canada on the sanctity of life, reflected in Canadians' rejection of capital punishment.

Each side also made use of testimony from expert witnesses on the relevant ethical issues. Among the submissions presented by the plaintiffs was that of bioethicist Margaret Battin. Justice Smith quoted a portion of that submission:

> Physician assistance in bringing about death is to be provided only when
> the patient voluntarily seeks it (autonomy) and only where it serves to avoid
> pain or suffering or the prospect of them (mercy). Because these principles

do not operate independently, it cannot be claimed that permitting physician-assisted dying would require assisting lovesick teenagers who are not suffering from a serious medical condition to die; likewise it cannot be claimed that permitting physician-assisted dying on the basis of the principle of mercy would require involuntary euthanasia for someone who is in pain but nevertheless desires to stay alive. Both principles must be in play; but when they are in play, they jointly provide a powerful basis for permitting and respecting physician aid in dying.

Those who oppose physician aid in dying must show that the principles of liberty and freedom from suffering that are basic to an open, liberal and democratic society should be overridden. This is the point of slippery-slope assertions about the potential for corrupting physicians and widespread abuse in the Netherlands and perhaps Oregon. Yet there is no empirical evidence that supports these claims, and substantial evidence to the contrary.[19]

Smith returned to the issue of empirical evidence of abuse later in the ruling.

Next she quoted another expert witness for the plaintiffs, physician and bioethicist Ross Upshur:

Based on my review of the empirical, psychological, and philosophical literature and my experience as a clinician, I believe that, under certain conditions, providing assistance with suicide or euthanasia can be an ethically appropriate course of conduct for a physician. The conditions that I support, on the same professional foundation, are that the request be free and informed and made by an individual when competent. I do not believe that assisted suicide and euthanasia should only be available to those who are diagnosed as terminally ill, but rather should be available to those for whom life has become not worth living to them.[20]

Given the broader scope of decriminalization sought by the plaintiffs in *Carter v Canada* (much broader than that sought in *Rodriguez v British Columbia*), Upshur's comment regarding assisted dying for the non-terminally ill is especially relevant.

Another witness for the plaintiffs was neurologist Sharon Cohen, also quoted in the decision in *Carter v Canada*:

I have witnessed a number of patients with grievous and irremediable neurological diseases who have already experienced prolonged suffering, die slow and terrible deaths. I have witnessed patients with grievous and irremediable neurological conditions at the end of life gasping for breath as they slowly drowned in their own secretions or choked on their own saliva. These patients appeared extremely uncomfortable, agitated and restless. Some patients explicitly told me that they were experiencing discomfort and pain. I have seen patients turn blue because they cannot get enough air. Some appeared terrified. For some of these patients, this slow and painful march to death lasted days. Some patients experienced multiple episodes of choking and a feeling of suffocation over a period of weeks. These deaths were extremely traumatic for both the patient and their family. Sometimes patients are provided sedation to the point of semi-consciousness so they are made more comfortable as they struggle for breath. Nonetheless, they may linger in a state of dying for hours to days with families standing by in distressed states that may take years to recover from. In my opinion, physician-assisted dying should have been an available treatment option in these situations. With all my training as a physician, I cannot accept that it is right to allow patients to die in this immeasurably cruel and useless fashion if to do so is against the patients' wishes.[21]

Two points here might have warranted further comment by the court. The first point is Cohen's admission that such grievous suffering is in fact capable of being relieved through palliative sedation (which I will discuss in Chapter 4). The second point is the role that Cohen assigns to the psychological state of the dying individual's family. Although her compassion for family members in this trying situation is admirable, and clearly born from the concrete experiences of a caring clinician, perhaps the court should have noted the potential complications (moral and legal) associated with taking *someone else's* suffering as a justification for euthanasia. This is especially the case insofar as there might be other ways of alleviating this psychological distress, methods that do not entail terminating the life of the patient.

Among expert witnesses put forward by the government side was ethicist and legal scholar John Keown, who reaffirmed the vital importance of the inviolability of human life in both medicine and criminal law and argued that the risk of abuse and a slippery slope was real and supported by empirical evidence (contra the testimony offered by Battin).[22] Another witness for the government was ethicist and gerontologist Thomas Koch, who questioned the plaintiffs' use of the notion of personal autonomy. Justice Smith quoted a portion of his submission:

This claim isn't about individual choice and autonomy. We cannot stop but we need not applaud suicide in the face of adversity. Ms. Taylor may kill herself. She seeks not the right to do that but instead the obligation of us to agree her life is so insufficient that we will assist or direct her termination. This claim is about whether we honour each other irrespective of individual characteristics or set up a sliding scale by which some conditions devalue life until the point where its termination is appropriate. It is about whether we place our priorities in the arenas of rehabilitation, palliation, and social service or agree with the simplistic assumption that state-supported, physician-assisted or directed termination is or should be a reflexive response to restrictive medical conditions.[23]

Relatedly, defence witness Harvey Chochinov, Canada Research Chair in palliative care at the University of Manitoba, argued that medical advances can mitigate substantially the stated concerns about patient suffering and the alleged need to resort to assisted death to allay it. In his affidavit to *Carter v Canada*, he stated that

in the vast majority of instances, palliative care is able to mitigate suffering. As such, even in the absence of death hastening options, good outcomes in palliative care are regularly achieved. Palliative care has made great gains over the last few decades and can now attend to most sources of symptom distress. In some instances, managing physical distress may involve having to sacrifice conscious awareness … However, palliative care should no more be seen as the perfect foil to suffering, than medicine should be pitched as the perfect foil to death.[24]

Another palliative care physician, Romayne Gallagher, raised the worry that decriminalizing physician-assisted death would radically change the nature of the medical profession and undermine trust between doctor and patient:

The goals of medicine are prolonging life, relieving suffering and improving or maintaining function and have been so since the Hippocratic Oath was written thousands of years ago. Even then there was the strong pronouncement about not doing harm and not administering a deadly drug nor counselling a patient to take a deadly drug. The Canadian Medical Association Code of Ethics notes the core activities of a physician as health promotion, advocacy, disease prevention, diagnosis, treatment, rehabilitation, palliation, education and research. In no way is administering a drug with the intent to end the life of the patient consistent with the goals or core activities of medicine. While drugs administered to treat patients can result in death, that is considered an adverse outcome and not the intention of the treatment. Giving a drug with the intention of causing the death of the patient does not relieve suffering but moves the patient to a state where we presume they are beyond suffering. In my opinion changing the law to allow physicians to administer a deadly drug would be to radically change the concept of what a physician is that has been held for over two thousand years. I believe it would also seriously undermine the trust that patients have in a physician to do what is in their best interest.[25]

The court also heard submissions from various organizations as intervenors, some of which raised ethical arguments as part of their submissions. For instance, the Christian Legal Fellowship argued that the intentional killing of an innocent person is always wrong and that recognition of this moral fact is foundational for all Western civilization. In contrast, the Canadian Unitarian Council emphasized the moral import of personal autonomy in medical decision making and argued further that society recognizes the moral legitimacy of some decisions to terminate life intentionally.

Justice Smith then turned to the issue of whether it is feasible to decriminalize assisted death while also providing safeguards to prevent abuses. This is relevant, of course, not only to the context of the ethical debate surrounding the plaintiffs' case but also to the legal reconsideration of the *Rodriguez* ruling, given the role that concerns about safeguards played in the majority decision penned by Justice Sopinka. The claim of access to relevant new empirical data on this issue, data unavailable to the Supreme Court of Canada in 1993, Smith saw as supporting her contention that the Supreme Court of British Columbia possessed the capacity to invalidate the higher court's ruling. A substantial portion of her ruling (p. 111–249) consists of a review and an assessment of expert testimony pertaining to the data. Smith discussed safeguards implemented in jurisdictions that had decriminalized one or another form of assisted death since 1993, including the American states of Oregon, Washington, and Montana, as well as the nations of Belgium, Holland, Luxembourg, and Switzerland. The criteria for legally obtaining assisted suicide and/or euthanasia varied greatly from one jurisdiction to another. For instance, in Oregon, assisted suicide is restricted to the terminally ill, whereas in Holland both assisted suicide and euthanasia are available to those who lack any physical ailment but suffer from a psychiatric disorder, and in Switzerland no medical condition at all is required to obtain assisted suicide – only consent by a legally competent individual. Accordingly, the safeguards put in place also varied. Still, Smith found that within each jurisdiction the state's rules were generally followed; crucially, she found that concerns about coercion and abuse of vulnerable individuals were unfounded, writing that "although none of the systems has achieved perfection, empirical researchers and practitioners who have experience in those systems are of the view that they work well in protecting patients from abuse while allowing competent patients to choose the timing of their deaths" (p. 197). Smith also determined that fears about a potential decline in the quality of palliative care services post-legalization, and fears about negative impacts on patient-physician relationships, were similarly unfounded. She concluded from this review that "the risks inherent in permitting physician-assisted death can be identified and very substantially minimized through a carefully-designed system imposing stringent limits that are scrupulously monitored and enforced" (p. 249). Thus, Smith deemed an important ground for the *Rodriguez* decision against decriminalization to be mistaken in light of new empirical data.

That portion of the ruling led into the next major section, in which Justice Smith assessed to what extent the prior ruling in *Rodriguez v British Columbia* was determinative of the new *Carter v Canada*. She noted that

> both Canada and British Columbia submit that *Rodriguez* is binding on this Court because the facts pertaining to Gloria Taylor are virtually identical to those in *Rodriguez,* and the *Charter* provisions upon which the plaintiffs rely in this case are the same as those raised in *Rodriguez.* They say that it is not open to this Court to do anything other than dismiss the plaintiffs' claim.[26]

Moreover, the government noted that just ten years previously, in 2002, the Supreme Court of Canada declined to reconsider *Rodriguez* when it denied the plaintiff in *Wakeford v Canada* leave to appeal. (In that case, the plaintiff argued before an Ontario court that section 241(b) of the Criminal Code violated his equality rights under section 15 of the Charter.) However, in Canada, rulings of the federal Supreme Court are not, of course, absolutely final (unlike the high courts of some other nations) and may be revisited both by that court and by lower courts should new facts emerge, should dominant societal values shift dramatically, or should it be shown that the new case (perhaps despite initial appearances) is substantially dissimilar to the precedent. The plaintiffs before Smith in *Carter* were arguing that there were multiple such legal grounds for the Supreme Court of British Columbia to reconsider *Rodriguez,* and Smith came to agree with some of their points.

First, she deemed that the relevant facts in the *Rodriguez* and *Carter* cases were not equivalent. Social and legal contexts pertaining to assisted death had shifted between 1993 and 2012; more importantly, a great deal of empirical data on the feasibility of decriminalization had become available. As Justice Smith wrote,

> the evidence as to legislative and social facts in this case, however, is different from that in *Rodriguez.* By evidence as to "legislative and social facts," I refer to all of the evidence tendered in this case on matters other than the adjudicative facts – regarding topics such as the legislation and experience in jurisdictions with legalized physician-assisted death or assisted death, palliative care practice including palliative sedation, end-of-life decision making, Canadian public opinion regarding euthanasia or physician-assisted death, Parliamentary and other reports since *Rodriguez,* and medical ethics ... The most notable difference between the records in this case and in *Rodriguez* is that the record in this case includes: evidence pertaining to the experience with legal physician-assisted death in Oregon, Washington, Belgium, Luxembourg and the Netherlands and with assisted death in Switzerland; opinion evidence of medical ethicists and practitioners informed by the experience in jurisdictions with legalized assisted death; specific evidence pertaining to current palliative care and palliative or terminal sedation practices; and evidence regarding prosecution policies in British Columbia and the United Kingdom formulated since *Rodriguez.* The evidence regarding the experience in jurisdictions permitting physician-assisted death was available neither at the time *Rodriguez* was decided, nor when *Wakeford* was considered.[27]

Second, since 1993, there had been developments in the Supreme Court's understanding of section 7 of the Charter, with its attendant reference to the principles of fundamental justice. The court had since clarified that those principles demand that criminal legislation not violate the notions of "overbreadth" and "gross disproportionality." Basically, the notions are that the law cannot restrict liberty in a more sweeping and extreme fashion than is necessary to accomplish its purposes. The Supreme Court did not explicitly recognize these notions as implications of the principles of fundamental justice at the time of *Rodriguez,* and the plaintiffs in *Carter* were effectively claiming that the blanket prohibition on assisted death was in fact overbroad and grossly disproportionate. Justice Smith maintained that this change post-1993 supplied adequate legal justification for reconsidering the constitutionality of that prohibition.

Third, the majority in *Rodriguez* had declined to consider whether section 15 of the Charter was infringed, on the ground that, even if it were, any associated deprivation would be counted as in accordance with the principles of fundamental justice (given the court's verdict on the section 7 challenge) and justified by reference to section 1 of the Charter. However, in *Carter*, the issue of section 15 infringement could legitimately be raised anew, given the aforementioned post-1993 developments.

And fourth, the majority in *Rodriguez* had not explicitly stated whether the right to life under section 7 of the Charter was engaged by the prohibition on assisted death. However, the plaintiffs in *Carter* were now arguing that this right was infringed because the prohibition served to drive people at risk of total physical incapacitation to commit suicide earlier than they would otherwise. Justice Smith also saw that as raising a new point of law not determined by the precedent, which further justified the reconsideration of *Rodriguez*.

Having concluded that the Supreme Court of British Columbia had the legal authority to consider revisiting this prior decision by the Supreme Court of Canada, Justice Smith then turned to the detailed consideration of the plaintiffs' relevant arguments. She began with the argument arising from section 15 of the Charter, observing that the dissenting justices in *Rodriguez* had likewise expressed concern that the prohibition on assisted suicide disadvantaged the physically disabled in a way not in accordance with the principles of fundamental justice. Although the Criminal Code prohibition on assisted suicide applied to everyone, and did not explicitly or intentionally single out the physically disabled,

> even distinctions created unintentionally and implicitly, through the disparate impact of the law on a particular group of persons, may infringe s. 15 and should be interrogated in the same way as are intentional or explicit distinctions. This is because the commitment to substantive equality entails consideration of the actual impact of the law on the persons it affects (p. 289)

The plaintiffs' claim was that the impact was truly grievous, insofar as "people with physical disabilities who are unable to end their lives themselves are forced into the dilemma of either continuing to suffer or exposing other persons to criminal sanctions. Some resolve this dilemma by taking their lives before their illnesses progress to a point where they are no longer able to do so" (p. 294).

Later in the ruling, Smith quoted Elayne Shapray, a witness for the plaintiff suffering from secondary progressive multiple sclerosis:

> I understand that suicide is no longer a crime in Canada. The irony of the current situation as I experience it is that an able-bodied person can commit suicide in a lawful manner but somebody such as myself, who is unable by reason of their disability to do so, cannot. The means available to me to terminate my life unassisted at this time, if I was so inclined, are extremely limited and would likely involve violent, painful or personally terrifying outcomes. I consider the option of taking my own life by conventional "suicide" means, assuming that I was otherwise physically and emotionally able to do so, not only to be dangerous and inhumane, but also likely to be extremely traumatic to my family and my friends. I live in dread of the day when I will have been robbed of all meaningful quality of life by the progression of my disease. I fear that I will not have the option that others have of ending one's own life. I wish to have the choice of a dignified, physician-assisted termination of my life at the time of my choosing rather than being terrified daily about how I may end up simply because at a future date there would be no one able to legally help me. The current state of the law deprives me of the freedom to choose how and when I would end my life. The current law may cause me to initiate a premature termination of my life simply because if I wait until I am ready to do so, I may be unable to do so, in any humane fashion, without asking my loved ones to put themselves at legal risk.[28]

In response, lawyers for Canada and for British Columbia replied that even those suffering from total physical incapacity could commit suicide without external assistance, insofar as they could refuse food and hydration to the point of expiration. As such, section 241(b) served at worst to bar the disabled not from suicide per se but from certain *methods* of suicide. The plaintiffs in turn countered that this method of suicide would be slow and excruciating, such that, even if available to the utterly physically disabled, that it would be the only method available to them only served to highlight the ways in which the law affected them in a drastically unequal fashion vis-à-vis the able-bodied.

Lawyers for Canada then argued that the mere fact that attempted suicide was no longer subject to criminal sanction did not imply a right to

suicide, a right supposedly infringed by section 241(b) and disproportion-
ally so for the physically incapacitated. Yet, Justice Smith pointed out,
whether or not there is any right to suicide, plausibly there is a right to
physical integrity and autonomous decision making with respect to important aspects of an individual's life, including aspects pertaining to medical
intervention. Autonomy, of course, was not the only relevant value under
consideration, and here Smith noted an argument by one of the intervenors:
"The intervenor Euthanasia Prevention Coalition submits that the principles of community interdependence and the sanctity of life justify the
Criminal Code provisions. Legalizing assisted suicide, it says, would erode
these principles by dehumanizing certain members of the community. The
EPC says the Court must weigh these values against the values of autonomy
and self-determination emphasized by the plaintiffs" (p. 328). Nevertheless,
Smith maintained that autonomy is

> among the values that are fundamentally important and central to person-
> hood and have long been affirmed in the common law and in the Canadian
> Constitution. It must not be overlooked that what is at stake for someone in
> Gloria Taylor's situation is not merely autonomy, nor is it simply autonomy
> with respect to physical integrity. It is the autonomy to relieve herself of
> suffering.[29]

Taking all of that into account, Justice Smith concluded that plaintiff
Taylor's equality rights under section 15 of the Charter were in fact infringed
by section 241(b) of the Criminal Code. The next question was whether that
infringement was legally justifiable, especially in light of some significant
post-1993 Supreme Court of Canada case law.[30] Keeping in mind the new
empirical data on the practical feasibility of safeguards to protect the vulnerable and wider society in jurisdictions that have decriminalized assisted
death, Smith found that section 241(b) was both overbroad and disproportionate; a complete prohibition was not necessary to meet the law's goal of
protecting the vulnerable from coercion to commit suicide. As Smith noted,

> the question, then, is whether there is an alternative means for the legisla-
> ture to achieve its objective in a real and substantial way that less seriously
> infringes the Charter rights of Gloria Taylor and others in her situation.
> Clearly, it is theoretically possible for the legislature to do so. Parliament
> could prohibit assisted death but allow for exceptions. The exceptions could
> permit physician-assisted death under stringent conditions designed to

ensure that it would only be available to grievously ill, competent, non-ambivalent, voluntary adults who were fully informed as to their diagnosis and prognosis and who were suffering symptoms that could not be treated through means reasonably acceptable to those persons.[31]

Moreover, a careful weighing of the alleged potentially deleterious effects of decriminalization (e.g., undermining respect for life, eroding trust between physicians and their patients, weakening the palliative care system, etc.) with the salutary effects claimed by the plaintiffs (e.g., preserving personal autonomy, preventing needless suffering, etc.) failed to show that the alleged societal benefit of outlawing assisted death outweighed the infringement of equality rights under section 15.

Justice Smith turned next to the issue of whether section 241(b) infringed the right to life, a question not taken up explicitly by the majority in *Rodriguez v British Columbia:*

> The plaintiffs submit that the right to life is also engaged because the provisions may cause her to end her own life earlier than she would otherwise want to, out of fear that the progression of her illness will prevent her from doing so later ... The defendant Canada argues, on the other hand, that the s. 7 right to life does not encompass quality of life issues, which it says may implicate security of the person, but not the right to life itself. Canada argues that the right to life does not include the right to choose death. It submits that such an interpretation would directly contradict the plain and obvious meaning of a right to life and would mark a significant departure from existing Supreme Court of Canada jurisprudence.[32]

Contra the submission from Canada, Smith concluded that plaintiff Taylor's right to life was engaged, in the sense that Taylor had a right not to die, which was being infringed by the prohibition on assisted death, insofar as it could force her (and those in comparable situations of progressive physical incapacity) into an act of suicide earlier than she would otherwise have desired.

The next question was whether that infringement was consistent with the principles of fundamental justice and counted as a reasonable limit on the relevant right (thereby constituting a *permissible* infringement under section 1 of the Charter). After reviewing relevant post-1993 case law pertaining to overbreadth and gross disproportionality, and with reference again to the new empirical data on the workability of safeguards in the context of decriminalization, Justice Smith inferred that the state's interest in protecting the vulnerable could not justify the section 7 infringement entailed by the blanket prohibition on assisted death. That prohibition was in fact both overbroad and grossly disproportionate and thus inconsistent with the principles of fundamental justice.

The plaintiffs had asked the court not only to invalidate section 241(b) and thus *Rodriguez* but also to adopt certain specific recommendations regarding the conditions under which assisted death would be permitted. With respect to the latter, Justice Smith wrote that "it is the proper task of Parliament, not the courts, to determine how to rectify legislation that has been found to be unconstitutional. However, in a case such as this, where the unconstitutionality arises from the legislation's application in certain specific circumstances, it is incumbent on the Court to specify what those circumstances are" (p. 384). Departing from the plaintiffs' specific recommendations in several ways (e.g., intentionally dropping any reference to "psychosocial" illnesses), Smith put forward the following as constitutionally mandated:

> A declaration that the impugned provisions unjustifiably infringe s. 7 of the *Charter*, and are of no force and effect to the extent that they prohibit physician-assisted suicide or consensual physician-assisted death by a medical practitioner in the context of a physician-patient relationship, where the assistance is provided to a fully-informed, non-ambivalent competent adult person who: (a) is free from coercion and undue influence, is not clinically depressed and who personally (not through a substituted decision-maker) requests physician-assisted death; and (b) has been diagnosed by a medical practitioner as having a serious illness, disease or disability (including disability arising from traumatic injury), is in a state of advanced weakening capacities with no chance of improvement, has an illness that is without remedy as determined by reference to treatment options acceptable to the person, and has an illness causing enduring physical or psychological suffering that is intolerable to that person and cannot be alleviated by any medical treatment acceptable to that person.[33]

Smith gave the government a one-year period of grace within which to enact new legislation before the invalidation of sections 241(b) and 14 would take effect (likewise related sections 21, 22, and 222), in the meantime granting plaintiff Taylor an immediate constitutional exemption allowing her to receive assisted death.

The governments of Canada and of British Columbia then appealed the decision to the BC Court of Appeal.

The 2013 BC Court of Appeal Ruling on *Carter v Canada*

In a two-thirds majority verdict (dissent by Chief Justice Lance Finch), the BC Court of Appeal reversed Justice Smith's ruling in *Carter v Canada*. Writing as part of his dissent, Finch concisely summarized the grounds for appeal claimed by the government of Canada:

> The AGC [attorney general of Canada] argues that Smith J. erred by finding that she was not fully bound by the decision in *Rodriguez* with respect to her analysis under ss. 7, 15, and 1. In *Rodriguez*, a majority of the Supreme Court of Canada found, on similar facts, that s. 241(b) of the *Criminal Code* did not infringe s. 7 or s. 12 of the *Charter*. Though assuming an infringement under s. 15, the Court found that it was saved under s. 1. The AGC further argues that the respondents' rights under ss. 7 and 15 of the *Charter* were not infringed; and that, in any event, any infringement was justified under s. 1. The AGC says that in finding that the law infringed the respondents' rights under ss. 7 and 15 of the *Charter*, Smith J. asked the wrong question, or applied the wrong test. In examining whether the impugned provisions were overly broad or minimally impaired the respondents' rights, Smith J. should have asked whether there was a reasonable apprehension of harm that Parliament could only address with an absolute prohibition on assisted death. On the issue of minimal impairment under s. 1, the AGC's fundamental position on this appeal, as it was before Smith J., is that the only issue before the Court is whether Parliament's absolute prohibition against physician-assisted death was within the range of reasonable legislative alternatives.[34]

The Canadian government thus argued that the precedent in *Rodriguez v British Columbia* should have been allowed to stand and that Smith had erred in the manner in which she applied the more recently enumerated principles pertaining to overbreadth and gross disproportionality. Parliament is not obligated to demonstrate minimal impairments when its criminal prohibition on an activity clashes with Charter rights; rather, it need only show that the prohibition is a reasonable legislative response to a genuine risk of serious societal harm.

The BC Court of Appeal also heard from various intervenors supporting the government's position, including the following, summarized from the submission by the Evangelical Fellowship of Canada, which

> contended that the sanctity of human life is a *Charter* value and merits special protection. One cannot consent to die. They argue that compassion is misdirected when it posits killing as an antidote to what is difficult about dying. There can be no assisted suicide without another moral agent engaged in the killing. It would also require the State to be complicit in the act. No one has the right to be killed.[35]

The opposing side replied that Justice Smith had been correct in her assessment that the Charter infringements entailed by section 241(b) and the related Criminal Code prohibitions on euthanasia and counselling suicide could not be saved under section 1 of the Charter; Smith had correctly applied the more recently recognized principles of fundamental justice (pertaining to overbreadth and gross disproportionality) in light of the empirical data available post-1993, which provided ample legal standing for a lower court to overturn *Rodriguez*.

In assessing Justice Smith's ruling, the BC Court of Appeal first held that Smith was in fact bound by the earlier precedent set in *Rodriguez* as it pertained to section 15 equality rights. In part, this was because her analysis of post-1993 case law (notably, the 2009 Supreme Court of Canada ruling in *Alberta v Hutterian Brethren of Wilson Colony Charter*) was flawed. This was maintained both by Chief Justice Finch in his dissenting opinion and by the majority opinion authored by Justice Mary Newbury (paras 107, 270).

The remaining question concerned whether the Supreme Court of British Columbia had ruled appropriately regarding infringement of the section 7 right to life (a point not taken up explicitly in *Rodriguez*). The government of Canada argued that the prohibition on assisted suicide could not be seen as infringing the right to life, insofar as there are many possible responses available to the prohibition and no direct causal link between the prohibition and someone taking her own life earlier than desired. "To establish a causal connection, the AGC suggests there must be a direct link between the state conduct and the actual consequences of the prohibition. The AGC argues that premature suicides are not caused by the law and its prohibitive effect, but simply the fear of living with a degenerative medical condition" (para 115). The plaintiffs replied that they had established a direct causal link by showing that there are cases in which patients at risk of complete physical incapacitation intend to kill themselves earlier than they otherwise would, precisely because they know that assisted suicide is illegal and that they cannot rely on help in the future. In his dissenting opinion, Chief Justice Finch accepted the plaintiffs' argument that the section 7 right to life was indeed being infringed:

> In my opinion, there is a sufficient causal connection between the impugned provisions and premature deaths. The standard advocated by the AGC, which would require showing a direct causal link between the legislation and its effects[,] is not the correct standard to apply. In *Canada (Attorney General) v PHS Community Services Society*, 2011 SCC 44, the Court accepted that depriving drug users of access to medical supervision amounted to depriving the users of the right to life.[36]

Whether or not this infringement was justified under section 1 of the Charter, Finch wrote that the absolute prohibition on assisted suicide was indeed broader than necessary to achieve the goals of the legislation (to protect the vulnerable and manifest the state's regard for the inherent value of life) because steps short of absolute prohibition could plausibly accomplish these goals just as well, especially in light of the empirical data assembled by Justice Smith. Likewise, it was grossly disproportionate. As such, Finch would allow the decision in *Carter v Canada* to stand.

In contrast, in Justice Newbury's decision for the majority, it was deemed that Justice Smith was mistaken about the implications of post-1993 case law relevant to the relationship between sections 7 and 1 of the Charter: "With all due respect to the trial judge, we believe that she was bound by *stare decisis* to conclude that the plaintiffs' case had already been determined by the Supreme Court of Canada" (para 316). Newbury went on to grant that, if a piece of legislation could be shown to infringe a section 7 right, that would be a strong reason for deeming it unjustifiable under section 1, and indeed the Supreme Court of Canada had never found a section 7 infringement to be saved by section 1.[37] However, the plaintiffs had not successfully shown this; moreover, issues of breadth and proportionality were in fact taken into account in *Rodriguez,* if somewhat obliquely, when Justice Sopinka determined that an absolute prohibition on assisted suicide was necessary, not only to protect the vulnerable from coercion, but also to discourage the terminally ill from choosing death:

> The trial judge was of the opinion in the case at bar that it was open to her
> to reconsider this "final step" because, she said, the Court had addressed it
> "only very summarily." (Para. 936; but see also para. 998.) With respect, her
> opinion of the sufficiency of the Supreme Court of Canada's analysis did not
> permit her to disregard its conclusion. As we hope we have demonstrated,
> it is inherent in the law relating to the *Charter* that it is not written in stone
> and that ways of assessing laws inevitably evolve. Again, the focus for pur-
> poses of *stare decisis* should be on what was decided, not *how* it was decided
> or how the result was described.[38]

The fact that Sopinka was making this point in the context of a discussion of section 15 rather than section 7 is not pertinent to the basic point at issue: namely, that the court had been properly cognizant of the issues of breadth and proportionality, even if the conclusion reached differed from that of Smith. Moreover, the new empirical data that Smith discussed (changes in ethical views and the new information on safeguards in nations such as Holland) did not suffice to warrant reconsideration of *Rodriguez*.

The plaintiffs then appealed this decision to the Supreme Court of Canada.

The 2015 Supreme Court of Canada Ruling in *Carter v Canada*

In a unanimous verdict, the Supreme Court of Canada granted the appeal, declaring that section 241(b) and section 14 of the *Criminal Code of Canada* violated the section 7 Charter right to life in a way inconsistent with the prin-ciples of fundamental justice and were irredeemable by reference to section 1. The blanket prohibition was overbroad, for the purpose of the law was to pro-tect the vulnerable from coercion to commit suicide but in fact it had a much wider impact, including on those who are at no risk of coercion but rationally wish to end their lives. In its ruling in *Carter v Canada*, the Supreme Court rejected the government's claim that preservation of life generally was a further goal of the legislation as understood in *Rodriguez v British Columbia*:

> First, it is incorrect to say that the majority in *Rodriguez* adopted "the pres-
> ervation of life" as the object of the prohibition on assisted dying. Justice

Sopinka refers to the preservation of life when discussing the objectives of s. 241(*b*) (pp. 590, 614). However, he later clarifies this comment, stating that "[s]ection 241(*b*) has as its purpose the protection of the vulnerable who might be induced in moments of weakness to commit suicide" (p. 595). Sopinka J. then goes on to note that this purpose is "grounded in the state interest in protecting life and reflects the policy of the state that human life should not be depreciated by allowing life to be taken" (*ibid.*). His remarks about the "preservation of life" in *Rodriguez* are best understood as a reference to an animating social value rather than as a description of the specific object of the prohibition.[39]

There is a problem with this particular portion of the Supreme Court's ruling in 2015 in *Carter v Canada*: namely, it does not convincingly account for a further statement by Sopinka, adjacent to the passage just cited, in which, in reply to the potential objection that a blanket prohibition was overly broad, he wrote in 1993 in the decision in *Rodriguez v British Columbia* that

> the foregoing is also the answer to the submission that the impugned legislation is overbroad. There is no halfway measure that could be relied upon with assurance to fully achieve *the legislation's purpose; first, because the purpose extends to the protection of the life of the terminally ill. Part of the purpose, as I have explained above, is to discourage the terminally ill from choosing death over life.* Secondly, even if the latter consideration can be stripped from the legislative purpose, we have no assurance that the exception can be made to limit the taking of life to those who are terminally ill and genuinely desire death.[40]

This certainly appears to be a "description of the specific object of the prohibition." At any rate, the court accepted the plaintiffs' argument that prohibiting assisted death had the effect of forcing some people to commit suicide prematurely, thus violating their right to life. At the same time, it also violated the rights to liberty and security of the person by depriving them of autonomy over the process of dying. The section 7 infringements being sufficient to invalidate the prohibition and overturn *Rodriguez*, the court declined to assess the issue of a section 15 equality rights violation.

I will not say much more about the arguments of the Supreme Court in the 2015 decision in *Carter v Canada* since they mostly agree with those of Justice Smith in the Supreme Court of British Columbia's ruling, already summarized above. Still, before turning to the legal remedy laid down by the Supreme Court (which not only held that the blanket prohibition was incompatible with the Charter but also laid out criteria for the constitutionality of any future replacement legislation), I will note a few additional points. First, in making this decision, the court was explicit that it did not see itself as departing entirely from the ethical reference points employed by the majority in *Rodriguez,* notably that of the sanctity of life:

> The sanctity of life is one of our most fundamental societal values. Section 7 is rooted in a profound respect for the value of human life. But s. 7 also encompasses life, liberty and security of the person during the passage to death ... And it is for this reason that the law has come to recognize that, in certain circumstances, an individual's choice about the end of her life is entitled to respect.[41]

Second, in its submission, the government of Canada attempted to undermine the assessment of empirical data made by Justice Smith in her Supreme Court of British Columbia ruling, presenting further evidence on the matter from Professor Etienne Montero, a bioethicist. The court did not consider this new evidence probative against Smith's position. But its statement on this point contains a passage that could be of considerable import for adjudicating an interpretive dispute that has since arisen concerning the court's criteria for constitutionally valid assisted death legislation:

> Canada says that Professor Montero's evidence demonstrates that issues with compliance and with the expansion of the criteria granting access to assisted suicide inevitably arise, even in a system of ostensibly strict limits and safeguards. It argues that this "should give pause to those who feel very strict safeguards will provide adequate protection: paper safeguards are only as strong as the human hands that carry them out" (R.F., at para. 97). Professor Montero's affidavit reviews a number of recent, controversial, and high-profile cases of assistance in dying in Belgium which would not fall within the parameters suggested in these reasons, such as euthanasia for minors *or persons with psychiatric disorders* or minor medical conditions. Professor Montero suggests that these cases demonstrate that a slippery slope is at work in Belgium. In his view, "[o]nce euthanasia is allowed, it becomes very difficult to maintain a strict interpretation of the statutory conditions." We are not convinced that Professor Montero's evidence undermines the trial judge's findings of fact.[42]

Third, the Supreme Court specified that nothing in its ruling could be taken as compelling physicians to participate in an assisted death procedure and that the Charter rights of both patients and physicians (to conscience and freedom of religion) need to be respected by future legislation and guidelines put forward by federal and provincial legislatures and likewise medical associations.

Having invalidated sections 241(b) and 14 of the Criminal Code, the court proceeded to lay down some foundational requirements that any future legislation pertaining to assisted death will have to meet:

> The appropriate remedy is therefore a declaration that s. 241(*b*) and s. 14 of the *Criminal Code* are void insofar as they prohibit physician-assisted death for a competent adult person who 1) clearly consents to the termination of life; and 2) has a grievous and irremediable medical condition (including an illness, disease or disability) that causes enduring suffering that is intolerable to the individual in the circumstances of his or her condition. "Irremediable," it should be added, does not require the patient to undertake treatments that are not acceptable to the individual. The scope of this declaration is intended to respond to the factual circumstances in this case. We make no pronouncement on other situations where physician-assisted dying may be sought.[43]

Those last two sentences might lead one to think that the Supreme Court intended the scope of its remedy to apply only to those in *precisely* the same circumstances as Taylor (and Rodriguez): namely, suffering from a grievous and irremediable medical condition such as ALS, which leads to profound physical incapacity. And, indeed, to interpret the intended scope of the remedy as restricted in this fashion would make better sense of the court's argument from the right to life (i.e., that people in such circumstances have a right to euthanasia because otherwise they are liable to kill themselves prematurely while still physically capable of doing so). However, subsequent public discussions of the court's ruling have not reflected such an interpretation, nor has the government's legislative response to *Carter* in Bill C-14 – and with good reason. Earlier passages of the ruling clearly indicate that, in the court's view, the relevant "factual circumstances" are not the circumstances of an ALS patient specifically but of a much broader range. For instance,

> an individual's response to a grievous and irremediable medical condition is a matter critical to their dignity and autonomy. The law allows people in

this situation to request palliative sedation, refuse artificial nutrition and hydration, or request the removal of life-sustaining medical equipment, but denies them the right to request a physician's assistance in dying. This interferes with their ability to make decisions concerning their bodily integrity and medical care and thus trenches on liberty. And, by leaving people like Ms. Taylor to endure intolerable suffering, it impinges on their security of the person.[44]

Or consider this passage: "For the foregoing reasons, we conclude that the prohibition on physician-assisted dying deprived Ms. Taylor *and others suffering from grievous and irremediable medical conditions* of the right to life, liberty and security of the person" (p. 371; emphasis added). The court could have written "and others suffering from ALS and comparable *incapacitating terminal* conditions" but clearly intended that its ruling encompass a larger range of ailments.

The Supreme Court suspended the declaration of invalidity for one year (from February 6, 2015), giving the federal government a period of grace within which to enact new legislation pertaining to assisted death.

Concluding Evaluative Remarks

With the summaries of the four key rulings now complete, I will conclude the chapter with some brief evaluative remarks. The Supreme Court of Canada, in seeking to redress a concern regarding the alleged overbreadth of sections 241(b) and 14 of the *Criminal Code of Canada,* made much the same mistake. The court ruled that those sections infringed section 7 Charter rights because they drove those at risk of utter physical incapacitation to premature suicide and likewise deprived them of a proper measure of autonomy over the process of dying. A number of terminal ailments gradually bring on a loss of fine motor control, notably ALS, the terrible disease suffered by both Sue Rodriguez and Gloria Taylor. Someone in the final stages of ALS would indeed be unable to engage in the minimal physical activity needed to commit suicide, such as the self-administration of a deadly narcotic. But the number of such ailments is relatively small, and the total percentage of Canadians who perish from them annually is far smaller still. As such, it is unclear why the court struck down sections 241(b) and 14 in the manner that it did instead of declaring those sections void for that limited class of individuals demonstrably at risk of physical incapacitation. In other words, if the criminal prohibitions on assisted suicide and euthanasia violated the section 7 rights of the physically incapacitated and those facing imminent physical incapacitation, then the proper scope of the legal remedy would seem to be that of allowing assisted suicide and euthanasia for people in those situations. Instead, the court opted to strike down these laws for a far broader class: namely, any competent consenting adult with a grievous and irremediable medical condition that he or she finds intolerable. One might argue, of course, that the court's vastly broader remedy is superior on moral grounds: perhaps there is an inherent right to die, and/or perhaps the values of autonomy and self-integrity justify the legalization of assisted suicide and euthanasia. Nevertheless, the reason provided by the court (securing the rights to life, liberty, and security of the person for those at risk of imminent physical incapacitation) is unsuited to the actual remedy that it laid down.

Furthermore, the Supreme Court seems to have adopted as a working principle something akin to the following: *If the government's doing or prohibiting something is realistically liable to drive a small class of individuals to suicide, then that government action or prohibition infringes the section 7 right to life.* Adoption of this principle could have untoward results. For instance, a small percentage of people who face lengthy prison sentences kill themselves before going to prison, or kill themselves while in prison, because they cannot bear the thought of spending twenty years there. This is a demonstrable fact, well known to criminologists and legislators: Lengthy prison sentences drive some people to commit suicide. Does that mean lengthy prison sentences are unconstitutional? One might reply that the law does infringe the section 7 right to life but that the infringement is necessary for the broader public good and is consistent with the principles of fundamental justice (precisely because the offenders are guilty of serious crimes). Perhaps. But has not something gone awry with a legal doctrine that would lead one to think that lengthy imprisonment for serious crimes (for, say, murder or rape) could be seen as infringing in any way an offender's right to life? Keown (2014, p. 17), in his initial published critique of the Supreme Court of British Columbia's ruling by Justice Smith, raises a related worry regarding the larger implications of such a principle: "And if this plaintiff is able to invoke the right to life against the law prohibiting assisted suicide, could another plaintiff invoke it against a law prohibiting assisting female genital mutilation, on the ground that she would rather kill herself than not be able to obtain assistance to mutilate her genitals?" The example, though gruesome, is hardly fanciful. In some cultures, the demand that women undergo cliterodectomy or even infibulation is pressing, and such mutilations are regarded as a moral or even religious imperative. Women in these oppressive social contexts routinely risk their lives to undergo them.

It became apparent later from some of the public debates and lower-court challenges emerging since *Carter v Canada* that the high court's stated legal remedy is multiply ambiguous. The language of "grievous and irremediable medical condition (including an illness, disease or disability)" does not specify whether physical conditions alone are to be included or whether mental illnesses qualify as well. I would argue that an earlier portion of the ruling (see the highlighted passage in the citation from p. 384–385) indicates that the Supreme Court rejected the claim that legalization of assisted death would lead to its availability for the mentally ill and thus indicates that the court intended at least implicitly to limit availability to those suffering from physical conditions. Still, this ought to have been made clearer; certainly, an explicit ruling out of psychiatric conditions in the statement of remedy on page 390 would have prevented the subsequent confusion about precisely this question.[45]

Another reason that the ruling does not allow for assisted death for the legally competent mentally ill is that mental illnesses will not meet the criterion of irremediability, on a properly stringent understanding of that criterion. Since *Carter v Canada*, two presidents of the Canadian Psychiatric Association (CPA) have spoken out on this. Kirkey (2015a) reports the views of President Padraic Carr:

> After practising for generations to prevent suicide, psychiatrists across Canada could soon be asked to help some people kill themselves ... "I have been approached by many psychiatrists who have serious concerns about physician assisted death being applied to mental illnesses," said Dr. Padraic Carr, president of the Canadian Psychiatric Association and a professor of psychiatry at the University of Alberta. "Legal definitions are extremely important here," he said. *Remediable* could be defined as treatable, or curable. In psychiatry, he said, "complete cures are quite rare." Most treatments are directed at relieving symptoms. "If *remediable* implies a cure, then almost all psychiatric illnesses could be considered *irremediable*," he said. If, on the other hand, *remediable* is defined as treatable, most psychiatric illnesses wouldn't meet the standard, "because there are almost always treatment options we can try," Carr said. *Intolerable* and *enduring* suffering are also problematic.

Carr's successor as president of the CPA, K. Sonu Gaind (2016), argued in a similar fashion, writing the following in an opinion piece published in the *Globe and Mail:*

Assessing irremediability in mental illness is very difficult. In neurodegen-erative diseases with continued decline, irremediability can confidently be predicted. Not so with mental illness; in most cases, we can't say when there is no chance of improvement. Remediability goes beyond biomedical symp-toms. Social isolation, underemployment, poverty or lack of housing all have an impact on the suffering from mental illness. It may be more a societal question, but the question is, at what point are these irremediable? These concerns aren't academic: In the Netherlands, most of the people receiving a medically assisted death for psychiatric conditions cited depres-sion and unresolved loneliness. The Canadian Psychiatric Association has cautioned that there is no established standard of care in Canada for defin-ing when typical psychiatric conditions are irremediable. We are not alone in struggling with this. I have spoken with leaders of psychiatric associ-ations from Australia, New Zealand, the United Kingdom and the United States, and none is any further ahead at defining this.

Given these difficulties and ambiguities, the most plausible legal interpreta-tion of *Carter v Canada* on this issue is to maintain that it does not open the door to assisted death for the legally competent mentally ill. In the interven-ing few years, other Canadian legal and medical scholars have sought to buttress the case for this claim.[46] Others disagree, however, and this issue might be the subject of future legal adjudication.[47]

The Supreme Court also could have been clearer on the operative under-standing of "consent." Debate has emerged regarding the legality of advanced directives – for example, cases in which someone facing descent into dementia signs an order requesting assisted death after the dementia has taken hold, at which point the person will no longer be legally competent. Moreover, it is not obvious that consent is a sufficiently strict criterion in the present context. The ruling appears to count the following two scenarios equally as instances of consent. First, the dying patient requests MAID from his family physician, with no prompting from that physician, or from family members, all of whom attempt to dissuade the individual from following through on his request. Second, the dying patient reluctantly agrees to undergo MAID after his family physician brought it up as an option repeat-edly over several months and after being strongly encouraged to consider

MAID by multiple close family members. Legally, both scenarios count as consent, provided that the patient meets criteria for legal competence. But might not this show that, when it comes to MAID, a criterion more robust than consent ought to be put in place?

This is debatable, of course, and one might reply that any attempt to tighten up the criteria here smacks of an objectionable paternalism and/or a lack of faith in the autonomy of the severely ill (i.e., a lack of faith in their ability to make rational decisions and evaluate arguments for and against receiving MAID). Moreover, given that MAID is now legal, what legal grounds could there be for objecting to a physician or family member suggesting (indeed repeatedly *encouraging*) a patient to receive it, provided that such attempts do not involve threats of force or other means that would meet existing legal criteria for coercion? Yet those inclined to oppose MAID in the first place might see the latter point as providing further indication that there is indeed a risk here of a slippery slope, insofar as legalized MAID will make it difficult to prevent the practice of persuading the dying to terminate their lives early, in cases in which they might not have requested it otherwise (i.e., absent the persuasion). Indeed, legalized MAID seemingly *guarantees* that such persuasion is legally unobjectionable. What could be problematic legally about suggesting to someone that she perform a legal activity or repeatedly attempting to persuade that individual (through rational argument) to perform that legal activity in the event that she seems to be reluctant initially?

Relatedly, the Supreme Court's acceptance of Justice Smith's interpretation of the new empirical data on safeguards is also questionable. Scholarly opinion regarding the efficacy of these safeguards remains divided. And, if one maintains that MAID for the mentally ill is morally and/or legally insupportable, then the fact that it is now legal and increasingly routine in Belgium, the Netherlands, and Switzerland should give one pause. Furthermore, the court assessed these safeguards in a medical context that undergoes frequent changes, some of which might prove to be crucial to issues of consent and coercion. For example, at the moment, the most common method of MAID the world over is the administration of lethal doses of certain medications, whether orally or intravenously. However, if that method is abandoned in favour of death by organ removal (with the organs then used for transplantation),[48] then subtle pressure on patients might increase and with it the risk of coercion and abuse. These might be grounds for future court challenges of *Carter v Canada* as the relevant empirical facts change.

It is important to observe as well that, in striking down sections 241(b) and 14 of the Criminal Code as infringing on a fundamental right, the Supreme Court established at best a negative right to MAID. It manifestly did not establish it as a positive right, with the state thereby obliged to provide it to patients who meet the necessary criteria. Nothing in this ruling obliges provinces to fund assisted death, and nothing implies that the failure to do so would put a province in contravention of the *Canada Health Act*'s requirement to fund medically necessary services.

Finally, it is worth recalling the legislative change that opened the door to *Carter v Canada:* namely, the decriminalization of attempted suicide in 1972. This change, undertaken with the most laudable of humanitarian motives, ended up weakening the legal authority of the state to discourage suicide – weakening it to the point where the Supreme Court of Canada could declare that a prohibition on assisted suicide infringes the right to life. Regardless of whether this resulting shift was proper and necessary (as proponents of MAID will maintain, not without reason), it will surely go down in Canadian history as one of the more striking examples of the law of unintended consequences.

2

Developments in Law and Policy since the Ruling

My aim in this chapter is to provide a concise overview of some important developments since *Carter v Canada*. In the first section, I lay out the reaction of the Conservative government of Stephen Harper in the immediate aftermath of the ruling, up to that government's defeat in the October 2015 federal election. In the following section, I examine how the Liberal government of Justin Trudeau dealt with the ruling, focusing in particular on the belated passage of Bill C-14 and the ongoing debate about its constitutionality. This section concludes with an important court ruling in Quebec striking down a key provision of the bill in the fall of 2019 and some further developments thereafter. In the final section, I look briefly at some representative responses from provincial governments, especially the Quebec government's passage of its own independent MAID legislation and the court battles in Ontario about freedom of conscience for physicians.

The Initial Reaction of the Federal Conservative Government

The justice minister at the time, Peter MacKay, put out an initial statement emphasizing the government's intention to review carefully the decision (which came down on February 6, 2015). He declined to respond to reporters' questions about whether the government might consider invoking the notwithstanding clause to overrule the court.[1] Subsequent reporting on the matter has not clarified whether that option was ever explored seriously by the Conservatives. After this initial reaction, the public heard very little from the government regarding how it intended to proceed. Given that it had been granted only twelve months to develop any new legislation (twelve months being the amount of time that the court suspended its judgment), perhaps it is surprising that nothing further was heard publicly from the government until July 17, 2015, when MacKay and Minister of Health Rona Ambrose announced that an expert panel had been formed to consider options for legislation and to consult with the public. The three-person panel consisted of Harvey Chochinov, Canada Research Chair in palliative care (also an expert witness for the government in the 2012 *Carter v Canada* case before the Supreme Court of British Columbia); Catherine Frazee, professor of disability studies at Ryerson University (who likewise served as an expert witness for the government in that case); and Benoit Pelletier, professor of constitutional law at the University of Ottawa. The intention was to have the panel report back to the government in the fall, possibly after the October federal election. The panel's mandate included examination of the methods to be used in MAID, the precise requirements for eligibility, and the best ways to safeguard freedom of conscience and religion for physicians who objected to the practice.[2]

In the wake of the panel's formation, the Harper government remained mostly silent on the issue, perhaps hoping to hold off on dealing with a controversial matter until after the federal election of October 19, 2015. As it turned out, of course, that election would see a new party and prime minister assume power and with it the responsibility of responding to *Carter v Canada*.

The Reaction of the Federal Liberal Government

On December 11, 2015, the new Liberal government passed a motion to form a special multi-party parliamentary committee on MAID, to consist of MPs as well as Senate representatives. Similar to the three-person expert panel that the Harper government had formed (which submitted its report in December 2016, after which it apparently had no further input with the new government), the intention was to conduct public consultations with stakeholders and to form recommendations for new legislation on assisted death. As of early January, however, no MP had actually been assigned to the committee, and the government formally requested an extension from the Supreme Court of Canada, asking that its suspension of *Carter v Canada* continue for an additional six months beyond the original deadline – that is, August 6, 2016, instead of February 6, 2016.[3]

In response, the Supreme Court granted the government a four-month extension, to June 6. That decision by the court was unanimous, but in a 5–4 split decision the court likewise granted Quebec an exemption during that interim permitting it to continue the implementation of its own legislation on assisted death, Bill 52 (which took effect in December 2015). For the rest of the country, anyone who wished to receive assisted death could seek a court order from a judge in the relevant provincial or territorial superior court.[4] Many such court orders were sought and granted across multiple provinces.[5]

The multi-party committee having completed its work, the Liberal government tabled draft legislation on April 14, 2016, the first draft of Bill C-14. The result of much contentious debate within that committee, the bill proposed to permit not only physicians but also nurse practitioners and pharmacists to participate in assisted suicide and voluntary active euthanasia. However, it added a notable restriction: namely, the procedure was to be permitted only for those whose "natural death has become reasonably foreseeable." This appeared to limit the availability of assisted death to those suffering from a terminal ailment, though it provided no further guidance regarding precisely how proximate the foreseeable death needed to be (unlike assisted death legislation in Oregon, for instance, which declares that the individual must have six months or less to live). The draft law was thus arguably narrower in scope than what had been laid down in the legal remedy prescribed by the Supreme Court in *Carter v Canada*. It was also much narrower in scope than what the multi-party committee had favoured; that majority-Liberal committee had recommended explicitly permitting assisted death for the legally competent mentally ill as well as for mature minors and the legally incompetent who had signed advanced directives before becoming incompetent (e.g., dementia patients). As such, the constitutionality of Bill C-14 was a matter of controversy from the outset, with the BC Civil Liberties Association (one of the plaintiffs in *Carter v Canada*) putting out a public statement saying that the draft bill was incompatible with the court's ruling. Minister of Justice Jody Wilson-Raybould noted that the issue of assisted death for the mentally ill, and the other contested issues, could be revisited in the future, but the key short-term goal was to pass the legislation before the June 6 deadline.[6]

After further and acrimonious debate in the House of Commons, the bill eventually passed there, yet its full passage into law was delayed by the Senate, which vowed to amend the bill in significant respects to bring it more closely in line with the legal remedy prescribed in *Carter v Canada*. Consequently, the June 6 deadline laid down by the Supreme Court passed while the legislation was still being studied in the Senate, leaving the stated provisions in *Carter v Canada* as the effective law of the land regarding assisted death. However, that state of affairs was not long permitted to continue. Intense pressure was placed on the Senate to compromise and pass a somewhat amended bill that still included the crucial provision at the centre of the controversy: namely, the restriction of assisted death to those for whom natural death was reasonably foreseeable. Bill C-14 received royal assent on June 17, 2016.

Its principal provisions can be summarized briefly as follows:

- "Medical assistance in dying" encompasses both assisted suicide and euthanasia. Provided that the proper criteria are met, assisting someone in dying, in either manner, will carry no criminal culpability for physicians or nurse practitioners or for any third party assisting those health-care professionals in the task. Pharmacists are similarly indemnified from their participation by way of writing prescriptions for the relevant medications used in these procedures.

- Providing information about assisted death will likewise not be subject to criminal culpability, at least for a broad range of health-care professionals: "For greater certainty, no social worker, psychologist, psychiatrist, therapist, medical practitioner, nurse practitioner or other health care professional commits an offence if they provide information to a person on the lawful provision of medical assistance in dying."[7]

- Criteria for receiving assisted death consist of being legally eligible to receive health services funded by a Canadian province or territory;[8] being at least eighteen years of age and legally competent; having made a formal request for assisted death without having been coerced to do so; and suffering from a grievous and irremediable medical condition, experienced by individuals only when

- they have a serious and incurable illness, disease or disability; (b) they are in an advanced state of irreversible decline in capability; (c) that illness, disease or disability or that state of decline causes them enduring physical or psychological suffering that is intolerable to them and that cannot be relieved under conditions that they consider acceptable; and (d) their natural death has become reasonably foreseeable, taking into account all of their medical circumstances, without a prognosis necessarily having been made as to the specific length of time that they have remaining.[9]

- Requisite safeguards include the individual's having to request assisted death in writing before two independent witnesses (neither of whom can knowingly be a financial beneficiary of the individual); that at least one other independent physician or nurse practitioner has verified that the criteria for legal eligibility are met;[10] and that there be a ten-day waiting period between the signing of the request and the termination of life, except in cases in which the two medical professionals "are both of the opinion that the person's death, or the loss of their capacity to provide informed consent, is imminent – any shorter period that the first medical practitioner or nurse practitioner considers appropriate in the circumstances."[11]
- Medical professionals who carry out an assisted death knowingly in breach of any of the requisite safeguards are "guilty of an offence and … liable (a) on conviction on indictment, to a term of imprisonment of not more than five years; or (b) on summary conviction, to a term of imprisonment of not more than 18 months"[12]
- Provincial and territorial governments are responsible for decisions regarding the funding of assisted death,[13] whereas the federal minister of health, in consultation with provincial and territorial authorities, is responsible for setting forth standards concerning information collection and storage, including whether and how assisted death is to be indicated on death certificates.[14]

As noted above, one of the key items of dispute pertaining to the bill involved the definition of "grievous and irremediable" as incorporating the reasonable foreseeability of natural death, in consequence of which various court challenges quickly ensued in multiple provinces. The first out of the gate was British Columbia, with the BC Civil Liberties Association mounting such a challenge just eleven days after the passage of Bill C-14. It filed a suit in the BC Superior Court challenging the law's constitutionality, precisely on the ground that the reasonable foreseeability requirement violated the Charter.[15] Other challenges followed in Ontario and Quebec, culminating in the September 2019 Quebec Superior Court decision mentioned in the introduction, in which Justice Christine Baudouin struck down the "reasonably foreseeable" provision of Bill C-14. She argued that it violated sections 7 and 15 of the Charter, and she made the same determination with respect to Quebec's prior legislation on MAID, which had restricted euthanasia to those at the "end of life."[16] Her ruling came down just as the fall 2019 federal election campaign was about to begin, and predictably it became a point of contention in that campaign, with Liberal

Prime Minister Justin Trudeau promising to let the ruling stand and Conservative Leader of the Opposition Andrew Scheer promising to appeal it.[17] With Trudeau's victory, and the active support of MAID by the New Democratic Party (whose votes on the matter might be necessary to push through amendments to Bill C-14, given that the Liberals now hold a minority government), the original "reasonably foreseeable death" provision of the bill is likely to be overturned. (Regarding relevant amendments via Bill C-7, please see the updated information provided on page 156, note 5.)

Developments at the Provincial Level

The government of Quebec had already put forward its own legislation pertaining to assisted death, maintaining that it possessed the legal authority to do so since health care was under provincial jurisdiction. Its Bill 52 came into force on June 5, 2014, prior to the ruling in *Carter v Canada*.[18] Its provisions, in certain respects, were more restrictive than those eventually laid down in *Carter*, notably in restricting assisted death to those at the "end of life" (a provision since overturned by the Quebec Superior Court, as noted above). Yet it also laid down that all provincially funded hospitals and nursing homes must offer the service, and it required that physicians who refuse to carry out the procedure provide referrals to those who will. By January 16, 2016, provincial officials were already confirming the first deaths under the new law.[19]

Meanwhile, the first recorded assisted death outside Quebec occurred in early March 2016 when a Calgary woman suffering from ALS obtained a court order permitting the procedure. However, she was unable apparently to find a physician in Alberta willing to perform the procedure, so she had to travel to British Columbia to receive a lethal injection.[20] After the passage of Bill C-14, these provincial court exemptions ceased of course.

As provinces and territories formulated policies regarding assisted death individually, there was a shared source of guidance in the form of the Provincial-Territorial Expert Advisory Group on Physician-Assisted Dying, whose final report was released on November 30, 2015. This advisory group had been formed in the summer of 2015 among eleven provinces and territories (excluding Quebec) and developed a set of recommendations for the conduct of assisted death. Some of them were mirrored in Bill C-14 (e.g., that not only physicians but also nurse practitioners be permitted to participate). Notable among the recommendations *not* explicitly included in Bill C-14 were the following pertaining to public funding: "All provinces and territories should ensure access to physician-assisted dying, including both physician-administered and self-administered physician-assisted dying ... Provinces and territories should require all regional health authorities to have an effective publicly-funded care coordination system in place to ensure patient access to physician-assisted dying ... Provincial/territorial governments should publicly fund physician-assisted dying" (p. 5).[21] The advisory group also recommended that health professionals who object on moral grounds to participation nonetheless be required to refer patients for assisted death:

> Conscientiously objecting health care providers should be required to inform patients of all end-of-life options, including physician-assisted dying, regardless of their personal beliefs ... Conscientiously objecting health care providers should be required to either provide a referral or a direct transfer of care to another health care provider or to contact a third party and transfer the patient's records (p. 9).

Subsequently, policies on these and other points have been worked out differently from one province and territory to the next, being formulated in part by relevant provincial professional associations and by provincial health ministries. Ontario, for example, went much the same route as Quebec on the referral requirement, with the College of Physicians and Surgeons of Ontario (CPSO) requiring that all members with a conscientious objection to performing MAID themselves nonetheless be willing to make effective referrals to colleagues providing the service. The constitutionality of this requirement was challenged in Ontario provincial court by a team of plaintiffs consisting of five individual physicians and three medical NGOs, who argued that the requirement violated physicians' Charter-guaranteed rights of conscience. However, in a January 30, 2018, ruling, the divisional court ruled in favour of the CPSO.[22] The plaintiffs filed an appeal to the Ontario Court of Appeal, which in a decision of May 15, 2019, also ruled in favour of the CPSO.[23] This issue at present varies to some degree from one province to the next.[24] It will likely be the subject of further provincial court challenges and possibly at some point a Supreme Court case.

Clearly, the constitutional status of Bill C-14 remains a matter of some contention, on multiple fronts, and issues remain to be adjudicated at the provincial level. I will examine some of these legal and policy issues in Chapters 5–8. I turn next to the moral controversies surrounding MAID.

3

Background to the Moral Debate over MAID

The ethics literature on assisted suicide and voluntary active euthanasia (jointly referred to here as medical assistance in dying or MAID) is substantial.[1] It is also highly diverse; a wide variety of arguments has been employed by each side of the debate, and various philosophical and theological perspectives have served to underlie those arguments. Consequently, it is difficult to provide a concise overview of this material, and it is more difficult still to make any progress on such well-trodden ground. However, one should attempt both tasks – the former because, for those unfamiliar with these debates, the size and diversity of the existing literature render a short, up-to-date introduction useful; the latter because there are in fact some areas of discussion that have received relatively little attention in the existing literature (e.g., the ethics of public funding for MAID). There are even some long-standing arguments that, in my view, could use some additional explication and defence. In the next several chapters, then, I will attempt both to provide an accessible introduction to core existing arguments for and against MAID and to make some new points.

In this chapter, however, I present a review of background ideas in ethics relevant to the arguments for and against MAID. It is intended for a general audience; ethicists working their way through the book will already be familiar with this chapter's material.

The chapter is divided up as follows: the first section covers some of the major competing views of the nature of human well-being; the second section does so for some of the major competing options in ethical theory. All of this is a necessary preliminary to the focused discussion of the ethics of MAID in later chapters, for certain arguments for and against euthanasia and assisted suicide are rooted in differences in underlying theoretical commitments.

There is a long-standing dispute among philosophers concerning the proper relationship between abstract ethical theory and debate on real-world moral problems. Although some hold that the key to resolving disagreements about the latter lies in reaching consensus about the former, others maintain that debate about concrete moral problems can and should be conducted independently of more theoretical issues. Those who advocate for the independence of concrete moral debate often do so on account of an underlying pessimism about our ability to attain demonstrable truths at the level of high moral theory (e.g., about the nature of human well-being or the ultimate grounds of moral obligation). I cannot attempt to adjudicate here this background dispute about proper methodology in applied ethics.[2] Suffice it to say that, in the applied ethics literature on MAID, some argue on the basis of explicitly stated theoretical commitments, whereas others develop arguments intended to be plausible independent of such commitments. Since I wish to provide the reader with an accessible introduction to a reasonably representative array of arguments for and against MAID, I should be prepared to summarize arguments made both by those who proceed using the first method and by those who proceed using the second. And the best way to fulfill the first part of that task is to provide the reader with an introduction to some of the major accounts of human well-being and some of the major ethical theories. Insofar as some ethical theories historically have had close ties to theological commitments, I will conclude the chapter with some brief observations on the relationship between ethics and religion.

Overview of Major Theories of Human Well-Being

Of what does human well-being consist? To help clarify the question, consider the so-called crib test: you are looking at your newborn baby in her crib. What hopes do you have for her? Perhaps you desire that she live a useful life, that she accomplish positive things for society. But that is not all you desire. After all, there are cases of people who make valuable contributions to society but are nonetheless miserable. So, presumably, you also desire that your child have a life that is good not just for society but also *for her.* But exactly what should you desire when you desire that? In other words, what would a good life for her actually involve? That is the question that theories of human well-being (sometimes referred to as theories of human happiness) set out to answer. Finding the correct answer is clearly important, both in and of itself (surely we all want to know what it really means to live a life that is good for the person living it) and because commitments here carry further implications both for ethical theory and for applied ethics.

There are four main types of theory concerning the nature of human well-being: hedonism, desire satisfaction theory (also known as desire fulfillment theory), objective list theory, and perfectionism. There are also hybrid views that combine elements of more than one theory. Let us briefly look at each of the four and some of the well-known arguments for and against each.[3]

According to *hedonism*, the only thing that contributes to human well-being is the experience of pleasure, and the only thing that detracts from human well-being is the experience of pain. Thus, a life that, on the whole, is a good one for the person living it is a life in which the total amount of pleasure exceeds the total amount of pain, and a supremely good life presumably would be a life in which the experience of pleasure is maximized and in which there is no pain. Which kinds of pain and pleasure matter? Here we encounter a division between different versions of hedonism: *sensory hedonism* and *attitudinal hedonism*. In the former, well-being consists solely of the experience of sensory pleasure and the avoidance of sensory pain. In the latter, well-being consists solely of pleasurable psychological states, which might or might not be associated with sensory pleasure and in fact be compatible with the experience of sensory pain. Although there is much to be said for each version, the latter might seem, at least prima facie, to be more plausible, insofar as it accords better with the common experience of sacrificing sensory pleasures in favour of attitudinal pleasures. That people are often willing to do so, and that we often consider them rational in making that choice, appears to indicate that we think attitudinal pleasures can contribute to human well-being. (Think, for instance, of the marathon runner who experiences great sensory pain but whose emotional joy at victory seems to outweigh that pain.) Accordingly, I will restrict my attention to attitudinal hedonism.

Here are two points in favour of this theory. First, it has a definite intuitive appeal, based on the important role that pleasure seems to have in well-being. People whose lives seem to be going well are typically (always?) people who derive much enjoyment from their lives, in particular more enjoyment than suffering. Indeed, one of the things that renders clinical depression so pernicious is that it robs its sufferer of pleasure – outwardly, the depressed individual's life might seem to be filled with good things (e.g., loving family, useful work, social prominence), yet (perhaps because of a malfunction of brain chemistry that makes the individual incapable of experiencing pleasure from those good things) her life might not be a good one for her. Second, attitudinal hedonism permits a great deal of diversity in specifying how one fleshes out a good life and thus is open to tolerant variation from person to person. Whatever gives one pleasure will properly be regarded as enhancing one's well-being, whether that is reading Shakespeare or playing hockey or learning a new language (or, for that matter, moderate heroin use).

Here are a few points against this theory. First, pleasure might be important for well-being, but one can argue that it is implausible to maintain that it is the *only* thing that counts toward well-being. Think of the well-known example of the deceived businessman. Call him Phil. Say Phil takes great pleasure from his life. He enjoys his work and the company of his wife and children, loves watching sunsets, and so on. Moreover, his life is basically devoid of serious pain. It seems that, in attitudinal hedonism, his level of well-being is extremely high. But let us say that Phil is being persistently and systematically deceived in important ways: his wife and children actually despise him, his co-workers mock him behind his back, his job (which he believes to be important and socially useful) is actually a mob front, et cetera. Now, in evaluating attitudinal hedonism, the question is not "would Phil be better off knowing the truth, even if it would fill his life with pain and anguish?" Maybe he would be, maybe he would not be. Rather, the relevant question for the hedonist is the following: "Wouldn't Phil be *at least a bit better off* in a hypothetical situation in which his pleasure quotient is identical to what he actually has but in which his family *really* loves him, his co-workers *really* respect him, and his boss *is not* actually a mafioso, et cetera?" Because the attitudinal hedonist is committed to claiming that pleasure is the only thing that counts toward happiness, he is committed to the seemingly implausible claim that Phil's life is going equally well in both scenarios.

Second, and closely related to the previous argument (possibly just a different version of the same point), is the much-discussed "experience machine" objection. Imagine that you are offered the chance at a long life reliably filled with nothing but great pleasures and wholly devoid of any pain. The only catch is that it would be a fake life. You are offered the chance to plug your consciousness into a computer simulation – you will not realize that you are living in a simulation, so that fact will not trouble you. (Your memory of agreeing to plug in will be erased, say.) Would you plug yourself in? And, more importantly, do you think that a person plugged into this machine and a person living an equivalently pleasant life in the real world (with pleasures derived from real friends and family members and climbing real mountains, etc.) have *equally* good lives? The attitudinal hedonist is committed to the claim that, as long as the amount of pleasure is equivalent, so is the level of well-being.

Third, person A is freely living a life of much continual pleasure and no pain. Person B is living with the same amount of pleasure, but all of his thoughts and actions (unknown to him) are being remotely determined by scientists manipulating his brain waves as part of a mind-control experiment. The attitudinal hedonist is committed to claiming that persons A and B are living lives that are equally good for them. But to some that seems to be false. Freedom might seem to be important to well-being, over and above pleasure, such that a freely lived pleasant life is better than an externally controlled pleasant life.

Fourth, person A is freely living a life of continual, reliable, great pleasure and no pain. Person B is also freely living a life of continual, reliable, great pleasure and no pain. Suppose that the quantity of pleasure experienced by persons A and B during their lives is identical. But person A is a morally upright individual with all of the important virtues and few vices, whereas person B is a moral reprobate. Are their lives equally good for them? The question now is not: "Would your life be better for you if you were a virtuous person suffering greatly or if you were a vicious person continually experiencing great pleasures?" Instead, it is: "Would your life be better for you if you were a virtuous person leading a life filled with pleasure or if you were a vicious person leading a life filled with the same amount of pleasure?" For the attitudinal hedonist, good character contributes nothing to a person's well-being – again, all that counts is pleasure. The jerk and the saint are living lives equally good for them, provided that the pleasure they experience is equivalent. Some readers might find this counterintuitive.

Much more can be said for and against hedonism.[4] The latter set of objections has prompted some critics to develop hybrid theories of well-being in which it is not pleasure per se that wholly determines the level of well-being but freely acquired pleasure, or virtuously acquired pleasure, or non-deceitful pleasure, et cetera. The disadvantage of such hybridization, from the perspective of the traditional hedonist, is the prospect of watering down the theory to the point where it might look more like an objective list theory – that is, a theory of well-being built on a diverse set of goods, of which pleasure is only one.

Let us turn now to the next major option, *desire satisfaction theory (DST)*. The basic idea behind versions of this theory is that well-being consists solely of getting what you want: that is, your welfare is enhanced when you satisfy a desire and lessened when a desire is frustrated. There are two main versions of the theory: *actualist DST* (according to which your life is going well for you to the extent that you are getting what you actually want) versus *hypothetical DST* (according to which your life is going well for you to the extent that you are getting what you *would* want if you were fully rational and well-informed).[5]

Here are two points in favour of DST, in either version. First, it is intuitively plausible to think that desire satisfaction plays an important role in well-being. We tend to think that life is not going well for people whose principal projects and goals are continually frustrated. Second, the theory sidesteps some of the problems faced by hedonism. For instance, DST claims that, if your desire is to climb Mount Everest, then your well-being is more greatly enhanced by actually achieving that goal than by plugging yourself into a computer simulation in which you can fake-climb it and experience the equivalent amount of pleasure.

Here are some points against actualist DST. First, sometimes getting what you want apparently decreases rather than enhances your well-being. My well-being will be decreased by my eating nothing but jelly beans, because doing so will damage my health. That plausibly remains true even if I happen not to care about my health, indeed even if I desire (for some reason) to damage my health. Along similar lines, sometimes getting something that you *do not* actually want *enhances* your well-being. Second, it is possible to desire silly or base things, and it is plausible to think that the satisfaction of such desires does not really enhance well-being. To take a well-known example, I might desire to count all the blades of grass in a certain soccer field, but the fulfillment of that desire plausibly does not really enhance my well-being. More realistically, consider the person with obsessive-compulsive disorder who has a strong desire to wash her hands continually. It might seem to be counterintuitive to think that indulging her illness by satisfying that desire really enhances her well-being.

Those common criticisms help to move some DST advocates toward the hypothetical version of the theory; after all, were I a perfectly rational, well-informed person, I would not desire an all-jelly-bean diet, nor would I desire to count blades of grass. *But there are also worries facing hypothetical DST.* Say that you obtain all that the fully rational, well-informed version of yourself would want (balanced diet, meaningful work, loving family, etc.), but as a matter of fact you do not actually want any of those things. Are you leading a life that is genuinely good for you? Would your life not be even better if you both achieved all of those things and actually wanted to achieve them?

As with the previous theory, one common response in the face of such criticisms is effectively to hybridize DST, such that well-being is posited as consisting not just of satisfying one's desires (actual or hypothetical or both) but also of satisfying those desires when they are for genuinely fulfilling things, with the task then being to specify just what counts as genuinely fulfilling. And, similarly, a worry about such hybridization, from the perspective of a DST purist, is that it will have been transformed into a version of objective list theory.[6]

Both hedonism and DST are monistic theories: that is, they posit that one and only one thing counts toward human well-being. In contrast, most versions of *objective list theory (OLT)* are pluralistic: well-being consists of the acquisition/achievement of many different sorts of goods. What sorts of goods might go onto such a list? Well, pleasure and desire satisfaction might legitimately be included, and they are by some OLT proponents. But many other things might be included as well, commonly liberty (personal, political, etc.), meaningful work, family, friends, health, virtuous character, education, religious faith/relationship with God (in religious versions of OLT), political participation, appreciation of great art, and so on.

Here are some points in favour of OLT. First, it sidesteps the principal objections facing attitudinal hedonism and DST. Second, provided that one's list is well constructed, OLT seems to carry a good deal of intuitive appeal.

Here are some points against OLT. First, what if there is disagreement over exactly what should go on the list? How are disputes about this to be adjudicated? Second, OLT seems to be incomplete by itself until one finds a way of ranking entries on the list such that one can manage conflicts. Ideally, a theory of well-being should provide guidance through such conflicts. For example, if your circumstances are such that the good of meaningful work blocks your having a large family or prevents you from furthering your education, then how are you to decide which good to pursue? OLT by itself does not seem to give such guidance. Third, and relatedly, another question left unanswered by OLT is just what the common denominator is linking the items on the list. That is, OLT by itself does not tell us *why* something enhances our well-being. What is the common denominator behind the seemingly diverse goods of education, virtue, relationship with God, et cetera, such that they are all genuinely good for us? Of course, that question assumes that there is such a common denominator, which in fact is open to dispute. Still, if such a common denominator could be found, then it might help in the construction of a rational ranking of goods and in the management of conflicts between them.

Those worries facing OLT, though hardly decisive against it,[7] have helped to motivate the fourth sort of theory, known as *perfectionism*. According to perfectionism, there is a common denominator uniting the various goods enumerated in OLT: the fulfillment of one's natural capacities. So, for the perfectionist, well-being consists of exercising the capacities definitive of the sort of thing one is. (The old US Army recruitment slogan "Be All That You Can Be" has overtones of perfectionism, implying that it is good for a person to fulfill her potential as a human being.) What sorts of capacities are definitive of human beings? Certainly, we possess a wide range of abilities, some of which we share with other sorts of animals. For example, we have biological capacities for carrying out metabolic functions, for movement, for experiencing basic emotions of fear and anger, for experiencing sensory pleasure, for engaging in reproduction, et cetera. These capacities are shared with other animals, and fulfilling them is indeed generally good for us, just as it is for other animals. Correspondingly, being prevented from fulfilling these capacities is generally bad for us and likewise for other animals. (A tiger kept in a small cage, which badly restricts its movements, is living a life that is worse for it than a tiger that can run about freely in the jungle; a tiger in captivity that never gets a chance to mate is living a life worse for it than a tiger in the wild that gets to mate, etc.) But we tend to think that capacities that we share with other animals, though important, are not our *highest* capacities and that fulfilling only the lower-level capacities is not sufficient for human well-being. Rather, a good life for humans also requires fulfilling our higher capacities for rational thought and free choice.

According to advocates of perfectionism, this notion of fulfilling human potential not only explains why various items listed as good for us by OLT theorists should be listed but also provides rational grounds for ordering those goods in a particular way. For instance, OLT theorists will often include education or knowledge acquisition on the list of goods. Perfectionists will agree that education is good for us, but they will add that what makes education good for us is that it helps us to fulfill our potential as human beings: namely, by fulfilling our intellectual capacities. The perfectionist can also explain why we tend to view education as a more important item on the list than, say, gourmet food. Enjoying one's meals is good and fulfills our capacities for nutrition and enjoying sensory pleasure. But these are not distinctively human capacities, and fulfilling them is not as important as fulfilling the capacity for knowledge acquisition or aesthetic appreciation or other capacities tied to rationality and freedom. Thus, we admire the university student who lives mostly on Ramen noodles in order to save money for textbooks or the "starving artist" who sacrifices some meals in order to have more resources available to fulfill her potential as a painter.

So one way to rank goods is to rank them based on whether they fulfill distinctively human capacities or those shared with lower animals. Another arguably compatible method of ranking employed by perfectionists is to rank goods according to their status as necessary conditions for other goods. Thus, though we admire the "starving artist" who sacrifices some meals to buy paints, we would consider foolish and imprudent an artist who *literally* starved herself to death in order to buy paints. A dead artist cannot paint. So biological life itself, and correspondingly the fulfillment of those capacities necessary for biological life (the capacity for nutrition and so on), can be seen as *foundational* goods that must be in place in order to fulfill various other goods. Thus, it is arguably the case that life itself will rank highly in any perfectionist list of human goods. (Whether it must rank more highly than any other good is a matter of dispute among perfectionists. Might it not make sense to sacrifice one's life for a noble cause or to preserve one's virtue or dignity? This will be crucial, of course, for the debate over MAID. Similarly, the question of whether biological life itself is an intrinsic good or whether it is merely an instrumental good – that is, a necessary condition for the realization of other goods – will be important.)

Within psychology, Maslow's famous "hierarchy of needs" carries perfectionist overtones and recognizes a comparable dual-ranking method. Thus, the realization of lower-order goods such as food and shelter and security is obviously important and foundational for the realization of other goods. Yet a life that realized only such goods would not really be a happy life. Plausibly, the goods of friendship and knowledge and artistic appreciation and romantic love, and so on, are higher and, in a sense, ultimately more important for human happiness. The fulfillment of lower goods can be seen as instrumental (though perhaps not *merely* instrumental) to the fulfillment of higher goods.[8]

Here are some points in favour of perfectionism. First, it sidesteps the principal objections facing attitudinal hedonism and DST. This is an advantage that it shares with OLT. Second, it seems to carry a fair amount of intuitive appeal – we do tend to think that it is good for people to fulfill their potential. Third, if it really has identified a common denominator that links the various goods referenced by OLT theorists, then it carries more explanatory power than OLT and sheds greater light on human happiness. And fourth, if it really has provided a rational method of ranking goods, then it provides an advantage over OLT (though the OLT theorist can certainly avail herself of the "instrumental goods versus intrinsic goods" distinction, and something like Maslow's schema is compatible with OLT).

Here are some points against perfectionism. First, some would object to the claim that the fulfillment of distinctively human capacities is more important for our well-being than the fulfillment of capacities shared with other animals, perhaps because they object to the claim that human beings are a higher form of life than other animals. In particular, some in the animal rights movement would argue that such a claim is guilty of speciesism, a form of irrational prejudice favouring our own species over others. Second, the method of ranking provided by perfectionism, even if helpful to some degree, might leave a great deal unresolved. Third, perfectionism claims that what constitutes well-being for a person is that which fulfills human nature, in particular our distinctively human capacities. But this too leaves a good deal of room for disagreement, in this case arising from disagreements about what human nature really entails. Consider, for instance, a physicalist perfectionist in dialogue with an Orthodox Jewish perfectionist.[9] They might agree that happiness consists of the fulfillment of human nature. However, the physicalist thinks that human nature is reducible to an aggregate of subatomic particles structured in a highly complex fashion – that is, he thinks that humans are purely physical beings. In contrast, the Orthodox Jewish believer maintains that human nature involves the duality of a material frame and a spiritual, immortal soul. Given this radical disagreement about what human nature entails, inevitably they will conceive differently the details of what is involved in fulfilling human nature. For instance, the believer in Orthodox Judaism will think that as humans we have distinctive spiritual capacities for prayer and communion with God, which must be fulfilled in order for anyone to achieve genuine happiness (in this life or an afterlife). In contrast, the physicalist will deny the reality of such spiritual capacities, the reality of God, and the reality of an afterlife. These disagreements can have profound implications for how perfectionism plays out in applied ethics debates. So one might argue that perfectionism, if abstracted from a detailed philosophical account of human nature, is liable to provide relatively little moral guidance – or at least that it leaves great scope for disagreement on many important questions about how to achieve human well-being. And fourth, it seems that sometimes it is bad for us to fulfill innate capacities. Our innate capacity as biological organisms for the experience of severe pain, for instance, is plausibly not good for us (at least when it has gone beyond its usefulness in alerting us to pain or injury). Perfectionists therefore need (at minimum) to find ways of circumscribing the set of human capacities the fulfillment of which contribute to human well-being. But that in turn carries the risk that perfectionism will end up being relinquished in favour of some other account of well-being.[10]

This has been a whirlwind tour of these four principal theories; I have tried to give the reader a brief look at them, each of which has been the subject of whole books. And, as noted above, there are hybrid theories that seek to combine elements of two or more of these four theories, but I have not delved into these hybrids here. The reader will now have a sense of the potential import of these underlying theories for debates on MAID.

Overview of Ethical Theory

Ethical theory is that subdiscipline of ethics devoted to discovering the *basic moral principle (BMP)*. What is meant by the BMP? It is the common denominator that determines when an action is morally permissible. Think of some examples of uncontroversial, morally permissible actions (i.e., actions not obviously immoral). Here are a few that spring to my mind: eating a healthy vegan sandwich during a lunch break, walking to a local corner store to purchase a newspaper, and pondering the purchase of a bicycle. Let us take it as given that these three actions are indeed morally permissible.[11] Yet they are clearly three very different kinds of action: eating a sandwich is a very different kind of action from walking to the store, both of which in turn are very different from thinking about a bicycle purchase. Yet, despite being very different actions, they share something in common: moral permissibility. What exactly is the shared factor, the common denominator, that renders these otherwise very different actions permissible? In other words, in virtue of what is a morally permissible action morally permissible? When one answers this question, one is proposing a BMP. Competing ethical theories offer competing BMPs.

Consider, for example, a first stab at a BMP. Looking at this set of three permissible actions, it might be plausible to suggest that the common denominator that renders them all permissible is that their performance does not hurt anyone. Eating a healthy vegan sandwich during a lunch break harms no one, and neither does walking to a corner store to buy a newspaper or thinking about purchasing a bicycle. So maybe non-harm is what makes something permissible.

Stating this suggestion more formally, we might get something like the following. *The non-harm BMP:* An action is permissible if and only if (and because) it does not harm anyone.[12] An advantage of this hypothetical BMP is that it does seem to be applicable to a wide range of cases, categorizing accurately many permissible actions as indeed permissible. However, it quickly runs into problems. For instance, by not providing further details about what is meant by "harm," this BMP seems to provide relatively little concrete moral guidance. At the least, it needs to be paired with a theory of well-being (with its corresponding theory of harm) to render it potentially useful as a moral theory.

A marginally better version of the non-harm BMP might be like the following. *The attitudinal hedonist non-harm BMP:* An action is permissible if and only if (and because) it does not harm anyone (where to harm someone is to cause that person to experience attitudinal pain). This is marginally more sophisticated than the non-harm BMP but still problematic (even if, for the sake of argument, we grant that attitudinal hedonism is the correct account of well-being). For instance, most people would agree that there are situations in which it is permissible to harm someone: that is, to cause the person to experience attitudinal pain. The judge who sentences a guilty murderer to prison causes that person to experience attitudinal pain, but few would maintain that she is thereby doing anything impermissible. Far from it, she is fulfilling an obligation. This by itself seems to show that the nature of moral permissibility is not accurately captured by that BMP, insofar as it labels impermissible some acts that are actually permissible.

It might also be faulty in the opposite direction, labelling permissible some actions that really are not. Consider a promise made to a dying friend: In response to my friend's dying request that a tree be planted in his honour, I solemnly vow to do so. But then, after his death, I never plant the tree, not because I have forgotten or cannot afford the seedling or lack a green thumb but because I am just lazy and callous. Now, let us say that no one else knows of the promise. So no one but me is ever aware that a promise has been broken, and as such no one is affected by the broken vow, and certainly no one is caused attitudinal pain by my negligence. (Assume that I suffer no pang of conscience for my neglect. Assume too for the sake of argument that there is no God or afterlife and so no divinity or disembodied soul of my friend to be pained by my callousness.) The attitudinal hedonist non-harm BMP would give this deliberate negligence a stamp of approval, which is (arguably) problematic.

I am sure the reader can think of further counterexamples to the non-harm BMP (i.e., can suggest further actions whose moral status the BMP seemingly miscategorizes); the point is just to illustrate how one goes about evaluating suggested BMPs. In what follows, I will provide a short overview of four commonly defended ethical theories: consequentialism, Kantian deontology, natural law theory, and virtue ethics.[13]

The basic idea behind *consequentialism* is that the permissibility of an action is wholly determined by its results. More precisely, the *BMP for consequentialism:* an action is permissible if and only if (and because) its consequences will be at least as good as the consequences of any alternative action that the agent might instead perform.[14] This is the central commitment shared by most versions of consequentialism.[15] It entails that they are *maximalist* (an action is impermissible if the agent could have done something that would have had even a slightly better result but did not);[16] *future oriented* (its concern is not just for immediate impact but also long-term results); *egalitarian* (its concern is for all those affected by the action, not just for its impact on the agent or the agent's family and friends or ethnic group, for instance); and that *motives are morally irrelevant for the evaluation of an action* (what the agent intended has no bearing on the moral status of his action – all that matters are the results of the action). A consequentialist can still maintain that motives are morally relevant in a broader sense: namely, in the sense that they play a role in our evaluation of the agent's personal character. It's just that motives won't be relevant for the moral status of the action itself.

Different versions of consequentialism are obtained when that central commitment is combined with one or another theory of value. The assessment of these different versions can thus involve two criteria: evaluating the shared central commitment (e.g., arguing for or against the maximalist or egalitarian components, etc.) and evaluating the theory of value with which it is combined. The need for more specific versions is obvious insofar as the meaning of "good consequences" must be specified by reference to one or another theory of which sorts of things are relevantly "good" – that is, one needs to specify which sorts of consequences are to be sought.

If one locates intrinsic value solely in states of human beings (such that what counts as valuable is only human pleasure or human desire, satisfaction, and so on), then one gets versions of consequentialism closely linked with one or more of the four major theories of human well-being laid out above. If one locates intrinsic value in things other than states of human beings (e.g., maybe the health of the ecosystem has some independent intrinsic value), then that close linkage will not obtain.

One of the most historically important and commonly defended versions of consequentialism pairs the central commitment with a hedonic theory of intrinsic value, according to which states of pleasure (whether sensory or attitudinal and whether experienced by humans or other animals) are the only fundamental units of value. The resulting ethical theory is a version of consequentialism known as *hedonistic act utilitarianism (HAU)*. The *BMP for HAU:* an action is permissible if and only if (and because) it would produce at least as high a net balance of pleasure (or less pain) as any other alternative action that the agent might perform instead.[17] We have already considered some of the pros and cons of hedonism as a theory of human well-being, and some of those points will carry over to the assessment of HAU. That is, one might reject HAU because one finds hedonism problematic as a theory of human well-being and correspondingly as a general theory of intrinsic value. Alternatively, if one finds hedonism a particularly plausible conception of well-being, then one might be more inclined to accept it as a general theory of intrinsic value, and HAU might be rendered more plausible.

Here are a few points in favour of HAU (and consequentialism more generally). First, it accords with a common-sense intuition that consequences matter a great deal in assessing the moral status of an action. When deciding whether or not to perform some act, we typically take into account its anticipated effects and would consider irresponsible someone who persistently disregarded potential consequences in decision making. Consider, for instance, a decision on whether to donate to Oxfam or the Salvation Army. Looking carefully at what each charity accomplishes, and how effectively each administers donations, will allow us to determine which charity will do the most good with the donation. And it makes sense to think that the conclusion of that inquiry should determine which charity gets the funds.

Second, the egalitarian component of HAU accords with the moral intuition that everyone matters. When deciding whether or not to do some act, it is not enough to consider its effects on us or our immediate circle. Everyone counts, even future generations. (This is one reason we worry about long-term environmental degradation – we are concerned not just about how pollution and climate change affect us now but also how they will affect future generations.)

Third, the theory clearly shows the irrelevance of personal tastes and non-rational, subjective preferences (except where they might bear on pleasure and pain and thus bear on the utility calculus). One might argue that moral inquiry should be a rational rather than an emotional enterprise and that consideration of future consequences involves rational calculation. For example, I would never eat rabbit because, having grown up with a pet rabbit, I find the very notion distasteful. But in evaluating the objective moral status of eating rabbit, according to consequentialism, I cannot let that personal background affect my assessment – what matters rationally is the utility calculus, not my personal history. Correspondingly, the fact that I do not find eating bacon distasteful indicates nothing about its moral status – if I had been raised with a pet pig, I would probably find myself unable to eat bacon.

Here are a few points against HAU. First, consequences are clearly relevant in assessing the morality of our actions, but is it correct to think that consequences are the only things that matter in that assessment? Are motives really irrelevant to the evaluation of an act? (Remember that consequentialists can grant that motives are relevant to our evaluation of the character of the actor, but they are committed to the claim that they are irrelevant to the status of the act itself.) One might argue that motives are not so easily separable from the nature of the act. For example, if person A gives money to the homeless because she wishes to help them, and person B gives the same amount to them because she hates the homeless and hopes to hasten their deaths by providing funds for drug overdoses, then some theorists would say that these are two fundamentally distinct *kinds* of action. It is not simply a case of person A performing an act from a good motive and person B performing the same act from a bad motive but two distinct acts – charitable donation versus malevolent scheming.[18]

Second, one might point to cases in which a moral duty has plausibly been violated, even though no bad consequences ensue. Think again of the example of breaking a solemn vow to the dead.[19]

Third, and relatedly, one might point to cases in which the cost-benefit calculus required by consequentialism leads to apparent injustice. Consider the well-known thought experiment involving the "island of sadists." A government has set up a remote island prison in which it deposits its most sadistic sociopaths. A commercial jet then crashes on the island, and there is one survivor. Assume that, if the one hundred sadistic inhabitants were to torture this surviving passenger over a period of weeks, the net amount of pleasure (sensory, attitudinal, or both) that they would gain from the activity would far exceed the amount of (horrific) pain that the victim would suffer. And, given that the island's inhabitants would videotape the torture for future viewing, the long-term results in terms of the pleasure-over-pain calculus would favour torture even more clearly. (Assume for the sake of argument that no one off island, including the victim's family, ever learns of his fate, so no one off island ever experiences any attitudinal pain on account of it.) Given those facts about the utility calculus, HAU seems to entail that torturing this person is not only permissible but also obligatory. All things considered, torturing this innocent person for weeks would result by far in the best consequences, as good as (indeed better than) any other alternative action that the sadists could carry out.[20]

Fourth, the maximalist criterion might be problematic. Imagine that I am trying to decide between going to see an action film and going to visit my aunt in the hospital. Say that an objective utility calculus would show that the pleasure that I would get from going to the action film is a bit higher than the pleasure that I or my aunt (or both of us) would get from the hospital visit. (Maybe she would really enjoy the visit, and so would I, but I *really* like action films, so the net utility of doing the latter instead would still be higher.) Consequentialism entails that it would be immoral to visit my sick aunt because an alternative action (going to the movie) would have better consequences for all those affected by the action. But that might seem to be counterintuitive.[21]

There is much more to be said for and against the core commitment of consequentialism, and the literature that has developed around the theory (both pro and con) is vast and ever expanding. And HAU as a specific version of consequentialism remains popular and widely defended. As noted, though, this is intended to be a brief introduction, skimming the surface of these theories and some of their more commonly discussed pros and cons.[22]

The next major ethical theory to consider is *Kantian deontology*. Immanuel Kant, for all his brilliance, was not always the most lucid of writers, and scholars of Kant continue to dispute exactly what his BMP amounts to or whether he even offers a single BMP or several incompatible BMPs. I will work here with what is sometimes called the "humanity" formulation of Kantian deontology.[23] The *BMP for Kantian deontology:* An action is permissible if and only if (and because) the action, to the extent that it bears on the treatment of persons, treats persons (including oneself) as ends in themselves and not merely as means.[24] The basic idea here is that persons are intrinsically valuable beings and that intrinsically valuable beings should be regarded as (and treated as) ends in themselves rather than as mere instruments for some other ends. When we interact with others, we typically assume that they are valuable beings with meaningful thoughts, plans, and goals of their own, such that it is wrong to use others in a way incompatible with taking proper account of their dignity and agency as persons. That is not to say, of course, that we can never make use of others' services – simply that in doing so we must regard and treat them as persons. When I shop at the liquor store, I am, in a sense, using the cashier as a means to my end of buying liquor. But I am not using him *merely* as a means; I continue to have a regard for his welfare, which I manifest by politeness, patience in line, et cetera. In contrast, when I rob the liquor store, flashing a gun in his face and threatening his welfare for the sake of cash, I treat him merely as a means to my goal of emptying the register. Kantian deontology thus locates its BMP in the intrinsic value of persons and the implication that they cannot be treated in a purely instrumental fashion.

Here are some points in favour of Kantian deontology. First, it seems to accord well with our deep intuitions about the value of persons and the implications of such value. Second, it sidesteps some of the problems allegedly arising for certain versions of consequentialism (Kantian deontology would never grant a stamp of approval to the island of sadists). Relatedly, it can make a much stronger claim to ground a notion of inalienable human rights than does consequentialism. For example, people have a right not to be tortured simply because they are people – valuable beings never to be treated merely as a means to an end, even a noble end such as preventing a terrorist attack (in so-called ticking time bomb scenarios). Third, it retains aspects of egalitarianism, insofar as one is obliged to treat all people with dignity, as ends in themselves, yet it does not imply the impossibility of certain people having greater moral claims on us. Thus, it can allow that parents, for instance, may rightly care more for their own children's welfare than that of strangers' children. And fourth, it admits the moral relevance of motivation in the evaluation of action. Treating someone merely as a means might involve not just outward behaviour but also how we think about him and our personal reasons for action. In this respect, it is very different from consequentialism, in which motives count for nothing in the evaluation of action (even if they might yet be relevant in the evaluation of an individual's character).

And here are some points against Kantian deontology. It might be too narrow in its stated sphere of moral concern, insofar as it rules impermissible only certain actions toward persons. Surely an adequate BMP should rule out animal cruelty and other forms of harm to non-persons. Yet the underlying Kantian notion of dignity or respect for persons might not be applicable to animals; arguably, they lack the dignity of persons, yet it is still wrong to treat them cruelly. So what other moral principle is at play here? Whatever it is, it does not seem to be captured by the Kantian BMP. One could maintain that the notion of dignity can simply be expanded to encompass at least other higher mammals. But that could lead to an evacuation of the weight of dignity as a philosophical notion. If one says that it is wrong to torture a cow because a cow has intrinsic dignity (rather than because of some other operative moral principle), but still thinks it okay to slaughter cows for food (if quickly and humanely), then apparently the possession of intrinsic dignity does not confer much in the way of robust rights. At this point, one could introduce a notion of *degrees* of dignity, such that, while both cows and humans possess intrinsic dignity sufficient to render impermissible various sorts of cruel acts (e.g., torture), nevertheless cows have *less* dignity than people, so we can treat the former as a food source but not the latter. That might be a way to preserve this BMP; however, it would then be controversial whether different degrees of the same moral trait could ground radically different sets of rights such as those possessed by cows and people – perhaps those differences suffice to show that we are dealing not with differing degrees of the same property but with a different property altogether and a different BMP flowing from it.

Second, Kantian deontology might be too ambiguous in its implications, failing to supply clear guidelines for action. Although Kantian deontology clearly renders a verdict of impermissibility in the island of sadists scenario, it might not disallow other cases of torture. Consider the example of torturing a terrorist for information about a hidden bomb shortly to explode in a crowded public square. Suppose that torture is always a gravely immoral act, never to be permitted even in such extreme situations. Yet the torturer could appeal to the Kantian as follows:

> Look, I am not treating this terrorist merely as a means to get the information. I care about his personhood and inherent dignity. But if I were in his position, having become so corrupted in character as to plant a bomb somewhere in a crowded city square, I would want to be tortured for the information. I would want to be spared the burden of becoming a mass murderer. I am in fact treating this terrorist just as I would wish to be treated. I have regard for his welfare, too, and I am not using him merely as a means to secure the safety of his potential victims.

Now, for my purposes here, the question is not whether this is a convincing line of reasoning. Rather, the point is that Kantian deontology might not provide sufficiently clear moral guidance in controversial cases. This might be because of an under-specification of just what human dignity consists of and by extension just what respect for human dignity demands of us. (This is at any rate a worry for many contemporary Kantians; Kant himself had a detailed conception of dignity and human nature rooted in Christian theological anthropology.)

Third, even if it gives clear guidance, Kantian deontology might take inadequate account of the moral weight of consequences. Assume for the sake of argument that to torture someone is to treat him merely as a means – still, is it *really* always wrong? What if thousands of innocent lives are at stake and the bomber is unambiguously guilty and likely to break under pressure?[25]

Moving on to the *BMP for natural law theory:* an action is permissible if and only if (and because) in performing the action one does not directly violate any of the basic human goods. This BMP, with its talk of basic human goods, can be fleshed out in terms of either OLT or perfectionism; historically, however, most advocates of natural law theory have adopted some version of the latter, so I will work with that understanding here.

The idea, then, is that certain core goods (i.e., the fulfillment of certain core capacities) are necessary for human well-being, such that intentionally to cut someone off from these goods is wrong. Examples of core goods commonly cited by perfectionists include life itself,[26] family, friendship, education, and so on. Natural law theory, like Kantian deontology, can thus claim to ground a robust conception of human rights: we have a right to the fulfillment of certain core capacities, such that in general others are obligated to refrain from intentionally preventing their fulfillment and might even be obligated actively to help us fulfill them (recall the distinction between negative and positive rights introduced in Chapter 1). And, though natural law theory is typically formulated in terms of human goods, it can readily be extended to provide an account of animals' rights.[27] Animals have intrinsic natures of their own, the fulfillment of which is a good for them, such that for us to interfere intentionally and gratuitously with that fulfillment is a violation of their rights.

The *doctrine of double effect (DDE)* plays an important role in natural law theory by supplying an explication of the BMP's terminology of "direct" violations.[28] (Some adherents of other ethical theories, especially deontology, also make use of the DDE, but it is not an essential component of the formulation of those theories in the way that it is an essential component of natural law theory.) The DDE is meant to clarify how we should act in cases in which the fulfillment of one core good involves what seems to be an infringement on another. Self-defence provides a classic example, much discussed in the natural law tradition. Someone breaks into your home with the intention of harming your family. The only way to protect them effectively is to strike the assailant on the head with a hockey stick. Here we have what seems to be a conflict between core goods. On the one hand, you have to take into account your own life and the lives of your spouse and children. On the other, you have to care about the life of your assailant. He, too, is an inherently valuable human being with the ability to fulfill certain core capacities. By striking him on the head, you risk blocking his fulfillment of those capacities – that is, you risk his chances of future education because of brain damage, and indeed if you hit him too hard you risk his ability to fulfill his most foundational capacity, that of continued biological life. How do you weigh these goods against each other? In a case like this, the consequentialist would ask you simply to run a numbers game – that is, calculate the long-term consequences of killing him versus allowing him to kill you and your family. To a Kantian, that calculation would smack of treating the assailant merely as a means to an end: namely, the protection of your family. Somehow your reaction in this situation must take proper account of the fact that the assailant himself is a human being with intrinsic dignity and correspondingly certain rights. The natural law theorist will want to say something like the latter too. But does that mean you are not allowed to protect your family? No. Natural law theory permits *indirect* violations of the basic human goods.[29] An indirect violation is distinguished from a direct violation by reference to the following four criteria: 1) The action itself is not *intrinsically evil* regardless of the broader context and consequences; 2) the action is necessary for the fulfillment of the goal (i.e., there is no feasible way of achieving the good aim without incurring the unfortunate side effects); 3) the unfortunate side effects of the action are genuinely *side effects* (i.e., not intended by the agent, whether in themselves or as means to the end);[30] and 4) the unfortunate side effects are proportionate to the good achieved.

Plugging these four criteria into the present example, the natural law theorist can argue that striking the intruder is permissible provided that 1) striking a guilty intruder is not an intrinsically evil act, which (arguably) it seems not to be;[31] 2) striking him is genuinely necessary for the protection of your family (i.e., in this scenario, there is no other way effectively to protect them – the intruder will not listen to moral argument, merely threatening him with the hockey stick fails to deter him, etc.); 3) you *foresee* but do not *intend* the possibility that your blow will severely injure or even kill the intruder (i.e., if you could subdue him without injuring him, you would);[32] and 4) the good achieved (saving yourself and your family from death) is proportionate to the unfortunate side effect of badly injuring or killing the assailant.[33]

Here are some points in favour of natural law theory. First, its BMP, supplemented by the DDE (itself simply an explication of the notion of "directness" employed in the BMP), allows it to sidestep some of the problems apparently facing at least certain versions of consequentialism (e.g., a natural law theorist could never entertain the island of sadists scenario). Second, its linkage to perfectionism will be appealing to those who find that account of well-being more plausible than its competitors. Third, by way of the DDE, it takes into account the relevance of intention in assessing the moral status of an action (though, if this is in fact an advantage, then it is one that it shares with Kantian deontology). And fourth, by way of the DDE, it also acknowledges the moral relevance of consequences (though, if this is in fact an advantage, then it is one that it shares with consequentialism). Although in natural law theory one cannot point to consequences to justify a direct violation of a basic good, consequences do play a role in assessing whether an indirect violation might be permitted (especially by way of the fourth criterion of the DDE, that of proportionality).

Here are some points against natural law theory. First, some question the notion of an "intrinsically evil" act – referenced in the first criterion of the DDE – and how such an act can be discerned. From the perspective of natural law theory, such an act must equate to a direct violation of a basic good, but this does not necessarily provide a clear criterion for determining when that is taking place. Striking the guilty intruder is not intrinsically evil, but striking the innocent neighbour is, even though the outward physical movement involved is identical and even though the overarching intention in both cases is to save one's family. Clearly, the idea is that the *justice* of the former act is taken to be an intrinsic part of the act itself, and the *injustice* of the latter act is likewise an intrinsic part of it. But exactly how is this to be cashed out? Presumably, it will be by reference once again to the violation of human goods, perhaps in this case core social goods (equal treatment, reciprocity, desert, etc.). Historically, however, there have been some differences on this point, resulting in somewhat different versions of natural law theory. And some will want to press the claim that the notion of an act as good or evil *intrinsically*, irrespective of context and consequences, is incoherent.

Second, although its linkage to perfectionism might seem to be an advantage to those who favour that account of well-being, to those who find the latter unconvincing, it will be of course a disadvantage. Yet, as noted, some natural law theorists flesh out the theory in terms of OLT instead of perfectionism.

Third, some question the implications of natural law theory. For instance, it would rule out the intentional killing of an innocent neighbour in order to save your own family. It would also rule out torture, even in a ticking time bomb scenario in which many innocent lives are at stake. The reason is that torture is intrinsically evil, even the torture of a guilty individual.[34] Whereas many natural law theorists see such prohibitions as an advantage of the theory, others view this as too absolutist or inflexible. For example, what if murdering your neighbour is the only way to prevent the destruction of your whole city? Consequentialists like to urge such extreme cases on deontologists and natural law theorists, arguing that, when the consequences are sufficiently dire, we will all show our true colours as consequentialists and abandon any notion of inviolable human dignity or intrinsically evil (and hence absolutely prohibited) acts.[35]

Fourth, some have argued that the distinction employed in the DDE between *foreseen* effects and *intended* effects is artificial or otherwise difficult to sustain and/or that the agent's intentions are irrelevant to the evaluation of the moral status of an action (as opposed to the character of the agent).[36]

Let us turn briefly to the fourth theory, *virtue ethics*. The status of virtue ethics within ethical theory is itself a matter of dispute; some argue that virtue ethics provides a radically different approach to the moral life, such that it does not even attempt to supply a BMP. Others classify it as structurally similar to other ethical theories, properly counting as another attempt to supply a plausible BMP (i.e., a plausible common denominator that explains why all morally permissible acts are in fact morally permissible). I will treat it in this second fashion here. The *BMP for virtue ethics:* An action is permissible if and only if (and because) it is something a virtuous and well-informed agent, acting in character, would not avoid doing in the circumstances under consideration.[37] The idea behind virtue ethics (certain forms of it anyway) is thus that we start with a notion of what a virtuous person is like, and then when evaluating a particular act we ask whether it is the sort of thing that the person would do. In this conception, then, the notion of virtue is prior to the notion of permissibility and supplies a criterion for the latter.

For instance, imagine someone whom you take to be a paragon of virtue, whether real or fictional. Would he or she hit the intruder with a hockey stick to save innocent others? If so, then the action is in fact permissible. How about torturing the terrorist in the ticking time bomb scenario, would he or she do that? If you cannot realistically imagine him or her doing so, then the action is impermissible. And so on.

Following are some points in favour of virtue ethics. First, it seems to accord with some facts about moral epistemology – that is, facts about how we come to know moral truths. Arguably, we learn such truths (or learn them most effectively) not from explicit instruction but from observing role models. Virtue ethics might be seen as a way of extending that insight into moral epistemology to the foundation of moral theory: facts about what a genuinely virtuous agent would or would not do are now seen not merely as *indicative* but also as *constitutive* of which actions are permissible. Second, virtue ethics might supply a more workable procedure for decision making than the other ethical theories and thus provide superior practical guidance. Just pick the right role model, think carefully about what this person realistically would or would not do in a certain scenario, and a practical upshot is obtained. The consequentialist, in contrast, has to weight up all of the long-term consequences for those who stand to be affected by an action, and such calculations are often difficult to make; the natural law theorist has to contend with disagreements about which acts count as intrinsically evil and why et cetera.

Here are some points against virtue ethics. First, the main worry about virtue ethics, conceived as attempting to supply a BMP (and again not everyone conceives it in this manner), is that it might seem to get the order of priorities reversed. Arguably, a person is virtuous because she has a character that reliably disposes her toward the performance of permissible acts and away from the performance of impermissible acts. That is, the notion of virtuous character is properly defined by reference to the notion of permissible acts and thus is *posterior* to the latter, not *anterior,* as claimed by advocates of virtue ethics. (From the perspective of the natural law theorist, robbing a liquor store is wrong because it directly violates core goods of the cashier and store owner, not because it is the sort of act from which Mother Teresa would have refrained.) Second, in direct reply to the second supposed advantage, it is disputable to what extent virtue ethics can consistently provide practical guidance and likewise to what extent it can provide such guidance any more effectively than the competing theories. What if you and I disagree about what Mother Teresa would do in a certain scenario? If you claim that she would torture a terrorist in a ticking time bomb scenario (say a particularly extreme scenario in which a whole city is shortly to be blown up), and I claim that she would not, how could we rationally adjudicate this?[38]

That completes the whirlwind tour of four of the major competing ethical theories. As noted, this tour has been brief and necessarily incomplete. Each theory could use additional explication, and many more arguments for and against each could be adduced. Moreover, there are other ethical theories on which I have not touched, and there are various ways of trying to combine insights from several ethical theories to produce hybrid BMPs.[39] However, remaining cognizant of space constraints, I hope that the preceding will suffice in understanding some of the background theoretical disputes at play in arguments concerning the permissibility of MAID.

Before presenting those arguments, though, I would like to discuss briefly the role of theology in ethical theory. Claims about God and the human soul and other theological ideas are sometimes relevant to moral disputes. *Here are some examples.* First, theology introduces factual claims the truth of which could have impacts on consequentialist calculations. Is there an afterlife that we need to take into account when considering long-term results? Is there a God whose reactions must be taken into account in those calculations? Second, religions supply factual claims about human nature – about what sorts of beings we really are and what sorts of capacities we have. The truth or falsity of such claims can have a bearing on precise conceptions of dignity (e.g., are we created in the image of God, or are we a fortuitously assembled collection of chemicals?). They also have a potential bearing on the range of capacities that a perfectionist account of well-being must consider and therefore must be taken into account by perfectionist consequentialism and natural law theory. For example, do we have a capacity for communion with God? Are we able to survive physical death, such that there might be further goods to be attained in an afterlife? Third, for the religious virtue ethicist, certain individuals might be taken as providing particularly reliable moral examples (e.g., the great saints or prophets), reliable precisely because inspired by God. Fourth, any theistic religion will raise questions about the special duties that we might have to God, irrespective of which specific ethical theory is at play. Fifth, a particular religion might be committed doctrinally to the acceptance of a particular account of well-being or ethical theory or to the rejection of certain such theories. I would argue that Christianity, for instance, is committed to the rejection of hedonism and by extension HAU. And, though I think that Christian moral theology is strictly compatible with any of the other accounts of well-being and ethical theory discussed above (though there is at least some tension with actualist DST), Christian theologians historically have tended toward one or another version of natural law theory combined with either perfectionism or OLT.[40] And sixth, religious revelations typically claim to provide authoritative moral guidance, such that – if we could establish that some such revelation is actually true – we would be provided thereby with an additional source of moral knowledge. That in turn would give us an additional means of settling moral controversies, at least among adherents of the same religion.

4

Moral Arguments for and against MAID

As noted in the introduction, voluntary passive euthanasia has long been legal in Canada and is relatively uncontroversial morally.[1] Non-voluntary passive euthanasia is complex on both counts. Few today would defend involuntary euthanasia, whether active or passive. Non-voluntary active euthanasia does have defenders, mainly in cases involving minors incapable of providing legal consent (e.g., severely disabled newborns) and people who have entered into severe dementia or apparently irreversible comas and whose lives are judged by some not really to be worth living.[2] Closely related is the issue of the permissibility of euthanizing someone who is legally incompetent at the time of the lethal injection but who signed an advance directive indicating that, on descending into dementia, he wished to be euthanized – should that count as voluntary active euthanasia or as non-voluntary active euthanasia? Regardless of how one classifies that last act, at present it is illegal in Canada, insofar as Bill C-14 requires legal competence at the time of death. That could change should public pressure increase on the government to reconsider this issue,[3] and the legalization of advance directives has been defended in the scholarly literature.[4] And there are still other potential grounds of expanded eligibility that have been and continue to be discussed in Canada, including expansion to the legally competent mentally ill[5] and from legal adults to mature minors.[6] (Regarding pertinent amendments contained in the follow-up Bill C-7, please see too the updated information provided on page 156, note 5.)

Nevertheless, my focus in this chapter is on the ethics of our current legal situation and thus specifically on the ethics of assisted suicide and voluntary active euthanasia (i.e., MAID) under the specific rubric laid down by Bill C-14 (while remaining cognizant of the fact that its original provision of "reasonably foreseeable death" will soon be formally removed, having been judged unconstitutional by a Quebec court).

Some arguments for and against MAID are linked explicitly to one or another of the four major ethical theories considered in the previous chapter; others, though not explicitly linked to any particular theory, seem to depend implicitly on one or another of them. Still others proceed on the basis of premises intended to be compatible with multiple ethical theories and thus at least partly independent of background theoretical commitments. I will attempt to keep these divisions clear as we proceed. Some of these arguments will have a familiar ring, having been encountered (if in truncated form) in the court rulings canvassed in Chapter 1.

In the first and second sections, I discuss the two most common sorts of argument in favour of the permissibility of MAID: namely, those focused on mercy and those focused on autonomy.[7] In the third section, I lay out the single most common sort of argument against the permissibility of MAID, the intrinsic wrongness of killing an innocent person. In the remaining sections, I delve into arguments that remain important but have been less central to the recent debate.

Arguments for the Permissibility of MAID: Mercy/ Alleviation of Suffering

For the sake of clarity, I will formulate the arguments under consideration in premise-conclusion form. The first is tied explicitly to hedonistic act utilitarianism (HAU):

Premise 1: If HAU is true, then MAID will be permissible in any situation in which these practices maximize[8] the lifetime pleasure-over-pain ratio of those affected by them.
Premise 2: HAU is true.

Conclusion 1/Premise 3: Therefore, MAID will be permissible in any situation in which these practices maximize the lifetime pleasure-over-pain
   ratio of those affected by them.
Premise 4: There are in fact such situations.
Final Conclusion: Therefore, MAID is sometimes permissible.

The justification for premise 1 is found in the fact that this proposition can
be deduced from the BMP under consideration. It is merely a particular
application of the BMP – for an advocate of HAU, *any* action that would
maximize the lifetime pleasure-over-pain ratio of all those affected by it
thereby counts as permissible. The justification for premise 2 is provided by
the various arguments in favour of HAU, some examples of which I covered
briefly in the previous chapter. The justification for premise 4 is found in its
alleged empirical plausibility, specifically in the plausibility of the idea that
there are at least some cases in which, overall, more suffering is avoided via
suicide than if the individual continues to live. Think, for instance, of a case
in which a person is in continual, serious, physical and/or emotional pain
not outweighed by corresponding pleasures. Moreover, the person has good
reason to think that this ratio will not be subject to improvement in the
future (perhaps the ailment that troubles the patient is terminal, and she
lacks access to effective pain relief or palliative care). In other words, there
is good reason for her to think that continuing to live will only rack up more
pain and less pleasure, such that her life, taken as a whole, will only get
worse. Finally, imagine that in this case the patient has no friends or loved
ones who derive enjoyment from her continued presence among them, in
fact that her life does not contribute to the positive enjoyment of anyone,
even indirectly (e.g., the patient donates no money to charity, pays no taxes
to contribute to broader social welfare, etc.). So her ending her life will not
diminish the overall well-being of others – or, if that seems to be too extreme,
assume that, even if her death will cause others some pain or deprive others
of some enjoyment, those negative consequences will be outweighed by all
of the future pain that the patient will avoid by receiving MAID. Remember,
for consequentialism, the happiness of all those affected by the act must be
taken into account long term. So assume, too, that anyone helping her to die
will suffer in no way from providing the aid – no pang of conscience et cetera. Or, if any such pang is suffered, then its import is again outweighed by
the good of the patient's avoiding much future pain.[9]
   Glover (1977) is among the prominent ethicists who have argued in this
fashion, proceeding explicitly from HAU to the permissibility of MAID.[10]

Others, without explicitly advocating HAU, make use of comparable lines of reasoning having to do with calculations about future quality of life and anticipated pleasure-over-pain ratios. For instance, in arguing that assisted death should be made available more widely than just for the terminally ill, Warnock and Macdonald (2008, p. xiii) write that "if at the heart of the debate is the rightness or wrongness of helping someone to die who can see no value to himself and no pleasure in his future life, the principle involved seems to be the same whether that life is to be long or short."[11]

An obvious objection to premise 4 is an epistemic one: How can we ever really be sure that the person's prospective future pleasure-over-pain ratio is so bleak or be sure about the broader impact on others of his suicide? Glover (1977, pp. 173–174) states the worry as follows:

> Where someone contemplating suicide is sufficiently in control of himself to deliberate about this course of action, two factors are relevant to the decision. What would his own future life be like, and would it be worth living? What effect would his decision (either way) have on other people? The difficulties in answering the question about one's own future life are obvious. If life is at present sufficiently bad to make a person think suicide may be in his own interest, he will need to have some idea of how likely or unlikely is any improvement in his state. This is often hard to predict (except in cases where the blight on his life is an absolutely incurable illness). Most of us are bad at giving enough weight to the chances of our lives changing for better or worse.

However, Glover still thinks that there are cases in which a rational assessment favours early death, and given his parenthetical proviso regarding incurable illness he would surely judge that the sorts of cases permitted by Bill C-14 as originally written (namely, an incurable illness in which death is reasonably foreseeable) would supply even clearer moral warrant.

Yet this sort of argument renders the morality of many instances of MAID heavily contingent on the quality of care received by people in these dire straits. Someone suffering greatly from a terminal illness but surrounded by loving family and friends and receiving quality palliative care (including pain relief and counselling) might yet judge that his remaining life holds out the hope of greater satisfaction than suffering. It could be that in a nation such as Canada, capable in principle of supplying such quality aid to the great majority of those experiencing terminal illnesses, the proponent of HAU will have to judge impermissible most such procedures.

(And, given that the "reasonably foreseeable death" provision of Bill C-14 has now been deemed unconstitutional via the Quebec Superior Court ruling in 2019, such that legal eligibility for MAID is set to expand to include those suffering from non-terminal ailments, proponents of HAU will presumably look with even greater suspicion at the moral status of many cases of assisted death.)[12] Moreover, when considering not merely the permissibility of individual acts of assisted death but also the legalization of these practices, the proponent of HAU must include in the calculus the broader societal impacts of such a legal change (e.g., impacts on societal attitudes toward death, on the medical profession, on relationships between doctors and patients, etc.).

So, though in principle HAU seems to provide a solid backing to many cases of MAID, in fact it might not be quite so permissive as some think. Still, if true, then it would apparently justify at least *some* such procedures and perhaps many of them, which is why in assessing the present argument it is important to consider the possible falsity of its second premise. According to some, HAU is a deeply problematic moral theory, for reasons explored briefly in the previous chapter (e.g., the "island of sadists" objection), among others.

Much the same can be said for a version of consequentialism that pairs it with actualist desire satisfaction theory as an account of intrinsic value and of human well-being.[13] As a moral theory, it appears to be vulnerable to some of the same problems. Other versions of consequentialism seem to be less vulnerable, but also less clearly liable to justify MAID, even in cases of terminal illness accompanied by severe physical and/or psychological suffering. That is the result of these alternative versions' inclusion of a broader range of goods in their calculations of consequences. For instance, if patiently borne physical suffering can greatly boost the sufferer's virtuous character (patience being an important virtue), and developing virtue is ranked by one's version of OLT more highly than the avoidance of physical pain, then a version of consequentialism paired with an account of intrinsic value and of human well-being that accords with OLT might hold little prospect for deeming suicide rationally preferable, even in cases of terminal illness. A great deal will depend on the precise details of how the consequentialist formulates these alternative accounts of value and of well-being, especially with respect to the ranking of goods included. And in cases in which adequate pain relief is available, such that goods of character, knowledge acquisition, and so on remain available while physical suffering is minimized, the calculus is still more likely to go against early assisted death. Even in extreme cases in which the patient must be kept persistently sedated for the sake of pain relief (i.e., no other method of pain relief is sufficiently effective), these versions of consequentialism are liable to decide against assisted death. After all, though in such cases the patient himself cannot pursue goods of knowledge acquisition and so on, the good of his family and caregivers must also be taken into account, and these individuals themselves might benefit in various ways from the opportunity to provide this care (e.g., in exercising and developing virtues themselves in the love, respect, and patience that they show). Recall that for the consequentialist the long-term consequences for all those affected by an action must be taken into account equally, not just the consequences for the patient.

With all of those factors in mind, advocates of these alternative forms of consequentialism might be faced with many scenarios in which the moral status of an act of MAID is simply inscrutable. The calculation of long-term consequences can be a tricky endeavour at the best of times; moreover, if one is uncertain about aspects of the relevant accounts of intrinsic value and of human well-being (e.g., if one is convinced that some version of consequentialism plus OLT is true but is less sure about which version of OLT to affirm), then the difficulty increases markedly.

How ought one to act when faced with such uncertainty? I suggest that the following general principle should be adopted, not only by the consequentialist but also by anyone faced with a situation in which there is no clear answer to a question about the permissibility of killing someone. *The inscrutability proviso:* in any case in which reasonable doubt persists about the moral permissibility of deliberately killing a person, one ought to refrain from doing so, and the law should refrain from permitting deliberate killing in such a case.

Just what is meant here by "reasonable doubt" in this context? I favour a meaning closely analogous to that employed in the Canadian criminal law. The English system of common law, in which the Canadian criminal law is rooted, has long accepted the idea that, if there is any reasonable doubt about the guilt of the accused on trial, even someone on trial for murder, then that individual must be set free and certainly cannot be subjected to lifelong imprisonment or capital punishment. I emphasize that the standard is reasonable doubt, not preponderance of evidence; provided that reasonable doubt is in place, the accused must not be executed, even if the jury thinks it more likely than not that he is guilty (and even if the accused submits willingly to the judgment of the court, *consenting* to be executed if found guilty). The moral gravity of deliberate killing by the state is so great that reasonable doubt is taken as properly sufficient to exonerate the accused. I am suggesting that, when dealing with moral arguments for the permissibility of deliberate killing, an analogous standard applies: if there is reasonable doubt about the soundness of the argument in favour of killing, then killing in that situation must not be permitted.

Even leaving aside the analogy with Canadian legal standards, I take the inscrutability proviso to be a plausible general decision-making procedure given the risks involved. To engage in an impermissible act of killing a person is to engage in an act that, plausibly, is *gravely* immoral. (It is the gravity of the immorality that carries the further legal implication; we do not think, of course, that all immoral acts ought to be illegal, but gravely immoral acts, in particular gravely immoral acts that involve killing persons, seem to be strong candidates for legal sanction.) The stakes are as high as they can get, such that a substantial level of confidence in one's moral judgment is required. This is significant, insofar as it places a heavy burden of proof on the advocate of assisted death. In contrast, opponents of MAID need only sow a measure of doubt.

In reply, some consequentialists (in particular advocates of HAU) might dispute the inscrutability proviso on the ground that sometimes the risks of not killing are equivalent to or greater than the risks of killing – for instance, in cases in which refusing to kill might leave the individual in a state of grievous and irremediable suffering. One might think that the moral risk of allowing such suffering is at least equally as great as the moral risk of engaging in a questionable act of killing. However, even granting that the goods involved are commensurable, in nations such as Canada with modern health-care systems this dilemma need not be actualized, insofar as there will usually be other methods of alleviating the patient's suffering besides killing[14] including, as a last resort, continual sedation.[15] Of course, to some patients, the prospect of continual sedation is unappealing or even distressing, to the extent that death appears to them to be a preferable option. The point here is not to dispute their personal assessments of this matter; obviously, the voices of the gravely ill must be taken seriously and heard sympathetically, and one can certainly empathize with those who find the thought of continual sedation frankly frightening. Rather, the point is to challenge a potential objection to the inscrutability proviso by noting that the risks associated with not killing someone, in cases in which serious moral doubts remain, might not be as great as initially supposed. Certainly, one is not left with a binary choice between killing a person or leaving that person in a state of unrelieved horrible suffering.

At any rate, there are reasons to question the soundness of a consequentialism-based argument for the permissibility of MAID. Moreover, there is reason to question related arguments that, though not relying on consequentialism as a foundational moral theory, proceed from premises centred on the need to alleviate grievous suffering. As Sumner (2011, p. 89) observes,

> the most familiar form of the argument from well-being is consequentialist: where assisted death would be in the best interest of the patient, by preventing further suffering, then providing it would have the best consequences. But it can also take a deontological form, working from a duty of care to the patient or a duty not to inflict or permit avoidable suffering.

Here is one way to formulate such an argument, stated in terms of rights (and thus consistent with various background ethical theories):

Premise 1: Anyone suffering grievously from an illness, disability, or disease has a positive right to the alleviation of that suffering.[16]

Premise 2: There are cases in which the only way to alleviate that suffering is to kill the sufferer.

Conclusion: Therefore, in such cases, the sufferer has a positive right to be killed.

Premise 1 seems to be plausible. We normally think that there is a duty to supply medical aid where needed, even in cases in which the individual arguably does not deserve it (e.g., we are obligated to provide medical treatment even to a murderer who has been shot by police during arrest). However, we can imagine cases in which this premise would be questionable: namely, cases in which the only available means of relieving suffering is itself impermissible. For example, imagine someone suffering from a bizarre psychiatric disorder whose emotional anguish can be relieved only by watching the torture of live kittens. In this case, his right to the alleviation of suffering is trumped by the obligation not to engage in animal cruelty. Or imagine a case in which someone is suffering badly from the effects of kidney failure, and the only means to alleviate that suffering is a kidney transplant. In this scenario, the standard methods of symptom relief are unavailable for some reason. Yet there is no willing donor. Does the sufferer's right to alleviation imply that it would be permissible to force someone at gunpoint to donate the organ? Seemingly not – again the sufferer's positive right to the alleviation of suffering is trumped by another's negative right to bodily integrity and freedom from assault. So, though there is a positive right to the alleviation of suffering (especially grievous suffering), that right is apparently not absolute. It can be overridden by other morally relevant factors. Some actions are impermissible, even if done for the sake of relieving grievous suffering – even, indeed, if done for the sake of relieving such suffering that cannot be relieved in any other way.

With that fact in mind, consider the proposition that it is always wrong deliberately to kill an innocent person. This proposition is widely affirmed, whether on independent grounds (i.e., as a stand-alone principle), as an implication of a background ethical theory (e.g., natural law theory or Kantian deontology), or derived from religious doctrine. However, it is also highly controversial among ethicists, and I will consider shortly in more detail its larger role in the debate on assisted death. For now, I simply observe that its truth (if indeed it is true), combined with the fact that the positive right to alleviation of suffering is not an absolute right, would itself undermine any argument in favour of MAID on account of relieving suffering. That is, this is not a case of weighing two rights of comparable import; rather, the negative absolute right to life of the innocent automatically overrides the non-absolute positive right to the alleviation of grievous suffering. (One might propose, of course, that the injunction against deliberate killing applies only to killing someone *against her will*, such that a person who consents to her own death thereby renders that killing unobjectionable. But that would take us into the realm of a different sort of argument for the permissibility of MAID in which the central focus is autonomy rather than mercy.)

So premise 1 of the present argument is disputable. And, as we have seen, premise 2 is likewise disputable on empirical grounds. In most cases, even the suffering associated with a dire terminal illness can be effectively controlled using the best tools of modern medicine and controlled in a way that allows the patient to remain lucid. In the small percentage of cases in which that is not possible, palliative sedation remains an option of last resort. Of course, we are considering this argument within the specifically Canadian context. Premise 2 would be more plausible if considered within the context of an impoverished nation where this sort of medical care is unavailable to the vast majority of its citizens and where people with terminal illnesses often do perish in horrendous, unrelieved suffering. In such nations, calls for euthanasia to be legalized are comparatively rare. In fact, future historians are liable to remark on the seeming oddity of euthanasia being legalized only in wealthy, technologically advanced nations where effective pain relief is widely available.[17]

Yet the apparent weaknesses of these first two arguments for the permissibility of MAID (both of them versions of one common sort: namely, arguments from mercy/alleviation of suffering) might not seem to be much of a loss to advocates of MAID. Although such arguments are employed in the ethics literature (in various forms), and though concerns about the alleviation of suffering were clearly a factor in *Carter v Canada* and the related court rulings, in fact concerns about suffering are not really at the core of the case for assisted death, at least not by themselves. This is sometimes noted by proponents, for whom the most important arguments generally centre on the notion of autonomy.

Arguments for the Permissibility of MAID: Autonomy

Discussing the claim that assisted suicide and euthanasia cannot be justified by reference to the alleviation of suffering (since palliative sedation is available as an effective alternative), Battin (2005, p. 32) writes that

> the unsatisfactoriness of recourse to terminal sedation shows that the avoidance of pain is not all there is to the debate. For some, maybe most, patients who seek assistance in dying, pain is not the issue as much as it's control ... Patients fear future pain and want to avoid future hard deaths; but for most of them, it is retaining control, remaining capable of being the architects of their own lives, that is central. Even if all pain could be controlled – as terminal sedation will do, though in a way that proponents find unacceptable – this would not resolve the issue. Rather, the issue has to do with respecting terminally ill patients' own choices about how they want to die, rather than – as proponents would put it – forcing them to accept their physicians' or health care institutions' models of appropriate terminal care.

Battin also provides a helpfully concise statement of the autonomy argument:

> Just as a person has the right to determine as much as possible the course of his or her own life, a person also has the right to determine as much as possible the course of his or her own dying. If a terminally ill person seeks

assistance in suicide from a physician freely and rationally, the physician ought to be permitted to provide it. (p. 20)

Warnock and Macdonald (2008, p. 8), describing what they see as the principal motivation of those who seek assisted death, write that

> there are many people who suffer acutely before the foreseen end of their life, and who ask that they be helped to die not on account of any principle but on account of the very nature of their suffering, what they see as the total indignity of being unable to do anything for themselves or have any control over the way their life is lived ... They could doubtless bear the pain, if there were any hope of regaining control of their lives. They hanker for autonomy, not so much as a matter of principle, applicable to everyone, but because they personally intensely prefer freedom to the slavery of illness in which they find themselves.

Although autonomy is the chief focus in this passage, the authors also mention the concept of dignity (via its converse, indignity), which they take to be a related notion having to do with the ability to control one's manner of life. This is somewhat different from the notion of dignity employed in the summary of Kantian deontology above, in which it functioned as a synonym for the intrinsic value of persons. Some advocates of MAID explicitly favour reducing the notion of dignity to that of autonomy or even dropping the former altogether in favour of the latter. Schuklenk et al. (2011, pp. 38–45) argue for dropping it because in their view the notion of dignity as an inherent property of human persons is so thoroughly rooted in underlying theological conceptions – the idea of humans as made in God's image – as to be inadmissible in the context of moral discourse about public policy in a modern democracy. Still, for those of us who already have theological predilections, a religiously buttressed conception of dignity carries the advantage of robustly reminding us that the loss of control involved in serious physical illness is no sign of indignity. LeMasters (2008, p. 61), an ethicist and Eastern Orthodox priest, writes that,

> by definition, those in need of healthcare are in some respects weak and dependent. Many have profound constraints on their freedom to live as they wish, and the human life-cycle includes periods of complete dependence and lack of rational self-awareness. Nonetheless, all human beings bear the image of God and are persons because they are created and redeemed for communion with the Persons who are the Holy Trinity.[18]

Gill (2014, pp. 369–371) advocates a position similar to that of Warnock and Macdonald (2008):

> Many ethical discussions that invoke the value of autonomy equate autonomy with the ability to make one's own decisions ... But if we want to be clear about what the value of autonomy in end-of-life issues really involves, we need to draw a distinction between the kinds of decisions a person may make. The distinction I want to draw is between what I will call "big decisions" and "little decisions." Big decisions are decisions that shape your destiny and determine the course of your life. Big decisions call on you to make a choice in light of things that matter most to you, in light of the things that give your life whatever meaning it has. Big decisions proceed from your deepest values. Little decisions, by contrast, concern matters that are momentary or insignificant ... To respect autonomy is, first and foremost, to respect a person's ability to make big decisions. It is to respect a person's ability to determine her own fate, to shape her own life ... Suicide may be an unreasonable end to the lives of some people with terminal diseases. But it may not be an unreasonable end for the lives of others. And everyone should be allowed to decide for herself ... It is a big decision, deciding what sort of ending is for you the fundamentally right one, maybe one of the biggest decisions of all. That is why everyone whose end is imminent should be allowed to make it for herself.

The further implication here is that, because the ability to make such decisions is so significant, and because suicide for some is a reasonable choice, others ought to be permitted to assist in carrying it out. Typically, when an act is permissible, it is likewise permissible to receive assistance in performing it.

Harris (1995, pp. 10–11), in fact, places autonomy at the centre of human well-being:

> No one could, I believe, claim coherently to have genuine respect for persons unless at the very least they were prepared to show concern for their welfare and respect for their wishes. Normally these two ideas are complementary, but sometimes, where people have self-harming preferences, these two dimensions of respect of persons come into direct conflict and we have to decide which is to have priority ... To answer this question we need to remind ourselves of the point of valuing liberty – freedom of choice. The point of autonomy, the point of choosing and having the freedom to choose

between competing conceptions of how, and indeed why, to live, is simply
that it is only thus that our lives become in any real sense our own. The
value of our lives is the value we give to our lives. And we do this, so far as
it is possible at all, by shaping our lives for ourselves ... We need welfare,
broadly conceived in terms of health, freedom from pain, mobility, shelter,
nourishment and so on, precisely because welfare is liberating. It is what we
need to be able to pursue our lives to best advantage. So that where concern
for welfare and respect for wishes are incompatible one with another, concern for welfare must give way to respect for autonomy.

Later Harris draws out the implication for euthanasia (pp. 19–20):
"Euthanasia should be permitted ... simply because to deny a person control
of what, on any analysis, must be one of the most important decisions of life,
is a form of tyranny, which like all acts of tyranny is an ultimate denial of
respect for persons."[19]
    Consider also Young (2007, pp. 21–22):

Respect for persons demands respect for their autonomous choices, as long
as those choices do not result in harm to others ... In exercising autonomy,
or self-determination, each of us takes responsibility for our life and, since
dying is a part of life, choices about the manner of our dying, and the timing
of our death, are part of what is involved in taking responsibility for our life.
It is quite natural for each of us to be concerned about what the last phase
of our life will be like, not merely because of fears that our dying might
cause us great suffering, but also because of our desire to avoid dependency,
to retain our dignity, and, more generally, to retain as much control over
our life as is possible during its final phase.

The "each of us" aspect of Young's statement is important here; a common
claim is that the legalization of MAID is important for everyone, regardless
of whether we are healthy or ill, young or near the end of life. In this view,
we all benefit from the increased autonomy (and accompanying peace of
mind) afforded by the availability of MAID, irrespective of whether or not
we would ever choose it for ourselves. As Palmer (2015, p. 194) puts it, "the
prospect of being able to retain some autonomy and control over the end-
of-life process is of value to more individuals than would ever choose the
option of an assisted death." With these passages fresh in mind, how might
one try to formulate more precisely an autonomy-centred argument for the
permissibility of MAID?

I think that the best way to frame such an argument is to take autonomy as a *central* good (or right) without taking it as the *most important* one. Many would be uncomfortable with the idea of *always* having to respect a person's free choice of suicide; with the possible exception of Harris (1995), who places autonomy well above other components of personal well-being, the authors just quoted wish to restrict support for assisted suicide and euthanasia to cases of terminal or at least grievous illness (and even Harris refrains from drawing a broader implication than that pertaining to the terminally ill). We are not bound to respect an autonomous choice by a competent adult who wants to die as a result of a marriage breakup or job loss, for instance. As Plaisted (2013, p. 205) puts it, "someone of a strong libertarian frame of mind ... may be willing to make PAS [physician-assisted suicide] available to everyone of sound mind who wants it. But for others this would constitute a reductio ad absurdum of the argument. Such widespread PAS would be unthinkable to many, including some proponents of the DWD [death with dignity] laws." Similarly, Devine (1990, p. 183) writes that "one might still want to hold that it is permissible to do *anything* to someone so long as his consent is obtained and the rights of third parties are not violated. On this view duels, human sacrifice with consenting victims, and voluntary enslavement ... would, contrary to most of our intuitions, be permissible." Or consider Yuill (2015, pp. 55–56), likewise writing in response to versions of the autonomy argument that privilege autonomy over other considerations:

> Assisted-suicide advocates leaning on the autonomy argument may truly honour autonomy only by approving of *all* suicides. They may not restrict assistance only to those ... of which they approve ... Such suicides as those of Marshall Applewhite and 37 of his followers in the Heaven's Gate Cult, who killed themselves in order to avoid the recycling of planet earth, should be respected – if we privilege autonomy – as much as that of an elderly man suffering from terminal cancer ... There is enough evidence that all these deaths occurred with the consent of the dead even if not by the hand of the dead person. Assisted-suicide supporters may well regard the People's Temple and Heaven's Gate cults as delusory but, as long as the members freely entered into the decision to kill themselves, their suicides should, under the logic of autonomy, be legal and receive widespread approval.

Gorsuch (2006, p. 100) also refers to that example:

> Changing the law to permit consensual homicide would effect such a sea change in our culture, and it is difficult to assess what other forms of con-

sensual conduct would or would not come to seem acceptable in such a very different world. But some hints do exist. In 1997, thirty-nine members of the Heaven's Gate cult systematically ingested Phenobarbital and vodka and asphyxiated each other in a belief that they were releasing their souls to meet with a UFO following in the trail of the Hale-Bopp comet. In a video-taped testament filmed shortly before the suicides, one cult member stated, "I am doing this of my own free will," and "it is not something someone brainwashed me into or convinced me of or did a con job on."

Yet it cannot be denied that some ethicists embrace what Plaisted, Yuill, Gorsuch, and others take to be the *absurdum*. Varelius (2007, pp. 78–79), for instance, argues that suffering should not be seen as a necessary condition for receiving euthanasia:

> In other words, unless we include the requirement of suffering into the definition of voluntary euthanasia, we have to accept that persons can be euthanized when they are merely tired of living, having continuous feelings of uselessness, etc. But why would it be a bad thing if we accepted this? If an autonomous person who is not suffering judges her life to be so bad for her that she wants to die, why would this not be enough to make it legitimate to speak about euthanasia in her case? … If the patient autonomously requests euthanasia, why should the physician have to have some objective criteria, other than the requirements of autonomous agency, on the basis of which she could check whether or not death really would be good for the patient? If the patient qualifies as an autonomous agent and makes an autonomous request for euthanasia, why should this not suffice?

Nevertheless, I believe that most readers are more likely to side here with Plaisted, Yuill, and Gorsuch rather than Varelius and correspondingly would wish to restrict the range of acceptable grounds for MAID. So granting that acts such as consensual mass suicide are immoral, precisely what *makes* them immoral? Why is there a tendency to think (rightly or wrongly) that where possible we should intervene to stop the suicide of the recently divorced, or the recently unemployed, or the cult member, but not (perhaps) the terminally ill?

Cholbi (2011, pp. 88–92) argues that one crucial distinction has to do with the rationality of the choice of suicide. Building on that idea, a proponent of MAID might argue that we are bound to respect the autonomous choice of the terminally or grievously ill individual but not the recently divorced individual because we rightly deem that the autonomous choice of the first individual is at least minimally rational (i.e., not positively irrational), whereas the autonomous choice of the second individual is not minimally rational.[20] Hence, we are not permitted to interfere with the terminally ill person's suicide (or assisted suicide or consensual active euthanasia) since doing so would be paternalistic and tyrannical (to use Harris's term), but we are obligated to interfere with the divorcee's suicide (e.g., if we saw the person readying himself to leap off a bridge, then we would be obligated to try to talk him out of it). If respect for a person's autonomous choice is contingent on our assessment of the rationality of that choice, and not merely the rationality (in the sense of legal competence) of the agent making the choice, then it is apparent that autonomy plays at best a supporting role in the argument for the permissibility of MAID. Autonomous choice for death is to be respected only when that choice is combined with a medical condition sufficiently grave as to render suicide a rational decision.[21]

In this connection, the reader will recall the criteria adopted in Bill C-14, section 3 (241.2 (2)), according to which competent adults are legally eligible for MAID in cases in which

> (a) they have a serious and incurable illness, disease or disability; (b) they are in an advanced state of irreversible decline in capability; (c) that illness, disease or disability or that state of decline causes them enduring physical or psychological suffering that is intolerable to them and that cannot be relieved under conditions that they consider acceptable; and (d) their natural death has become reasonably foreseeable, taking into account all of their medical circumstances, without a prognosis necessarily having been made as to the specific length of time that they have remaining.

Note especially the wording in (c). The issue is not whether the suffering can be alleviated, as a practical medical matter; as a last resort, continual sedation can always be employed as an effective step to eliminate suffering without killing the patient. Rather, the issue is whether the suffering can be alleviated "under conditions they consider acceptable." And some prefer not to receive sedation. They would rather die than remain alive in a state of continual unconsciousness.

Since suicide is not rendered permissible by its being *necessary* to alleviate grievous suffering (it is not), the advocate of an autonomy argument for MAID needs to add the idea that autonomy and relief of suffering comprise sufficient grounds to guarantee the permissibility of MAID *where the range of a patient's autonomous choices with respect to how exactly that suffering is relieved properly extends to deliberate termination of his or her own life.* That is, what needs to be claimed is that the patient is exercising autonomy and suffering greatly from a terminal (or at least a grievous) ailment and rationally chooses death as one among several available means of ending that suffering. Death might not be the only way to end the suffering; however, if it is the method that the patient has freely chosen, then provided that this choice is not positively irrational we are duty bound to respect that free choice, whether through assistance or at least through non-interference (which would include neither criminalizing the act nor others' assistance in it). Taking all of this into account, an autonomy-focused argument for the permissibility of MAID might be formalized in the following manner:

Premise 1: A terminally ill patient, suffering grievously, may permissibly choose among any efficacious means of alleviating that suffering, provided that no one else is badly harmed thereby.[22]

Premise 2: MAID is an efficacious means of alleviating suffering that badly harms no one else.

Conclusion: Therefore, a terminally ill patient, suffering grievously, may permissibly choose MAID.[23]

The justification for premise 1 is to be found in the high value placed on personal autonomy, especially in the context of life's most important decisions. The justification for premise 2 is based on the obvious empirical point that MAID ends suffering by ending the life of the sufferer, combined with the less obvious claim that it causes serious harm to no one else. Of course, some harm might attend others – as noted earlier, for instance, there can be a deleterious psychological impact on the health-care practitioners involved. But one can argue that such harms are not of sufficient severity to outweigh the good obtained by the patient in carrying out his final wishes.

I believe that something like this captures the core idea of most of the autonomy-based arguments for the permissibility of MAID. And it is a forceful line of reasoning. The thought that those in the final stages of life deserve to be granted maximal control over their medical treatment, in particular over the means of pain relief, is a plausible justification for including MAID among the list of alternatives available to them. I understand and respect this perspective, and I sympathize with those who find themselves faced with such painful decisions at the end of life. The debate over the permissibility of MAID is a difficult one, and there are people of good conscience on both sides.

Still, I view MAID as morally impermissible. Everything possible should be done to alleviate grievous suffering, especially for the terminally ill, and those in this position should be given the choice among every available means – except deliberately killing them. Let us turn now to consider what is probably the single most common sort of argument against the permissibility of MAID, one that can also be seen as a direct challenge to the autonomy-based argument.

Arguments against the Permissibility of MAID: Inviolability of Life

Until the passage of Bill C-14, the Canadian criminal law (and the English common law on which it is based) had always prohibited any such killing. As Keown (2014, pp. 4–5) puts it,

> the principle of the inviolability of life is a fundamental principle of the common law ... The principle is grounded in an understanding of each human being as having an intrinsic and ineliminable dignity. The essence of the principle is the prohibition on the intentional taking of human life, intention used in its ordinary sense of aim or purpose ... Historically the law has been profoundly shaped by recognition of the intrinsic worth of the life of each human being and the principle that it is always wrong to intentionally kill innocent human beings (that is, those not involved in unjust aggression).

Modern Canadian law had taken the principle even further, abandoning capital punishment in favour of the view that even those guilty of horrific crimes ought not to be deliberately killed.

Of course, the fact that allowing MAID constitutes a departure from the Canadian legal tradition of prohibiting intentional killing of innocent persons does not automatically mean that it is a mistake. I would argue, however, that it is a mistake because that legal tradition was based on an important truth: it really *is* wrong deliberately to kill an innocent person, even oneself. As noted earlier, that proposition is widely affirmed, whether on independent grounds (i.e., as a stand-alone principle), as an implication of a background ethical theory (e.g., natural law theory or Kantian deontology), or as derived from religious doctrine. Sometimes it is parsed in terms of the right to life being inviolable, or in terms of the sanctity of life, though the basic idea need not be framed in terms of rights or theological language. Here is one way of formulating the argument:

Premise 1: It is impermissible to kill an innocent person deliberately.
Premise 2: MAID consists of killing an innocent person deliberately.
Conclusion: Therefore, MAID is impermissible.

The second premise is uncontroversial, so an assessment of the argument must focus on premise 1. That premise might be upheld as a plausible stand-alone proposition, one compatible with multiple ethical theories (though not all of them) and defensible independent of an explicit commitment to any one theory. Its intuitive plausibility might rest on nothing more than our pre-theoretical sense of the *profound* value of human life. Human life is precious. Most of us share an inherent revulsion at the thought of deliberately killing another human being, and this revulsion is arguably indicative of that important moral fact.[24]

Indeed, one might argue that part of how we assess the plausibility of background ethical theories is by checking whether they are compatible with the affirmation of intuitively plausible pre-theoretical principles of this kind. For instance, one might claim that one of the problems with HAU is that it is incompatible with premise 1; to see this, all one has to do is imagine a case in which the deliberate killing of an innocent person produces the greatest long-term happiness-over-unhappiness ratio. Such examples are a staple in the literature on HAU.[25] They do not, of course, disprove the theory – HAU advocates can simply grant this as a (perhaps surprising) implication of the theory, without admitting that the theory is thereby falsified. Conversely, those who find premise 1 compelling will take this as a mark against HAU. The weighing of conflicting intuitions is a necessary exercise in ethics, and many advocates of HAU will take the advantages of that theory as outweighing, in the end, the initial plausibility of premise 1. Others will engage in the same weighting exercise and judge that, whatever the advantages of HAU, its allowing for the deliberate killing of the innocent is a decisive mark against it.

I am not attempting here to pick on HAU; as I have stated before, it is an interesting and important theory with many prominent defenders in the ethics literature. I am simply using it as a foil to illustrate the point that one could plausibly claim that the only justification needed for premise 1 is its substantial intuitive appeal, to the extent that theoretical backing for it is not required – indeed to the extent that it can be used as a sort of criterion to help weigh the advantages and disadvantages of broader moral theories.

Still, though one can argue that premise 1 is not in need of additional theoretical support, such support can be, and has been, offered by way of grounding its truth in specific theories. Thus, a Kantian deontologist might justify premise 1 in terms of the killing of an innocent person being incompatible with regarding and treating that person as an end in himself; even killing him from a desire to end his suffering, even in a case in which killing is the only way to end that suffering (rarely if ever the case in a nation where advanced medical technology is available), would again be to treat him merely as a means: namely, a means to the (admittedly admirable) goal of stopping the pain. Cholbi (2011, p. 65) concisely summarizes (without endorsing) the Kantian position on this:

> Not only must we not treat other people's autonomy as a means to our own happiness, we must not treat our own autonomy as a means to our own happiness. But that, Kant says, is exactly what suicide often is: a person destroys herself, and thereby destroys the autonomous self that makes her have value or dignity, for the sake of her happiness (or more exactly, for the sake of putting an end to unhappiness). A person suffering from persistent depression, a painful illness, or a succession of devastating setbacks has understandable reasons to want to end her life, but to do so would be to destroy the autonomous self that gives our lives their importance. To take one's life because of the bleakness of the future is to reduce oneself to nothing more than a means for the realization of one's interests, or as David Velleman vividly puts it, to treat oneself "like a stick of dynamite, which realizes its nature by blowing itself up."[26] Suicide, in Kant's view, denies human beings the very dignity that makes them human.

Cholbi goes on to object to this argument, in part on the ground that, when people rationally choose to kill themselves (or consent to be killed by others), they "do not seem to be making themselves tools or instruments of anyone's happiness, including their own. They are determining that their lives are better if those lives are shorter, and Kant's claim that suicide is wrong because our autonomous selves are priceless simply does not seem to take that fact into account" (p. 67). I am not sure that quite answers the Kantian point. The claim of the deontologist is that a person cannot permissibly be treated merely as a means to some end. To do so contradicts the profound intrinsic value or dignity of a human being. Now, a person who makes an allegedly rational choice for MAID is doing so in order to achieve some end. As with any rational choice, there is a goal in mind. In most cases (all cases?), the person's overarching goal is not actually self-annihilation. What the person wants is an end to suffering, and self-annihilation is a method for achieving that goal. It is not the only method (as noted above), but it is one available method. Yet, unlike other such methods, it completely cuts off the person's ability ever to make further choices, ever to engage in additional autonomous activity. The agent himself will be no more.[27] In choosing to reject his very existence for the sake of achieving an end to suffering, he acts in a manner contrary to a proper respect for his own inherent dignity as a person. Palliative sedation, in contrast, lacks this feature. The suffering ends while the agent himself persists with the inherent capacity to exercise rational autonomy should the situation somehow change for the better. No doubt in the vast majority of cases in which palliative sedation is applied, the patient is mostly beyond hope of recovery. But last-minute reprieves, spontaneous remissions, and so on have been known to occur even in the direst of medical situations. A further oft-noted worry about MAID is that it eliminates all such hope. This provides one way of resisting the common claim (e.g., Sumner, 2011, p. 59) that there is no normatively relevant difference to the patient between MAID and palliative sedation, given that both entail unconsciousness.

A natural law theorist can justify premise 1 by reference to the idea of human life itself being the most foundational human good. In addition to life itself being valuable, the possession of any other good (e.g., autonomy or pleasure) can be seen as dependent on being alive; accordingly, it makes no sense to destroy life for the sake of realizing some other good of the agent. There will be no agent left in whom the realization of that good will be found. Paterson (2008, pp. 105–106), a natural law theorist, puts the point as follows:

> A person simply cannot be harmed or benefited when they cease to exist, for there is no *ontological existent* to be harmed or benefited. To assign a meaningful benefit or loss to a person requires the continuing existence – the beingness – of the person. The real evil inflicted upon a person by death is to terminate the very existence of the person, rendering a person non-existent. It is this radical ontological change from personal existence to non-existence that crucially explains why it is that death *per se* is considered to be a primal evil for persons. When we assert that a person is harmed or benefitted by some state, this requires that there is actually a

person in existence who is capable of being the bearer of the value or dis-value. If it is good to be without pain and suffering, as indeed it generally is, this presupposes the existence of a person in order to instantiate that good (or any good).

Garcia (2007, p. 254) expands on this sort of idea, employing the distinction between *relief* of pain versus *cessation* of pain:

> The way in which someone's dying puts a stop to her pain, etc., is not by bringing the sufferer something that can properly be called *relief* of pain, or even release from it, but instead only its cessation. Ending her pain cannot be a benefit to her for the usual reason, then, because here the patient does not experience relief and thereafter live pain-free. As the end of her pain here does not improve her experience neither does it improve her life, her condition. Rather, she (her integrated human life) ends along with the pain, and she is in no condition at all during the period when she is lifeless. We cannot, then, meaningfully compare it with her condition over the same time had she lived.

Colwell (1996, pp. 11–12), though not proceeding specifically from natural law theory, makes a similar point:

> When a boy's broken arm is mended he usually lives to enjoy the cure. But if we try to mend a man's miserable life by removing it, he is no longer around to enjoy the help. Here the choice is not between living in pain and living in peace; rather, it is between living in pain and not living at all. To be in pain, or not to be: that is the question. If we say that extinguishing a life which is terribly painful has more value than sustaining that life, we must ask a further question: For whom does it have the greater value? We can scarcely answer, "For the man who dies," for he exists no more. Can the extinguished life enjoy its painless state?

Again this assumes, for the sake of argument, that physical death is really the end of the agent. If, conversely, death is not the end, then that fact will likewise be relevant to the assessment. But then the prospect of an afterlife will not necessarily lend support to MAID, as Colwell rightly goes on to note (more on that shortly).

Of course, the natural law theorist must be careful here not to draw unwarranted inferences from this, such as the inference that an incurable,

terminally ill patient has no right to consent to the refusal or the withdrawal of life-preserving treatment (e.g., a terminal lung cancer patient
who opts out of being hooked up to a respirator). So natural law theorists
who employ the present justification for premise 1 recognize the related
idea that, though the good that is human life must not be *directly violated*
by intentionally destroying it, there is no obligation *to pursue* that good
under any and all conditions. The profound good that is human life cannot
be deliberately attacked; nevertheless, nature can be permitted to take its
course, such that life is allowed to cease on its own. Life, after all, does
have a natural and unavoidable end. Watt (2015, p. 222) observes that "to
say that life has value is not, of course, to say that this value must be pur-
sued on every occasion. This is no more true than it is true that we must
seize every opportunity to pursue any other basic good: every opportunity
to learn something, for example, or to make another friend."[28] Nevertheless,
natural law theorists typically agree that, even in the withdrawal or refusal
of treatment, death should not be an intended goal but a foreseen side
effect of another goal (e.g., ceasing a course of care that has become bur-
densome to the patient).

The notion that human life retains intrinsic value and dignity even in its
final stages, and indeed even in a state of unconsciousness prompted by
palliative sedation, is resisted by some. But Pruss (2010), quoted in Watt
(2015, p. 219), presses the point:

> Consider the attitude one might have towards someone that one loves who
> has fallen dreamlessly asleep – say, one's child or one's spouse. One may
> fondly kiss the beloved's head, recognizing the beloved's present value –
> fondness always involves an element of taking the beloved to have value. If
> the value of humans essentially requires consciousness, there is either a
> mistake here or else the value is entirely constituted by the expected future
> consciousness. It is implausible to say that a mistake is being made, so let us
> consider the future-consciousness hypothesis. Suppose that the beloved is
> going to be executed by a tyrant as soon as she is about to regain conscious-
> ness. There is no future consciousness (except in the afterlife, and I do not
> think the attitude depends on beliefs about the afterlife). But the tragic
> absence of a future consciousness does not make one less fond – it does not
> make one value the person less – but the very opposite. Nor is one's attitude
> as it is towards a corpse. In the case of the sleeping person who will be exe-
> cuted, one dreads and mourns a *future* loss; in the case of the corpse, one
> mourns an already *present* loss.

If one shares Pruss's intuitions about these situations, and thinks that such intuitions track normative truths, then one will have additional reason to resist opting for MAID over and against palliative sedation, insofar as one will recognize the remaining value even of the unconscious human being. That the latter possesses rights and interests is further supported by powerful intuitions concerning the inviolable right of those in a comatose state to freedom from assault.[29]

One might also justify premise 1 of the inviolability argument by reference to underlying theological notions. These notions can take several forms. One might buttress, for instance, the claim that human life is profoundly valuable by adverting to the Judeo-Christian doctrine that human beings are made in the image of God. Furthermore, besides being intrinsically wrong, the deliberate killing of the innocent might also be wrong because, as our creator, God has some legitimate rights over our lives (whether one wants to cash out those rights in terms of "ownership" over our lives or more plausibly in some other fashion), which can be infringed when we deliberately take someone's life. Note that this moral consideration should weigh on the mind of anyone who takes theism seriously as at least a live option – not only theists but also agnostics should be concerned about violating God's rights over our lives. If, for all we know, there might be a God with some legitimate rights over our lives, then that is an additional reason to worry that deliberate killing of the innocent might be morally impermissible, even when the person consents to death. To put the point a bit differently, if there is a God, then perhaps no one really has a legitimate right to consent to her own deliberate killing. (In contrast, the incurable, terminal patient who consents to the withdrawal of life-sustaining treatment might not intend her own death and in fact might conceptualize the act as one in which she leaves the situation in God's hands.)

It is important to emphasize that agnostics as well as religious believers ought to take such an argument seriously, insofar as it is often erroneously claimed that arguments proceeding from theological premises cannot legitimately be employed in moral debates within modern, pluralistic democracies. For instance, Schuklenk et al. (2011, p. 42) write that

> the underlying premise – namely that all humans are possessed of dignity in virtue of a special relationship to a God – is, however, incapable of being used as a basis of public policy proven in the context of a democratic, multicultural and multi-faith society that must cleave to the strictures of public reason in ethical deliberation. In the absence of a societal consensus in

favour of, or incontrovertible proof of the existence of the God in question, and therefore, the absence of overwhelming societal support for the metaphysical claims underlying this grounding of dignity, this account of human dignity cannot be relied upon to justify normative guidance on assisted dying on a societal level. Religious people might choose to avail themselves of the guidance provided by their respective religions, but it is unreasonable to enforce normative views, derived from claims about a God, uniformly on a societal level given the multicultural and multi-faith nature of Canada in the twenty-first century.

Sumner (2011, p. 74) concurs:

> Life is a gift from God, one of the familiar arguments runs, and so should not be destroyed. Or: it is up to God, and not to us, to decide when we quit this life. However, theistic arguments of this sort are ... faith-based, [so] they are not susceptible of rational refutation and cannot serve as the ethical basis of public policy.

But that seems to imply not that public policy must be religiously *neutral* but that it must presuppose *the truth of atheism*. Only the committed atheist can safely ignore the potential moral relevance of the existence of God. In contrast, someone genuinely unsure about the reality of God will have to take such potential moral implications seriously as a matter of simple prudence. If there is a realistic possibility of the existence of God, which could have a bearing on the morality of suicide, then the agnostic cannot rationally ignore this possibility in his or her moral assessment of suicide. Relatedly, polls consistently show that a majority of Canadians believe in God. For instance, a 2015 Angus Reid survey of more than 3,000 Canadians found that 73 percent profess belief in a God or higher power.[30] One might question why the spiritual beliefs of the majority of the citizenry must be studiously ignored when debating public policy.

So far, I have discussed the moral relevance of theism and agnosticism only in terms of the possibility of the existence of another agent, namely God, whose rights and interests must be taken into account in discussions of deliberate killing. One might also reference a more self-interested theological point: namely, the possibility of an afterlife in which one might conceivably be punished for deliberately killing an innocent person. Most theistic religions affirm the reality of something like heaven, hell, and purgatory in which people are judged for their actions during their lives on Earth.

For an agnostic uncertain about the reality of such afterlife states, the possibility that one's final act on Earth (namely, suicide) could be a sin subject to punishment ought rationally to give one pause. Such concerns might motivate something akin to a Pascalian wager: given that one is undecided between theism and atheism, one ought prudently to weigh the possible benefits and risks of suicide. The benefits might include the expression of personal autonomy and the ending of physical and emotional suffering. (Again, though, one would also have to bear in mind the fact that death is not the only available means of ending that suffering or, for that matter, the only way of meaningfully expressing autonomy at the end of life.) The risks might include the prospect of postmortem punishment, whether temporary or eternal (depending on which model of the afterlife one considers most probable). If killing an innocent person (even oneself) might be gravely immoral, and if there might exist postmortem punishments for gravely immoral acts, then that possibility ought to give one an additional reason to question the rationality of suicide.[31]

I emphasize again that, in making these theological points, I am not arguing in the following manner: because God exists, one ought to worry about infringing God's rights and/or worry about experiencing divine postmortem justice. The point is more like this: because there is a chance (even if only a slim one) that God exists, one ought to worry about infringing God's rights and/or worry about experiencing divine postmortem justice. The latter sort of argument must be taken seriously by a sincere agnostic and can be rationally dismissed only by someone very confident in his or her atheism (or someone very confident that, if God does exist, then God has no relevant rights over our lives). And, of course, to dismiss a moral argument by reference to the truth of atheism is to adopt not a theologically neutral stance but a committed *atheological* stance. It is unclear to me why a settled atheism should be seen as a more appropriate stance for the sake of public moral discourse than an agnostic stance.[32]

Those are some of the reasons that have been put forward in support of premise 1. Criticisms of that premise engage those supports and concentrate on demonstrating points such as the following: the right to life is a forfeitable right properly ranked below other rights; in killing oneself, one is not treating oneself merely instrumentally; the good of human life is not so profoundly good as the premise supposes, such that it can properly be viewed as subordinate to other goods (e.g., autonomy); on the most plausible accounts of human well-being, it is better for someone to be deprived of existence than to be alive and in pain, even should the pain be treatable (remember that I am thinking of scenarios in which the terminal, grievously suffering patient rejects palliative sedation in favour of MAID);[33] and either atheism is demonstrably true or, if there is a God, then we can be very confident that God approves of MAID. Demonstrating the truth of any one of these critical points, let alone all of them, is a daunting task in my opinion.

I have now reviewed the two most common sorts of argument for the permissibility of MAID and the single most common sort of argument against its permissibility. I have provided samples of the diverse argumentative strategies by which the key premises of these arguments have been buttressed – an incomplete sampling, I should emphasize. The literature on these arguments is decades old and massive, and here I cannot hope to summarize its full contours while keeping this introduction accessible and of a reasonable length.

The moral arguments considered thus far, though the most prominent types regarding MAID in the recent literature, are certainly not the only ones available to consider. What follows are some further lines of reasoning.

Arguments for the Permissibility of MAID: *Carter v Canada*

Recall that the Supreme Court of Canada in its 2015 *Carter v Canada* ruling reasoned that the right to life enshrined in the Charter entails the legal permission of MAID. Why? Because criminalizing MAID likely has the effect of driving to premature suicide those at risk of future physical incapacitation. The court did not put forward this line of reasoning as an explicitly *moral* argument; however, a moral argument does seem to be implicit in the legal reasoning deployed on this point. This moral argument did not receive much attention in the prior ethics literature,[34] but no doubt it will in the future, having now played such an important role (if only implicitly) in jurisprudence on MAID. At any rate, it will be interesting to subject it to formalization and assessment.

Premise 1: Everyone possesses a negative, non-absolute (i.e., forfeitable) right to life.
Premise 2: If everyone possesses a negative, non-absolute (i.e., forfeitable) right to life, then everyone possesses a negative right to freedom from anything that could plausibly drive a person to premature suicide.

Conclusion 1/Premise 3: Therefore, everyone possesses a negative right to freedom from anything that could plausibly drive a person to premature suicide.

Premise 4: Those at risk of future physical incapacitation (incapacitation sufficiently severe as to risk blocking even the minimal physical activity needed to commit suicide) could plausibly be driven to premature suicide under conditions in which voluntary active euthanasia is prohibited.

Final Conclusion: Therefore, those at risk of future physical incapacitation (incapacitation sufficiently severe as to risk blocking even the minimal physical activity needed to commit suicide) have a negative right to freedom from the prohibition on voluntary active euthanasia.

Of course, as an exegesis of the Supreme Court's actual line of reasoning, this is not accurate since the court reached a much broader final conclusion, such that its actual argument seems to run more like the following:

Premise 1: Everyone possesses a negative, non-absolute (i.e., forfeitable) right to life.

Premise 2: If everyone possesses a negative, non-absolute (i.e., forfeitable) right to life, then everyone possesses a negative right to freedom from anything that could plausibly drive a person to premature suicide.

Conclusion 1/Premise 3: Therefore, everyone possesses a negative, non-absolute (i.e., forfeitable) right to freedom from anything that could plausibly drive a person to premature suicide.

Premise 4: Those at risk of future physical incapacitation (incapacitation sufficiently severe as to risk blocking even the minimal physical activity needed to commit suicide) could plausibly be driven to premature suicide under conditions in which voluntary active euthanasia is prohibited.

Final Conclusion: Therefore, every competent adult suffering from a grievous and irremediable disease, illness, or disability that causes enduring suffering intolerable to the individual has the negative right to freedom from the prohibition on assisted suicide and voluntary active euthanasia.

This second, seemingly more accurate, formulation is a non sequitur. The final conclusion simply does not follow from the premises since the category of those eligible for euthanasia is mysteriously extended from those at risk of future physical incapacitation to a far broader category.

Perhaps it is uncharitable to attribute such a manifestly invalid line of reasoning to the Supreme Court. Maybe the justices were thinking more along these lines:

Premise 1: Everyone possesses a negative, non-absolute (i.e., forfeitable) right to life.

Premise 2: If everyone possesses a negative, non-absolute (i.e., forfeitable) right to life, then everyone possesses a negative right to freedom from anything that could plausibly drive a person to premature suicide.

Conclusion 1/Premise 3: Therefore, everyone possesses a negative right to freedom from anything that could plausibly drive a person to premature suicide.

Premise 4: Those at risk of future physical incapacitation (incapacitation sufficiently severe as to risk blocking even the minimal physical activity needed to commit suicide) could plausibly be driven to premature suicide under conditions in which voluntary active euthanasia is prohibited.

Conclusion 2/Premise 5: Therefore, those at risk of future physical incapacitation (incapacitation sufficiently severe as to risk blocking even the minimal physical activity needed to commit suicide) have a negative right to freedom from the prohibition on voluntary active euthanasia.

Premise 6: If those at risk of future physical incapacitation (incapacitation sufficiently severe as to risk blocking even the minimal physical activity needed to commit suicide) have a negative right to freedom from the prohibition on voluntary active euthanasia, then every competent adult suffering from a grievous and irremediable disease, illness, or disability that causes enduring suffering intolerable to the individual should also have the negative right to freedom from the prohibition on assisted suicide and voluntary active euthanasia.

Final Conclusion: Therefore, every competent adult suffering from a grievous and irremediable disease, illness, or disability that causes enduring suffering intolerable to the individual should also have the negative right to freedom from the prohibition on assisted suicide and voluntary active euthanasia.

This restores logical validity to the Supreme Court's argument; then the challenge is to find some plausible justification for the truth of premise 6. I find myself unequal to that challenge; this premise is a conditional proposition, and I do not see any easy way of establishing a relevant tie between antecedent and consequent.

Bracketing that problem, let us consider the remainder of the argument. Premise 1 is true and would be granted by proponents of at least those major ethical theories that admit rights language. (The status of "rights" in consequentialism is much disputed.) However, the precise interpretation of this premise will vary somewhat. Think, for instance, of disagreements over whether the forfeiting must always be voluntary; the debate about capital punishment can be seen as a debate in part about whether the murderer has forfeited his right to life, even though he does not wish to be executed. Other details will likewise vary; restricting the range to those not guilty of a capital crime, natural law theorists will argue, for instance, that the right to life can never be *deliberately* violated, though there are cases in which, in accordance with the doctrine of double effect, one can carry out an act that, though not directly killing an innocent person, will have the foreseeable though not intended result of death. That is the only sense in which they will admit that the negative right to life of an innocent person can be "forfeited." For instance, imagine that someone sees a child fall onto the subway tracks just as the train is approaching and jumps down to rescue him even though she knows that she will only have time to push him off the track and will be fatally struck herself. Here the rescuer carries out an act that in itself does not directly violate a basic good, so it is not intrinsically evil (i.e., jumping onto the subway tracks does not of itself count as an evil act, considered independently of context and consequences). The good effect (saving the child) is intended, and the bad effect (the rescuer's own death) is foreseen but not intended. Moreover, it is the only way to achieve the rescue, and the bad consequences are proportionate to the good consequences. So the act meets the four criteria for the DDE.

Premise 2 is more problematic. Leaving aside the tricky issues involved in the notion of a "premature" suicide,[35] the claim appears to be overly broad, insofar as many things are known to drive people to commit suicide, whether singly or (especially) in combination: divorce, job loss, death of a loved one, recurrent clinical depression, cyberbullying, an extended prison sentence, untreated drug addiction and alcoholism, spousal abuse, et cetera. For some such factors, a person clearly has the negative right to be free from them – a person has the negative right to freedom from abuse, cyberbullying, and so on (i.e., others are obligated to refrain from abusing him or subjecting him to cyberbullying). But, for other major risk factors, there is no such right. That job loss is correlated with suicide does not imply that it is morally wrong to lay off an employee; that divorce is correlated with suicide does not imply that it is morally wrong to divorce a spouse; that an extended prison sentence is correlated with suicide does not imply that the state is duty bound to refrain from imprisoning convicted murderers. (Of course, employers, spouses, and the state are obligated to treat people with kindness and respect, which should cut down on the corresponding risk of prompting self-harm in such situations.)

Premise 4 is likewise problematic. The idea here is that the individual at risk of future physical incapacitation will not want to wait until that incapacitation sets in because he will be unable then to commit suicide. And he will be reluctant to have his doctor or friends engage in active euthanasia because he will not want them to face the risk of future pros-ecution. So this is taken to imply that the state should decriminalize euthanasia in such situations. But notice the intermediate layer that this introduces into the allegation that the state is driving the individual to premature suicide. It will have that effect only on those who care about the future prosecution of their doctors or friends. It will not have that effect on those who, for whatever reason, lack that concern. (They need not lack it because of unconcern; they might have a well-founded belief, for example, that the doctor is unlikely to be caught or unlikely to face jail time if caught.) This is potentially significant, insofar as it introduces the prospect of multiple ways to rectify the problem of the legislation driving people to suicide (granting, for the sake of argument, that it has this effect and that the Supreme Court is obligated to rectify it somehow). One way, the way adopted by the court, is to drop the legislation entirely and make assisted death available to a broad range of applicants. Another way is a narrower judicial exemption for those at risk of imminent total physical incapacitation. Yet another way is to introduce diminished criminal pen-alties for those who engage in active euthanasia for people in this situa-tion. (I am not endorsing either alternative but simply pointing out that alternatives do exist.)

The Supreme Court's argument thus appears to be unsound. One might question, of course, my reconstruction. Perhaps my interpretation of the court's implicit moral reasoning is off base; maybe a better, more compelling reconstruction could be made available. Given that the court's argument is a somewhat novel one, not having been developed in detail in previous pub-lished moral reflections on assisted death, I am operating in something of a vacuum. Still, I hope that this brief discussion is not wholly deficient as a first stab at trying to understand and assess the moral argumentation under-lying the court's legal reasoning.

Arguments for the Permissibility of MAID: Virtue Ethics

Let us turn now to another argument for assisted death, this one arising from a specific ethical theory: virtue ethics. Begley (2008) presents a version of such an argument; however, since her understanding of virtue ethics is rather different from the one laid out earlier (she sees virtue ethics not as providing a basic moral principle but as providing a vision of ethics in which the attempt to find a BMP is misguided), I will consider an alternative formulation.[36]

Premise 1: If a fully informed exemplar of virtue would engage in MAID, then MAID is morally permissible.
Premise 2: A fully informed exemplar of virtue would engage in MAID.
Conclusion: Therefore, MAID is morally permissible.

Premise 1 would be justified by reference to the truth of virtue ethics. Premise 2 would be justified by reference to examples of incontrovertibly virtuous agents whom we can easily imagine participating in MAID.

Premise 1 will be disputed by those who find virtue ethics objectionable as an ethical theory. Premise 2 seems to be vulnerable to seemingly intractable disputes about which exemplars can or cannot be pictured giving lethal injections to willing patients. The advocate of assisted death might think, for instance, of Mother Teresa as an exemplar of virtue and say that, given her remarkable commitment to compassion, she could easily be pictured providing such an injection to a suffering person (or at least she could be so pictured provided that one also imagines her first becoming fully informed and thus giving up her religious scruples on the matter). The opponent of assisted death will reject the claim on the grounds that the act is not really expressive of compassion correctly understood and that Mother Teresa cannot plausibly be pictured deliberately giving someone a lethal injection. In the absence of agreement on this example, other paradigms of virtue could be put forward and intuitions about them tested. But again it is difficult to see how this could contribute much to resolving the dispute, for the disagreements are liable to persist.

Nor can one rely on the claim that in performing MAID certain virtues are plausibly being exercised (e.g., the virtue of compassion) at a high level. Apparently, there are cases of impermissible actions in which virtues are nonetheless being exercised (e.g., the soldier fighting an unjust war might exhibit great courage, the mobster organizing his empire might exhibit prudence, etc.). Although it is certainly a disputable point, at least prima facie it seems that virtues can be manifested even in the commission of vicious acts, such that the manifestation of virtue is not a sufficient condition for the moral permissibility of an action.

Arguments for the Permissibility of MAID: Self-Ownership

Cholbi (2011, pp. 84–88) discusses (without endorsing) another interesting argument for the permissibility of suicide, one proceeding via the concept of self-ownership. He summarizes the basic line of reasoning as follows:

> Our bodies are our property, and just as with anything else we own, we have the right to do with our bodies what we please. I own the laptop computer used to write this book, and because I own it, I am morally permitted to treat it in certain ways. I can improve it by adding additional software to its hard drive or by painting colorful designs on its case. I can sell it if I determine it no longer meets my needs or if I purchase another laptop. And if I so desire, I can even throw it in the trash. The same is true of anything else that is my property, including my own body. I can improve my body through physical exercise, surgery, or (arguably) tattoos. Some would argue that I am morally permitted to sell my body (or at least parts of it, such as my blood or my kidneys). And if the circumstances appear to me to warrant it, I can do to my body the equivalent of throwing my laptop away: I can destroy my body through suicide. (p. 85)

The argument is compatible with multiple ethical theories and might be formalized in perhaps the following manner:

Premise 1: It is permissible to do with one's own property whatever one wishes, provided that it harms no one else.
Premise 2: One's body is one's own property.
Conclusion: Therefore, it is permissible to do with one's own body whatever one wishes, provided that it harms no one else.

The first premise might be explicated further in terms of an underlying notion of rights (in this case, property rights), but it can also be treated as an independent principle. Initially, it seems to have some intuitive appeal, as shown via Cholbi's example of the laptop.

However, it runs into some potential problems since we often think that certain actions taken toward one's own property are in fact morally questionable. For instance, we often condemn the practice of wasting food. If I buy a bagel, then it is my property. I have the right to eat it, to give it to someone else to eat, et cetera. I could also just leave it on the kitchen counter for days, deliberately letting it become mouldy and inedible. Yet that seems to be a morally troublesome waste of a good. We also consider it wrong to abuse or neglect a pet or farm animal. Some would question that example, arguing that an animal cannot rightly be considered property because no one can really own a living thing. But then that would only strengthen a critique of premise 1: if the human body is a living thing, and it is impossible for a living thing to be property, then it is impossible for the human body to be property – *even one's own body*. We might even be bothered by someone who purchases a houseplant only to stomp it to death or purchases a lovely painting only to deface it. Wanton, gratuitous destruction seems to be problematic, even if one is destroying one's own property. In most cases at least, destroying something prima facie requires justification, some adequate reason for destruction. More strongly, one might argue for a position directly contrary to that taken up by premise 1: namely, that we have a moral responsibility to use our own property wisely; it is not permissible to do whatever we wish with our property, and in fact we have special duties of stewardship in that context. The more valuable the piece of property (whether in monetary terms or in some other respect), the greater the obligation of stewardship.

The second premise likewise seems to be questionable. Even if you grant that your own body can be regarded as property (in some sense), it is not immediately clear that you are actually the owner of that property or at least the sole owner. Bringing to mind the theological justification for premise 1 of the inviolability argument above, if God exists and through his causal power conserves your body in existence (along with the rest of creation), then it might seem that God is the real owner of your body or at least a co-owner (if indeed "ownership" is the right way to think about this). If your body is granted to you by God, then it might be regarded as something merely on loan or a responsibility placed under your care, perhaps temporarily, and over which you have resultant duties of stewardship.[37] Note that I am not criticizing premise 2 by saying that "God exists, so your body is not wholly your own." Rather, I am criticizing premise 2 by saying that "unless you are very sure that there is no God, you cannot be very sure that you have sole ownership rights over your body." This criticism is enough to undermine premise 2 and can be taken on board as effectively by the agnostic as by the theist.

Cholbi (2011, pp. 86–87) goes on to criticize the self-ownership argument based on some significant disanalogies between ordinary property and the body and on the grounds that a metaphysical naturalist[38] would not grant the implicit claim that a person is distinct from her body (implicitly required since one cannot be identical to one's own property); rather, the naturalist would want to identify (in some sense) the person with the physical organism.

Arguments against the Permissibility of MAID: The Slippery Slope

Another worry commonly cited by opponents of MAID, one that played an important role in the court rulings canvassed in Chapter 1, is that of the so-called slippery slope. Manning (1998, p. 61) concisely summarizes a distinction between two different types of slippery slope argument:

> There are really at least two forms of the argument: the psychological form and the logical form. The psychological argument claims that if an exception is made to a traditional rule, there will be a tendency for unwanted exceptions to follow. The logical form of the argument speaks to the grounds available for denying any further exceptions to the rule. If we allow *this*, then we have no rational grounds for not allowing *that*.

One might worry about both forms of slope in this context. With respect to the first, one might worry that any weakening of the widespread taboo against deliberately killing the innocent might have a profound, long-term impact on our broader moral intuitions, an impact difficult to predict in advance. Colwell (1995, p. 44) writes that

> their concern is that although we may *start* with VAE [voluntary active euthanasia] for such unfortunates as terminal cancer patients, it will not be long before we slide morally to the place where we are promoting the practice of VAE on non-terminal patients, such as the chronically depressed. And if we permit that, the slide will continue until eventually we shall be killing people without their permission. At the bottom of the moral slope it

will be *we,* and not the patients, who are determining who is a "burden" to society and whose life is "not worth living." In the name of mercy, says this moral causal slope argument, we begin with what appears to be a lofty respect for human life and slide to a position of profound disrespect.

Regarding the second sort of slope, some relate a concern that the kind of autonomy plus suffering, dual justification argument for the rationality of suicide laid out earlier could prompt some to extend the eligibility for MAID on the grounds of what some might see as a logical difficulty in maintaining consistently that both aspects are needed. That is, some maintain that such an argument carries the risk of rendering acceptable *autonomous suicide by the non-suffering* and/or *non-voluntary (or even involuntary) euthanasia of the suffering.* Meilaender (2013, pp. 63–64), for instance, writes that

> if self-determination is truly so significant that we have a right to help in ending our life, then how can we insist that such help may rightly be offered only to those who are suffering greatly? Others who are not suffering may still find life meaningless, the game not worth the candle. They too are autonomous, and, if autonomy is as important as the argument claims it is, then their autonomous requests for euthanasia should also be honored, even if they are not suffering greatly. Similarly, if the suffering of others makes so powerful a claim upon us that we should kill them to bring it to an end, it is hard to believe that we ought to restrict such merciful relief only to those who are self-determining, who are competent to request it. Surely, fully autonomous people are not the only human beings who can suffer greatly. Thus, from both directions, from each prong of the argument, there will be pressure to expand the class of candidates for euthanasia. Those who suffer greatly but cannot request relief and those who request help even though their physical pain is not great will begin to seem more suitable candidates. That is, in fact, the logic of the argument currently being played out in our public policy disputes.

Somerville (2001, p. 43) makes a similar point pertaining to the non-competent: "But if one focuses on the fact that permitting euthanasia for competent people recognizes that the intentional infliction of death is legitimate in some circumstances (for example, to eliminate suffering), it could set a precedent for the legitimation of avoluntary euthanasia of incompetent people whose circumstances are similar to those of competent people who die through euthanasia."

One can always dispute slippery slope arguments, of either the first or the second variety, on the ground that they proceed on the basis of uncertainty. In the first case, can we be sure that common moral intuitions will actually be weakened? In the second, can we be sure that people will draw out the larger, more permissive implications of pro-MAID arguments, if indeed there are such implications? Yet Colwell (1995) argues that past experience and rational reflection on the weaknesses of human nature provide good reasons for taking such risks seriously. Indeed, the passage from his work is particularly striking in the present context since, at the time that he was writing (twenty-five years ago), it was largely taken for granted by the various parties to the debate that extending euthanasia to the non-terminally ill (in his example, the chronically depressed) should be regarded as a step down the moral slope. In contrast, by 2020, a number of Canadian academics and activists were arguing that those suffering solely from mental illnesses share the right to MAID.[39] Discussions on such an extension continue. Moreover, assisted death for psychiatric patients has been practised in Belgium and the Netherlands for some time now and for a wide range of conditions: depression, anorexia, personality disorders, drug addiction, autism, et cetera.

In those nations, some individual cases of MAID for the mentally ill have leaked out into the realm of public discussion and received substantial media attention. For instance, O'Gara (2015), writing in *Newsweek*, reported the following:

> Doctors in Belgium are granting a 24-year-old woman who is suffering from depression but is otherwise healthy the right to die as she qualifies for euthanasia under the Belgian law, even though she does not have a terminal or life-threatening illness. The 24-year-old woman, known simply as Laura, has been given the go-ahead by health professionals in Belgium to receive a lethal injection.

Aviv (2015), writing in the *New Yorker*, likewise related some fairly striking recent cases. Among her interview subjects was Dirk De Wachter, a psychiatrist and professor at the University of Leuven:

> De Wachter believes that the country's approach to suicide reflects a crisis of nihilism created by the rapid secularization of Flemish culture in the past thirty years. Euthanasia became a humanist solution to a humanist dilemma. "What is life worth when there is no God?" he said. "What is life

worth when I am not successful?" He said that he has repeatedly been confronted by patients who tell him, "I am an autonomous decision-maker. I
can decide how long I live. When I think my life is not worth living anymore, I must decide." He recently approved the euthanasia of a twenty-five-
year-old woman with borderline personality disorder who did not "suffer
from depression in the psychiatric sense of the word," he said. "It was more
existential; it was impossible for her to have a goal in this life." He said that
her parents "came to my office, got on their knees, and begged me, 'Please,
help our daughter to die.'"

Aviv reports that public support for MAID in Belgium remains high, and
press coverage is broadly supportive:

> The Flemish media have adopted a mostly uncritical approach to eutha
> nasia, running numerous articles about the courage of people who have
> chosen to die. Last year, *De Standaard*, a prominent Flemish newspaper,
> published a long tribute about a depressed mother who was euthanized
> after being abandoned by her boyfriend and becoming disillusioned by her
> psychiatric care. "I am forever grateful to her that she handled this so well,"
> her twenty-four-year-old son told the paper.

Cases of that sort are not new, and in the Netherlands one of the important early court decisions pertaining to MAID involved a psychiatric patient.
Hendin (1998, pp. 63–64), a psychiatrist specializing in the study of suicide,
recounts some of the details and then relates the situation back to slippery
slope concerns:

> In the Dutch city of Assen in the spring of 1993, a court of three judges
> acquitted a psychiatrist who had assisted in the suicide of his patient, a
> physically healthy fifty-year-old woman who had lost her two sons and had
> recently divorced her husband. The court ruled that the psychiatrist, Dr.
> Boudewijn Chabot, was justified in his actions because his patient was
> competent to make the decision to die freely, her suffering was irremedi
> able, and the doctor met the Dutch criteria for *force majeure* ... The court's
> landmark decision in the Assen case gave legal sanction for assisted suicide
> and euthanasia for patients who were not physically ill. Assisted suicide and
> euthanasia are not yet advocated in the United States for physically healthy
> patients regarded as having purely psychiatric ailments. But the ruling in
> the Assen case seems to justify warning of a "slippery slope" that descends

inexorably from assisted suicide to euthanasia, from those who are terminally ill to those who are chronically ill, from those who are physically ill
to those who are mentally ill, and from those who request euthanasia to
those whose lives are ended at the doctor's discretion.

It is also worth noting that Belgium in 2014 extended the legal availability of
MAID to children.[40] We might also think of the support within some quar-
ters of academia for killing incompetent, non-consenting dementia patients,
as in Warnock and Macdonald (2008, pp. 134–136), who likewise advocate
MAID for legally competent consenting psychiatric patients (ch. 3). Recall,
too, the position of ethicists such as Varelius (2007), who argue that MAID
should be made available to those who suffer from no medical condition
whatsoever.

Besides these concerns about the risk of extending MAID to new groups,
there is the perennial concern that those currently eligible legally will be
subtly (or not so subtly) pressured to consent to it, contrary to their real
inclinations, and that legalization might spark increased use of non-voluntary
euthanasia. The court in *Carter v Canada* was confident that effective safeguards could be implemented, but this remains an area of active debate.[41]
Even aside from the risk of person-to-person pressure, one can also argue
that the mere legal availability of MAID itself results in a kind of pressure on
the dying or even the long-term disabled (especially now that the provision
of "reasonably foreseeable death" has been struck down by the Quebec
Superior Court ruling in 2019). This latter concern is often raised by opponents of MAID, including Bishop (2016, p. 267):

> Thus, the social apparatus of palliative care will be fundamentally altered
> when assisted death is legally sanctioned. The patient will soon find herself
> in a situation in which the option of death is always at hand. Soon she will
> be forced to defend to herself why she continues to stay alive – one more
> burden, to be relieved in choosing death. In short, there are logics that are
> created within the auspices of our institutions and apparatuses, whether
> adjudicated by physicians or by judges ... These procedural logics will shape
> our social imagination about dependency, care, and the meaning of com-
> passion, and the meaning of life at life's end.

Yet, for opponents of MAID, it is becoming increasingly difficult to know
when and how to deploy slippery slope arguments; what they might regard
as an obvious bottoming-out point, or near-bottoming-out point, of a dan-

gerous slope the proponent of MAID might regard as entirely unobjectionable. The moral divide between certain parties to this debate has grown so
radical that slippery slope arguments might no longer be worth the effort,
insofar as just about everything now appears to be regarded as a legitimate
option by at least some proponents of MAID.

Put differently, for a slippery slope argument to be pragmatically useful in
a public policy debate, at least two requirements must be met. First, the person pushing the argument must convince her interlocutors of the plausibility
that the feared outcome might really come to pass; second, both parties to
the argument must agree that the feared outcome really is to be feared. My
worry is that slippery slope arguments about assisted death have become
mostly useless because there is no longer sufficient agreement about which
outcomes are to be feared. Time would be better spent, perhaps, attempting
to resolve the more foundational questions about the value of life and when,
if ever, an innocent person may be killed. That being the case, I will not consider slippery slope arguments any further here.[42] Instead, I will just observe
that, if the reader already agrees with me in opposing the extension of MAID
to psychiatric patients, then the recent history of Belgium and the Netherlands
should give her serious concern about *any* legalization of MAID. Are we
Canadians so morally superior to the Belgians and Dutch that we can be
confident we will not fall down the same slopes as them?

Arguments against the Permissibility of MAID: The Loss of Goods

Another sort of argument against MAID is that, even when carried out on
those in the final stages of a terminal illness, it can deprive them of certain
important goods. Although suffering is not a good in and of itself, it can
function as an instrumental good, providing the sufferer with an opportunity to exercise certain virtues (e.g., patience, humility, courage). It likewise
provides caregivers with opportunities to exercise a variety of virtues. And,
for some, a prolonged experience of dying might provide a final opportunity
to reflect on certain deep questions (e.g., to reflect on God and the afterlife)
and to settle important affairs (e.g., reconciliation with alienated family
members).

Replying to arguments of this sort, Gill (2014, pp. 370–371) writes that

> in response to this objection, let me say first of all that it is true that *some*
> people may have profound, life-changing experiences at the very end of life.

The very end of life may be the time when *some* people achieve a new awareness or forge new relationships that cast all their previous years in an entirely different light. What is crucial to realize, however, is that this may not be true for all people. There may also be people who have settled all their worldly and spiritual affairs a month or two before they are expected to die. Some people may have no need to make financial arrangements or pursue any sort of interpersonal reconciliation in the final months of life because they may already have done all the work on their wills and their relationships that they believe they need to do. Some people may not need to experience any more suffering and dying because they may believe that they have learned all the lessons about themselves and the human condition that they are ever going to learn. Some people may have already achieved exactly the relationship with God to which they aspire. So while PAS [physician-assisted suicide] may be the wrong thing for *some* people, it is not necessarily the wrong thing for *all* people.

This seems to me to be a convincing reply. The argument from end-of-life goods is overly ambitious if its proponents attempt to use it to establish the impermissibility of assisted suicide and euthanasia in all cases; Gill is correct in thinking that the argument should be seen as having a more limited application.

Nevertheless, the points raised in this context are worth keeping in mind, insofar as the discussion of end-of-life matters can focus so much on the pain and suffering associated with this stage of life as to neglect more positive aspects of the process of dying, aspects that many might risk missing out on once MAID becomes common practice in Canada. Psychiatrist M. Scott Peck (1997, p. 152), for instance, writes that

no work I ever did as a psychotherapist was as fulfilling to me as that with a number of dying patients. People tend to learn best when they have a deadline. (What a wonderful word!) Mind you, the majority seem to deny that they are dying up until their final breath. But those who are not in denial, who know they have little time left, tend to speed up their development. They may choose to face issues they have been avoiding for a lifetime. It is a pleasure and a privilege to work with them at such a moment. Deathbed confessions and conversions do happen, as do forgiveness and reconciliation and leaps of learning that never seemed possible.

Moreover, the religious believer can raise certain relevant points about the meaning and import of the process of dying, which will carry no purchase for the settled atheist but which might be worth pondering by those open to theological concepts. For instance, Meilaender (2013, p. 65), a Lutheran ethicist, writes that

> were our goal only to minimize suffering, no doubt we could sometime achieve it most effectively by eliminating *sufferers*. But then we refuse to understand suffering as a significant part of human life that can have meaning or purpose. We should not, of course, pretend that suffering in itself is a good thing, nor should we put forward claims about the benefits others can reap from their suffering. Jesus in Gethsemane – who shrinks from the suffering to come but accepts it as part of his calling and obedience – should be our model here. The suffering that comes is an evil, but the God who in Jesus has not abandoned us in that suffering can bring good from it for us as for Jesus. We are called simply to live out our personal histories – the stories of which God is the author – as faithfully as we can. Our task, therefore, is not to abandon those who suffer but to maximize care for them as they live out their own life's story.

Or consider Engelhardt (2000, pp. 331–332), who had doctorates in both medicine and philosophy and who wrote from the perspective of Eastern Orthodoxy:

> Traditional Christianity is fundamentally opposed to physician-assisted suicide and euthanasia. The traditional Christian life has always experienced such a death as a separation from the humility and holiness of the life and death of Christ. This opposition to suicide, assisted suicide, and euthanasia is rooted in the experience of the Christian life as a life directed to humility. To be a Christian is to take on Christ, not only His life, but also His submissive death on the Cross (Romans 6) ... The life and death of Christ with which Christians unite themselves conflict radically with secular culture. Because the times have changed with the emergence of a vigorous, post-Christian, post-traditional, indeed neo-pagan culture, the Cross is ever more a stumbling block. It is the epiphany of an undignified death, a humiliating death, a death of submission. Traditional Christianity provides bioethics a language out of step with a culture of self-determination and pride. It sees matters of suffering, dying, and death without a central focus on considerations of rights, dignity, and self-satisfaction. Instead, the focus is on how life in the body of Christ teaches us to live and die. At stake is a goal beyond freedom, dignity, and virtue: union with the transcendent God

through taking on Christ's divinity, as He took on our humanity. The culture of traditional Christian belief focuses on life regained through the humiliation of death on the Cross.

Conclusion

My treatment of arguments for and against the moral permissibility of MAID has been necessarily incomplete – again, given the decades of literature on the topic, I cannot supply a full review here.[43] Hopefully, though, the preceding has provided at least a reasonably clear idea of some of the main lines of discussion.

Perhaps the reader will find the pro-MAID arguments wholly convincing and not be moved at all by the anti-MAID arguments. Yet I suggest that, if the reader is at all moved by one or more of the anti-MAID arguments, such that her confidence in the permissibility of MAID is weakened and a measure of doubt sown, then she should oppose both the commission of MAID and its legalization. The demands of the inscrutability proviso are such that, if the success of the pro-MAID arguments is less than complete, then opposition is required. Recall *the inscrutability proviso:* in any case in which reasonable doubt persists concerning the moral permissibility of deliberately killing a person, one ought to refrain from deliberate killing in that case, and the law should refrain from permitting deliberate killing in that sort of case. I believe that there is some reason to adopt this principle, both for its intuitive plausibility and for its similarity to a principle of the Canadian legal system that most readers would accept. If this principle obtains, then the burden of proof is greater for the proponent of MAID. So, if the reader is less than convinced by the pro-MAID arguments, then the fact that MAID involves deliberate killing means that it should be opposed. The burden of proof here is properly a high one. Personally, I believe that the burden is unmet.

Yet the Canadian government has now legalized MAID. Via Bill C-14, the federal government has implemented *Carter v Canada* (though, of course, there remains ongoing controversy about whether it has done so fully and adequately). If my assessment is correct, then we appear to be in a situation in which the law is badly out of step with the demands of morality. Where do we go from here?

5

Invoking the Notwithstanding Clause

Opponents of MAID might look at the current legal situation and assume that there is nothing more to be done: the Supreme Court of Canada has spoken, and the legislature has acted accordingly. But in Canada this need not be the end of the debate. With respect to rulings on the *Canadian Charter of Rights and Freedoms,* of which *Carter v Canada* is a clear case, the court is not the highest authority in the land. The notwithstanding clause (found in section 33 of the Charter) allows the federal government or any one of the provinces or territories to pass and enforce laws in open contravention of sections 2 and 7–15 of the Charter. All that the federal government, or any provincial government, need do is declare in an act of the legislature that it is doing so. Any such instance of overriding the Charter must be renewed by the government after five years, but in principle there is no limit on the number of renewals that can be made. So, in theory, the federal government could retain those sections of the *Criminal Code of Canada* struck down by the court in *Carter* by declaring that they will be reinstated notwithstanding that ruling. Because *Carter* was striking down sections of the Criminal Code, the situation facing the provinces is more complicated, for they do not have constitutional authority to write new criminal laws, so no province on its own could directly reinstate the relevant sections of the Criminal Code. Nevertheless, even in a situation in which the federal government refrained from invoking the notwithstanding clause, there remains a great deal that an individual province could do by way of unilateral action to void, in its own way, the ruling of the court. For instance, given provincial authority over health care, a province could pass legislation to the effect that any health-care practitioner who participates in assisted death would have his or her licence to practise medicine in that province revoked. Or it could pass legis-lation to the effect that any such practitioner would be ineligible to receive payment for services from the provincial government.

At first glance, these might seem to be rather extreme measures; even someone who agrees with the moral assessment put forward in the previous chapter might find the prospect of invoking the notwithstanding clause troubling. After all, its invocation over the past several decades has been rare, and a fairly strong presumption against its use is found at both the federal level and the provincial level, arising in part from regard for the Charter. Yet it has been invoked multiple times, specifically by Quebec, Saskatchewan, Alberta, and Yukon. So the presumption against its use hardly rises to the level of a taboo. The notwithstanding clause is an import-ant part of Canada's constitutional structure, affirming the principle of par-liamentary supremacy (in sharp contrast to the United States, where the Supreme Court is not subject to direct check by the other branches of fed-eral or state government). Adoption of the clause was a crucial factor in the provinces' acceptance of the Charter. And, if there was ever an issue of suf-ficient moral gravity to warrant serious consideration of its use, surely it is the debate over MAID.

On the (obviously controversial) assumption that the moral assessment laid out in the previous chapter is correct, I would argue that it implies the state is obligated not to permit assisted death. Given that *Carter v Canada* imposes a legal (though not a moral) requirement on the state to do just that, the state is obligated to override *Carter* by invoking the notwithstand-ing clause. I will state the argument more formally:

Premise 1: The federal government is morally obligated to criminalize MAID.
Premise 2: The only way for the federal government to meet that obligation is to invoke the notwithstanding clause (and invoking the notwithstand-ing clause is not itself immoral).
Premise 3: When the performance of some act is the necessary condition for the fulfillment of an obligation, the performance of that act itself becomes obligatory (provided that the fulfillment of the necessary condition is not itself immoral).
Conclusion: Therefore, the federal government is obligated to invoke the notwithstanding clause.

Given that the federal government has the proper authority in matters of criminal law, the duty to override *Carter v Canada* of course falls chiefly to it. However, should the federal government fail to fulfill this obligation, it will fall to individual provinces to institute their own methods of effectively voiding the court ruling; they cannot do so directly (i.e., by passing criminal laws), but they have various indirect means at their disposal via their constitutional authority over health care.

How realistic politically is any of this? I will not venture a judgment. At any rate, my concern in this chapter is with ethics. If I am correct in my moral assessment of MAID, then the claim that the government is obligated to invoke the notwithstanding clause to recriminalize these practices follows readily enough. For readers who disagree with that moral assessment, that suggestion is liable to seem not merely unrealistic but itself morally objectionable – especially my suggestion that physicians who kill consenting patients could legitimately have their licences revoked by the province. To those readers, I address the following question: To what *extent* do you disagree with that assessment? Do you think, for instance, that assisted death is morally licit under the circumstances laid out in Bill C-14? Well, let us grant that for a moment. What if in the future the Supreme Court rules that those suffering solely from a psychiatric condition must be eligible for assisted death? (I think that the legal case for this would be weak and not in accord with the current court's opinion, but for the moment suppose that I am wrong. Suppose, that is, that future Canadian courts will shift toward the legal position adopted by Belgians, the Dutch, and the Swiss.) Readers who accept the permissibility of assisted death for the terminal physically ill, or even the non-terminal seriously physically ill, might be uncomfortable with its extension to the physically healthy mentally ill. Let us assume that this moral stance is correct (i.e., that Bill C-14 as it stands is morally unobjectionable but that MAID for the mentally ill is impermissible). Would the reader accept that the federal government could legitimately invoke the notwithstanding clause to override the Supreme Court on the issue of assisted death for psychiatric patients? And would the reader accept that, in the absence of such an invocation, provinces could rightly sanction physicians who killed the consenting, legally competent, mentally ill? If she is willing to entertain such measures to prevent the extension of MAID to the mentally ill, then she has no absolute objection to the use of the notwithstanding clause in the context of the MAID debate or to provinces' resorting to seemingly harsh measures against physicians. Rather, the disagreement lies in differing assessments of the conditions under which MAID is morally permissible. The (hypothetical) reader maintains that assisted death for the non-terminal mentally ill is immoral; I agree but add that so is any deliberate killing of innocent persons. If the reader shares my assessment of the latter, then presumably she would share my assessment regarding the obligation to invoke the notwithstanding clause under current circumstances.

If the state is obligated not to *permit* MAID, then obviously it is still more obligated not to *provide* MAID. Nevertheless, at present the provinces and territories have all opted in favour of public funding even though nothing in *Carter v Canada* or Bill C-14 legally requires that they do so. In the next chapter, I lay out a comprehensive argument against public funding for assisted death – comprehensive in the sense that I claim that public funding should be rejected not only by those who share my moral assessment of assisted death but also by those who think its provision permissible or even obligatory. There has been virtually no discussion of the ethics of public funding in the existing literature on MAID, so here we are heading into relatively uncharted territory.

6

The Ethics of Public Funding for MAID

Consider four scenarios regarding the moral status of MAID under the rubric laid out by Bill C-14:

- Its availability is morally impermissible.
- Its availability is morally permissible (but not obligatory).
- Its availability is morally obligatory.
- The moral status of its availability is inscrutable.

In what follows, I will argue that in each case provinces should refrain from funding MAID. On the assumption that the four alternatives constitute a complete disjunction, the resulting conclusion is that provinces should refrain from funding it. That is, whichever stance one adopts concerning its moral status, provinces should refrain from funding it. I will proceed through each scenario in turn.

Its Availability Is Morally Impermissible

If the first scenario is true, then we would have cause to reject public funding, insofar as we normally think that governments should not deliberately carry out or facilitate impermissible acts.

Premise 1: If a type of action is morally impermissible, then governments should refrain from deliberately funding that type of action.

Premise 2: MAID is morally impermissible.
Conclusion: Therefore, governments should refrain from deliberately fund-
    ing MAID.

The truth of premise 2 can be taken for granted here since it is merely the
first of our four disjuncts. The truth of premise 1 should be relatively
uncontroversial but might require further explication. One might object
that governments routinely fund immoral activities deliberately but that
they do so permissibly when that funding is provided in the interests of fulfilling more important duties. Consider, for instance, the practice of decep-
tion in state intelligence services: one might argue that lying is wrong but
that intelligence officials must lie in the course of performing their duty to
protect the public. So governments deliberately fund the deceptions practised by spies on their payrolls, but they do so morally – a lesser evil is deliberately facilitated in order to prevent a greater evil. One might conclude
from this example (and analogous cases) that premise 1 is false.

However, purported cases of that sort are best analyzed not in terms of
doing a lesser evil in order to prevent a greater evil but in these terms: first,
the distinction between prima facie and ultima facie duties (i.e., acts or
omissions that are duties "at first glance" but, under certain circumstances,
can be outweighed by more important concerns versus acts or omissions
that really are duties all things considered); second, double effect reasoning.
In the first option, lying is morally okay in the context of legitimate espio-
nage because the duty not to lie is merely a prima facie duty here outweighed
by a more important duty. In the second option, the relevant acts of decep-
tion are not intrinsically evil and meet the other standard criteria for the
application of the DDE (proportionality, necessity, and foreknowledge without intent). The performance of genuinely impermissible acts (i.e., *ultima
facie* wrong acts or acts that fail to meet the criteria of the DDE) should not
be deliberately undertaken by governments or enabled by public funds. So I
think that premise 1 stands.

A manuscript reader put forward another interesting counterexample to
premise 1: government-funded needle exchanges for drug addicts. On the
assumption that heroin use is immoral, premise 1 seems to entail that governments should not provide funding to facilitate such use. In reply, I would
argue that the best way to conceptualize what the government is doing here
is not that it is funding or facilitating heroin use but that it is funding HIV
prevention (and likewise the prevention of other diseases transmitted
through injection drugs). That heroin use is facilitated is a foreseen but not

intended consequence of the government funding, such that this case is amenable to plausible analysis using the DDE.

If one really takes the first option seriously and maintains that MAID is morally impermissible, then that could be seen as a ground for advocating something stronger: namely, that it should be recriminalized. But here I am concerned only with the issue of whether the procedure should be publicly funded, not whether it should be legally permitted.

Its Availability Is Morally Permissible (but Not Obligatory)

In this disjunct, it is morally permissible that MAID be made available but not obligatory. Assuming the truth of this, consider the following argument:

Premise 1: If a type of action is permissible but not obligatory, yet rationally rejected as grievously immoral by a substantial portion of the population, then governments should refrain from deliberately funding that type of action.

Premise 2: MAID is permissible but not obligatory yet rationally rejected as grievously immoral by a substantial portion of the population.

Conclusion: Therefore, governments should refrain from deliberately funding MAID.

The claim in premise 1 is a general point concerning the ethics of taxation: When a type of action that is permissible but not obligatory is rationally thought to be grievously immoral by a substantial portion of the population, governments should refrain from funding that activity. Individuals should not be forced to pay for activities that they rationally (even if erroneously) think grievously wrong unless there is an overriding reason to compel such payment. Since (by hypothesis) the performance of the action is merely permissible but not obligatory, that is warrant for thinking that there is not an overriding reason to compel payment.

Why, exactly, should individuals not be thus coerced? Here various justifications might be developed. One might formulate, for instance, the point in terms of harm avoidance. Being forced under penalty of law to facilitate activities that one considers grievously wrong can strain an individual's conscience in various ways (e.g., confronting the apparent dilemma of having to choose between disobeying a legitimate government and knowingly facilitating grievously wrong acts). Such a strain is plausibly construed as a harm, and governments should not harm substantial numbers of their citizens unless there is an overriding reason to do so. Still, I am not wedded to this formulation and remain open to other ways of grounding the claim that, where possible, people should not be compelled by the state to pay for activities that they rationally think grievously immoral. The claim itself seems to me to be intuitively plausible though of course subject to disagreement.

Several other points raised in premise 1 require clarification. First, the claim made here applies to erroneous but *rational* moral beliefs. The argument has nothing to say regarding moral beliefs that fail to meet a minimal standard of rationality. Arguably, it is permissible for governments to compel citizens to fund activities that those citizens think grievously wrong when the relevant belief fails to meet that standard. This assumes that there is a minimal standard of rationality and that, in at least some cases, it is possible to distinguish beliefs that meet it from those that do not. Those assumptions are controversial but plausible.

Second, the claim pertains to erroneous but rational moral beliefs upheld by a *substantial portion of the population*. I will not attempt to specify precisely what is meant by a "substantial portion" – I am not sure where the borders lie here. Is 10 percent a substantial portion? Or must it be higher, say 25 percent? I do not see any easy way to adjudicate the matter. Intuitively, I am inclined to think that anything over 10 percent would count, but I expect that many would think that percentage too low. Certainly, the closer the number comes to 50 percent, the more plausible it will be to think that a substantial portion of the population is in play.

Third, the claim pertains to beliefs that an act is not merely immoral but also *grievously* immoral. I think that the argument above could be run on the weaker formulation. But it is still more convincing to think that governments should refrain from compelling payment for activities that people rationally consider not merely wrong but also gravely wrong.

Fourth, this premise maintains that governments should simply refrain from funding MAID altogether. There are other ways, of course, of attempting to accommodate individuals who do not wish to pay for activities that they think are grievously immoral; for instance, a government could include an opt-out provision on tax forms, allowing individuals to direct their tax dollars away from certain programs on the basis of conscientious objection.[1] However, from a government's perspective, such an alternative faces practical concerns (e.g., the potential for fraud as some taxpayers opt out simply to save money). From the perspective of the objecting taxpayer, it also raises the concern that he will still end up funding the activity indirectly (e.g., the government might choose to redirect funding originally designated for other programs to the allegedly immoral activity). Another option might be to administer funding for hospitals in a manner analogous to how public schools are funded in provinces such as Ontario and Alberta. There taxpayers can designate whether they wish their taxes to go to the Catholic school system or the "public" school system (though in one obvious sense both systems are public because both receive funds from taxpayers). One can likewise envision a scenario in which taxpayers can designate whether they wish their taxes to go to Catholic hospitals (or other religious hospitals) or public hospitals, the former being exempt from performing assisted death. This would be a reasonable compromise but hardly ideal given that not all cases of assisted death are carried out in hospitals. Certainly, nothing in Bill C-14 requires that these procedures be done in a hospital rather than, say, a hospice or the patient's own home. Taking all of these complications into account, it is better that the government simply refrain from funding the activity given that (by hypothesis in the second disjunct) it is not an activity that the government is obligated to fund in the first place.

To illustrate further the claim of premise 1, consider a concrete example from the United States: state funding in Texas for the lethal injection of those convicted of premeditated murder. Assume for the sake of argument that the death penalty for premeditated murder is a penalty the imposition of which is morally permissible but not morally obligatory. Justice allows for lethal injection in these cases but does not demand it (perhaps because other penalties, such as life imprisonment, also meet the demands of justice). Now assume further that a substantial portion of Texans considers the death penalty grievously wrong morally (however "substantial portion" is to be cashed out) and that their belief, though erroneous (under the present supposition), is still rational. Applied to this scenario, the truth of premise 1 would entail that the government of Texas should refrain from funding the death penalty for premeditated murder. This would further imply that, since the state is the only agent that can legitimately carry out the death penalty, the government of Texas should desist from the use of the death penalty for premeditated murder.

To employ an example in the Canadian context, consider federal funding for our Olympic boxing program. Let us say that boxing is a sport that can be engaged in permissibly. Let us further assume that a substantial portion of the population believes, erroneously but rationally, that competitive boxing is grievously immoral (perhaps on the grounds that it is grievously wrong deliberately to subject another human being to some degree of traumatic brain injury for sport and for an audience to enjoy watching two people deliberately subjecting each other to some degree of traumatic brain injury). Should these individuals be compelled to pay for our Olympic boxing program? No. Where possible, governments should respect the consciences of their citizens, respect shown in part by refraining from funding *optional* activities that a substantial portion of those citizens rationally reject as grievously immoral and thus do not wish to be implicated in (even indirectly by way of paying for the activity). As such, unless the government is obligated to fund Olympic boxing, it should not do so but leave the funding of that sport to private individuals or private (non-publicly funded and non-tax-exempt) charities.

With premise 1 of the argument having been explicated, let us turn to premise 2. The first portion of that premise reads "MAID is permissible but not obligatory." This portion of the premise needs no defence since it is merely a statement of the second disjunct. It is the latter portion of premise 2 that will require defence: namely, the claim that assisted death is "rationally rejected as grievously immoral by a substantial portion of the population."

The first point here (that it is rationally rejected) is a weak claim: namely, that this moral belief is not irrational, that it meets the standard (however exactly that standard is to be formulated) of minimal rationality. Given that assisted suicide and active euthanasia have been against the law in Canada for most of the nation's history, and that *Carter v Canada* reverses the Supreme Court's own relatively recent previous decision on the matter (in *Rodriguez v British Columbia*), it seems to be uncharitable to claim that opposition to MAID is not merely incorrect but also irrational. That conclusion is buttressed when one recalls that MAID is also considered grievously immoral by many professional bioethicists and physicians and explicitly condemned as grievously immoral by multiple major world religions (e.g., Orthodox Judaism, Islam, Jainism, Roman Catholicism, the Eastern Orthodox Church, the Oriental Orthodox Church, Evangelical Protestantism, etc.).

The second point, that assisted death is rejected as grievously immoral by a substantial portion of the population, is an empirical claim. It is also an ambiguous claim, insofar as it is debatable just what constitutes a "substantial portion." One might try to defend the empirical claim by reference to Canada's religious demographics and the opposition among major world religions to assisted suicide and active euthanasia – that is, opposition will be high among observant Muslims, Orthodox Jews, Jains, traditional

Christians, et cetera. Or one might point to polling data showing that those who fail to approve of assisted death (even for the terminally ill) constitute about a quarter of the Canadian population.[2] I would consider that number sufficient to constitute a substantial portion for my purposes here, but intuitions will differ, and my view on this is open to question – that number arguably might not constitute a substantial portion.

Opposition to assisted death rises when respondents are asked specifically about assisted death for the mentally ill. This will become relevant should this aspect of Bill C-14 be struck down by future court rulings in favour of a more permissive regime, of the sort seen in Belgium and the Netherlands (though I take that to be unlikely). As part of a comparative international study on behalf of the *Economist* in June 2015, the polling firm Ipsos MORI polled citizens of fifteen nations concerning their views on assisted death. In Canada, 2,129 people were polled. Regarding mental illness, participants were asked: "Do you think that it should be legal or not for a doctor to assist a patient in ending their life, if they are not terminally ill, but are mentally or emotionally suffering in a way that they find unbearable and which cannot be cured or improved with existing medical science, and they are still 'of sound mind'?" In response, 31 percent chose the answer "yes," 41 percent chose "no," 25 percent chose "don't know," and 2 percent chose "prefer not to say." In fact, of the fifteen nations polled about assisted death in this study (Australia, Belgium, Canada, Germany, Spain, France, Britain, Hungary, Italy, Japan, the Netherlands, Poland, Russia, Sweden, and the United States), only Belgium and the Netherlands had a majority of respondents approve of assisted death for the mentally ill.[3]

A poll in 2016 of 1,517 Canadians by Angus Reid found a stronger level of disapproval of MAID for the mentally ill, though importantly its question focused on *morality* rather than *legality*. Specifically, 78 percent of respondents rejected the permission of MAID for those suffering solely from a psychological ailment, agreeing with the statement that "psychological suffering on its own should not be considered a reason to obtain doctor-assisted suicide."[4]

Similarly, a 2016 survey specifically of Canadian psychiatrists found that, of the 528 respondents, more than 61 percent disapproved of the extension of MAID to those suffering only from a psychiatric condition, with another 9 percent expressing indecision, such that only about 30 percent approved of the idea.[5]

Importantly, when it comes to assisted death for the terminally ill, among those polled from fifteen nations, those who failed to answer "yes" (i.e., those who answered "no," "don't know," or "prefer not to say") in most cases constitute at least 20 percent of the population, the exceptions being again Belgium and the Netherlands, plus France.[6]

Its Availability Is Morally Obligatory

Premise 1: If there is an obligation to make available a service, yet a substantial portion of the population rationally considers that service grievously immoral, then where possible that obligation should be met without recourse to the use of public funds.

Premise 2: There is an obligation to make MAID available, yet a substantial portion of the population rationally considers that service grievously immoral.

Conclusion 1/Premise 3: Therefore, where possible, MAID should be made available without recourse to the use of public funds.

Premise 4: In the present context, it is possible to provide MAID without recourse to the use of public funds.

Final Conclusion: Therefore, in the present context, MAID should be made available without recourse to the use of public funds.

The first premise relies in part on a claim that also appeared in my treatment of the second disjunct, according to which people should not be forced to pay for activities that they rationally (even if incorrectly) believe are grievously immoral. The application of this point in that disjunct was easier since it was stipulated there that the provision of assisted death is permissible but not obligatory, which rendered easier the defence of the claim that the compulsion of payment by those with conscientious objections should be avoided. In the context of the third disjunct, the employment of this intuition is more problematic since it is stipulated that making available this service is actually obligatory. Nevertheless, premise 1 makes the point that this duty might yet be fulfilled, even while accommodating the conscientious objections of those who do not wish to pay for this service, by making the service available *by some means other than taxation* (e.g., private insurance, private charities, etc.). Not all duties must be performed by the government. Consequently, if there is a duty whose performance by the government would constitute a hardship for a substantial portion of the population (in this case, those who erroneously but rationally think that assisted death is grievously immoral), then, if possible, that duty should be met by some other means. Note the "if possible" – premise 1 grants that, since the provision of the service is stipulated to be a duty, if public funds are necessary to fulfill that duty, then those with conscientious objections will simply have to "take the hit," as it were.

For the sake of further clarification, let us think about premise 1 in light of the previous examples of the death penalty in Texas and of Olympic boxing. Let us assume that there is an obligation to execute those convicted of premeditated murder – no other penalty is adequate. Let us say further that a substantial portion of Texans erroneously but rationally believe that capital punishment is grievously wrong morally. What should the state of Texas do? In this scenario, those with conscientious objections might simply have to absorb the hardship of paying for what they take to be a grievous wrong. The reason is that the state is the only agent that can legitimately carry out capital punishment. There is thus no proper alternative available – the provision of capital punishment must be made out of public funds. (I suppose that in theory one could propose volunteer executioners as an alternative to the use of public funds, but that proposal would obviously raise moral complications of its own in that unique context. Alternatively, one might suggest an opt-out provision on tax forms, as mentioned earlier, but such suggestions carry practical problems.)

Note, too, that on this point we find an important disconnect between the existing literature on taxation, conscientious objection, and civil disobedience, on the one hand, and the present debate over the public funding of MAID, on the other. The former body of literature has been formulated mostly in terms of whether pacifists can rightly refuse to pay taxes toward military expenditures. Military defence is an activity that, if legitimate at all, is legitimate only insofar as it is conducted by the state. In contrast, assisted death in principle could be legitimately carried out by non-state actors, as are many other health-care services. Military defence is also an activity that, practically speaking, can only be funded via public taxation. Modern militaries are simply too costly to be paid for by any other means (e.g., private charities). In contrast, assisted death could be funded by other means. Consequently, two arguments made against exempting pacifists from military-related taxation (namely, that military defence is the sole purview of the state and that it can only be funded via public taxation) will be inapplicable to the debate over the public funding of MAID.

Contrast this with the funding of Olympic boxing. Even on the (dubious) assumption that there is a duty to fund Olympic boxers, there is still no corresponding requirement that this duty be fulfilled by the use of public funds. It is not the case that the government is the only agent morally or practically capable of providing the requisite funds. Perhaps private charities can step up to fund Olympic boxing, such that those with conscientious objections need not be compelled to fund an activity that they believe is grievously immoral. At the least, in such a scenario, *the attempt should be made first* to fund the boxing program via private charities or other such means; should that attempt fail, and it is shown that Olympic boxers are receiving inadequate support, then and only then should the government consider stepping in to fulfill the duty by recourse to public funds.

Turning to premise 2, its first portion needs no defence since it is simply a statement of the third disjunct. The second portion of the premise is an empirical point whose defence I undertook in the previous subsection. Premise 3 follows logically from premises 1 and 2. The key premise is thus 4, which consists of the empirical claim that the demand for assisted death can be met adequately without the use of public funds. Unfortunately, this empirical claim is difficult at present to assess thoroughly, and it constitutes a weak point of the argument. Multiple questions would need to be answered here, notably the numbers involved. How many requests for MAID will each Canadian province receive annually in the coming years? Complicating matters is the fact that the numbers might differ from one province to the next. They are likewise liable to shift over time in response to demographic changes (recall Canada's rapidly aging populace) and to other relevant public policies (e.g., a reform of our palliative care system might succeed in keeping demand for MAID lower than it otherwise would be). Similar questions could be raised, of course, with respect to the funding situation in Britain or other jurisdictions that have recently contemplated allowing MAID. In Belgium and the Netherlands, extensive data are available regarding annual rates of assisted death; in the Netherlands, the rate has been rising somewhat, such that now about 3 percent of all deaths there result from MAID. In Belgium, 4.6 percent of all deaths are from MAID. (To give some additional context, Belgium, for instance, had about 61,000 deaths from all causes in 2013.)[7] The most recent numbers on the frequency of MAID in Canada come from Health Canada's spring 2019 interim report, which noted that, since its legalization, 6,749 Canadians had received MAID, so about 1 percent of deaths in the country are now attributable to it. More than 90 percent of the procedures were performed by physicians, less than 10 percent by nurse practitioners. Euthanasia has proven to be far more popular than assisted suicide, with only 6 of the 6,749 people opting to end their lives by self-administering a prescribed drug.[8] With those data in mind, in terms of the total number of deaths, the cases of MAID seem likely to remain manageable, and one can envision these deaths being successfully funded by private means. Moreover, the fact that MAID is carried out in Switzerland by private charitable organizations provides further indication that such a model is in fact workable as an alternative to public funding.

If the present argument is correct, then the attempt might be made to meet that demand without recourse to public funds – that is, see what private charity and private insurance can accomplish; if they prove to be inadequate, then provincial governments might consider stepping in and compelling those with conscientious objections to pay for an activity that they rationally consider grievously immoral. Even so, if the third disjunct is the actual moral status of MAID, then one must admit that it will be more difficult to maintain a case against public funding, especially if demand rises substantially.

The Moral Status of Its Availability Is Inscrutable

Each of the previous disjuncts adopted a definite stance toward the moral status of MAID. The fourth disjunct, in contrast, is the claim that we cannot know its moral status. If indeed that were the case, then that would have an implication for the moral status of public funding.

Premise 1: If the moral status of a type of action is inscrutable, then the performance of that type of action should not be publicly funded.
Premise 2: The moral status of MAID is inscrutable.
Conclusion: Therefore, MAID should not be publicly funded.

Premise 2 is just a statement of the fourth disjunct and thus in need of no defence since it is stipulated for the sake of argument. Premise 1 should be uncontroversial. If we really have no idea whether a certain type of action is morally permissible, then we should certainly not ask people to pay for it (especially against their strong objections). For all we know, we might be asking them to subsidize a grievously immoral type of action.

To sum up, governments should not fund MAID because it might be gravely wrong morally; even assuming that its provision is permissible, or indeed obligatory, there remains room to deny that it should be publicly funded. However, one must grant that the argument against public funding is stronger with respect to the second disjunct than the third disjunct. Finally, if the moral status of assisted death is inscrutable, then governments should err on the side of caution and refrain from funding it.[9]

7

Freedom of Conscience for Health-Care Providers

In *Carter v Canada,* the Supreme Court of Canada specified that physicians who objected to MAID on moral and/or religious grounds could not be compelled to participate in it directly. However, it left open the question of whether they might be obligated to refer patients to other physicians willing to engage in MAID.[1] Bill C-14, in turn, leaves it up to individual provinces to regulate referral. The Provincial-Territorial Expert Advisory Group on Physician-Assisted Dying recommended that physicians with such objections be required to engage in referrals. As of the time of writing, not every province has adopted the same requirements on this front, with Ontario and Alberta, for example, providing starkly opposite pictures of how the health-care system is to manage MAID. As we have seen, Ontario courts have mandated that physicians cannot claim the freedom of conscience exemption from making referrals for MAID, whereas in Alberta physicians with conscientious objections are not obliged to provide referrals (the province having set up a telephone hotline for patients wishing to receive confidential advice on MAID and referrals to willing physicians).

One advantage of the argument laid out in Chapter 6 is that it would provide additional support for the claim that physicians (or nurse practitioners)[2] with moral objections cannot legitimately be placed under legal or professional constraint to make referrals to willing colleagues: if a medical "service" is not even funded by the province, then it is more difficult to maintain that a physician could be obligated legally to make referrals for such a service.

Still, let us assume that MAID will continue to be publicly funded. Here is one way to formulate an argument against a legal or professional obligation to make referrals, even in that scenario:

Premise 1: If it is morally impermissible to do or obtain *x*, then it is morally impermissible to provide advice to others on how to do or obtain *x* (and in other ways to facilitate deliberately their doing or obtaining *x*).

Premise 2: It is morally impermissible to assist in suicide, to perform active euthanasia, and to obtain either.

Conclusion: Therefore, it is morally impermissible to provide advice to others on how to assist in suicide and to perform active euthanasia and to obtain either (and in other ways to facilitate deliberately their doing or obtaining these procedures).

Premise 1 seems to be plausible. If it is immoral to hire a hitman to kill one's boss, then it is immoral to give a friend the phone number of a quality hitman for the sake of killing his boss. (The law recognizes this by its provision for prosecuting not only those who commit murder but also those who are accessories to murder.) If it is wrong to commit adultery, then it is wrong to create a website designed to enable other people in their adultery. If it is wrong to compete in brutal mixed martial arts tournaments, then it is wrong deliberately to facilitate competition in those tournaments by purchasing tickets to them as a spectator. If it is wrong to engage in hunting for sport, then it is wrong deliberately to advise others by authoring a *Dummies' Guide to Hunting for Sport*.

Premise 2 will be denied, of course, by anyone who approves of MAID. But what is really relevant here is that this argument allows us to see why a physician or nurse practitioner who objects on moral grounds to assisted death would be rational in thinking that she is morally implicated by referring a patient to someone else to obtain the service or even providing information directly related to it. So, if we are sincere about respecting the consciences of health-care professionals (even when we think that their moral views are erroneous), then we ought to refrain from punishing those who refuse to provide referrals for assisted suicide and euthanasia. Moreover, in the modern information age, in which most people have access to the internet, the refusal of one physician to provide a referral hardly prevents the average Canadian from obtaining the desired information. This is particularly the case in provinces that have tried to make such information readily available, such as Alberta, which has set up a special phone number specifically for consultations on MAID.

Against this sort of claim for freedom of conscience, Schuklenk et al. (2011, p. 46), for instance, write that

> such objecting healthcare professionals are required to transfer an assist-ance seeking person on to other healthcare professionals who will provide the required service in a timely manner. The underlying rationale for this procedural solution lies in this kind of reasoning: If only healthcare profes-sionals are permitted to provide assistance but they are not obligated to do so, then their autonomy is not limited but the autonomy of those seeking assistance could potentially be unfairly limited. Hence the requirement on conscientious objectors to refer assistance seekers to colleagues who are prepared to oblige them. If individuals other than healthcare professionals are permitted to provide the assistance, then the autonomy of healthcare professionals and those seeking assistance is not limited. However, there could be legitimate concerns over how society could regulate the actions of non-healthcare professionals in this context in order to limit the risk of abuse.

The principal argument here is one from autonomy: Given that only health-care professionals are permitted to provide MAID, by not requiring phys-icians to make referrals for MAID the autonomy of patients is unfairly limited.[3]

I do not believe that the conclusion follows. Even if one granted that autonomy guaranteed the patient's right to request MAID, and even granted that autonomy guaranteed a negative right to receive MAID (such that others are obligated not to interfere), autonomy cannot guarantee a positive right to receive MAID. It is not always the case that a right to exercise auton-omy – to make important free choices bearing on one's own fate – obliges anyone to provide one with anything, whether we are talking about phys-icians or some other profession or sphere of life. For instance, when one freely proposes marriage to a potential spouse, one is exercising the right to autonomy. That does not oblige him or her to accept the proposal – on the contrary, he or she can refuse and, in making that refusal, in no way disre-spects one's status as an autonomous agent. As Yuill (2015, p. 48) puts it, "if we refuse to honour a suicidal wish, no one's freedom – not even that of the would-be suicide – is diminished. In the refusal to act on a suicidal wish, society refuses to become part of the suicide, to validate it and affirm it as correct." Autonomy rights are not a bludgeon by which one can force others to bend to one's will, especially when doing so would violate others' deeply held moral convictions. Trigg (2017, pp. 35–36) writes that "my autonomy does not give me the right to ignore the right of others to autonomy or dignity. Appeals to such rights, like all appeals to human rights, assume the existence of objective standards that all must accept. The exercise of conscience implies the obligation to respect the conscience of others." From a more judicial and legislative perspective, neither *Carter v Canada* nor Bill C-14 explicitly asserts a positive right to MAID. The ruling struck down prior criminal prohibitions, but it made no claim to assisted death as a medically necessary service that the state was obligated to supply. Bill C-14 also leaves such matters up to the provinces in accordance with their constitutional mandate for health care.

Sumner (2011, p. 173) puts forward a different sort of argument for the moral requirement of all physicians to make referrals for MAID, one focused on the notion of care rather than autonomy:

> Some physicians will have no religious or ethical objection to providing this service for their patients, while for others it will violate the dictates of their conscience. A policy must include a "conscience clause" that enables providers to decline to offer the service on grounds of personal conviction. However, it must also require that they not abandon patients who indicate a desire to request an assisted death; in such circumstances they must at a minimum inform their patients where they might find a provider willing to help them.

However, it is not clear why the requirement of non-abandonment would entail a duty to make a referral for assisted death. A physician might reasonably maintain that a requirement of non-abandonment instead entails that she not give up on her patients, that she work with them to ensure an excellent level of care (both physical and psychological) right to the end, including palliative sedation if need be. Declining to participate in a patient's killing, directly or indirectly, *while at the same time continuing to offer steadfast support with every other form of care,* should not be condemned as abandonment.

Moreover, it is worth recalling just how recent all of this is and what a massive change in professional ethics is involved in the shift to legally permitted MAID. One might think that this would motivate a greater degree of official tolerance of those who have been working within the traditional professional paradigm for their previous careers in medicine. In commenting on the requirement by the Ontario College of Physicians and Surgeons that its members make effective referrals for MAID, Kelsall (2018, p. E181) writes that the

> failure to comply with these policies puts doctors at risk of discipline for unprofessional conduct, even though participating in MAiD would have been culpable homicide in this country until 2015. For physicians who object to MAiD on religious or other grounds of conscience, providing a direct referral makes them complicit in the procedure. This is not mere semantics – to be blunt, the physician must ask another health care provider to consider killing their patient.

As a final point, it is worth noting that, if Canadian physicians and nurse practitioners are required by law to make referrals for MAID, then in the future observant Muslims, Orthodox Jews, Jains, Evangelicals, Roman Catholics, Eastern Orthodox, or indeed anyone else whose religion expressly prohibits any form of suicide could be barred effectively from pursuing careers in medicine. That would be a tragic loss to the profession and constitute a potentially Charter-violating instance of religious discrimination.

One manuscript reader wrote that

> this is a rather extreme conclusion, and I don't think many would swallow it. Only the most severely dogmatic of individuals would avoid an entire career in medicine due to a requirement to provide *referrals* on procedures to which they object. Many might dislike being forced to provide such referrals, but very few would ever allow it to limit their career prospects – they would just grumble and deal with it.

This response underestimates the depth of opposition to assisted death among faith groups with a doctrinal opposition to MAID. Some members of these groups currently going through medical school are very worried about freedom of conscience, and they are willing to consider moving to other provinces (or even relocating to the United States) on account of this, should the need arise. For example, in the wake of the January 30, 2018, Ontario divisional court ruling in favour of requiring physicians to make referrals for MAID, a representative of one of the plaintiffs in the court challenge (the Christian Medical and Dental Society of Canada), Larry Worthen, made the following statement: "We heard from our members and other doctors with conscientious objections over and over again that they felt referral made them complicit and that they wouldn't be able to live with themselves or stay in the profession if effective referral is still required."[4] More recently, Dr. Ramona Coelho was interviewed by the *Globe and Mail* in the wake of the Ontario Court of Appeal's upholding of that divisional court decision. As Grant (2019a) reports,

> Ramona Coelho, a family doctor in London, Ont., is still hopeful a solution can be found that would allow her to avoid formally referring MAID patients. She is a practising Catholic whose work with refugees and other vulnerable patients has reinforced her opposition to presiding over – and referring for – physician-assisted death. "I feel like the decision is going to exclude from mainstream medicine most people of faith," Dr. Coelho said. "Almost all world religions, all their moral theologians agree that a referral creating that direct pathway is not permissible."

I have focused in this chapter on freedom of conscience rights for individual physicians and nurse practitioners. A separate question, which has received substantially less attention in the scholarly literature, has to do with whether they might have other – professional but non-moral/non-conscience-based – grounds for the refusal to provide MAID (or other services, for that matter). If so, then what precise legal and normative standing might such alternative grounds have? See Pruski (2019) for an accessible recent contribution to that discussion.

Another question not addressed here, but which is receiving increased attention, pertains to conscience rights for institutions. For example, can a Catholic hospital (especially one that receives public funding) be permitted to opt out of having MAID performed on its premises? Moreover, just as individual physicians and nurses might invoke non-conscience-based professional objections to providing MAID, so too institutions might do so. For an incisive discussion of the latter points, see Shadd and Shadd (2019). Currently, many Catholic hospitals across Canada have opt-out privileges allowing them to refuse to offer MAID on site, but this is liable to be challenged.

8

Additional Legal and Policy Issues

In the first section of this chapter, I look at the potential legal risks to Canadian health-care professionals arising from the disconnect between Canadian criminal law and the rest of the world, in particular the disconnect with the majority of US states that still count assisted suicide and active euthanasia as forms of criminal homicide. In the second section, I discuss matters related to privacy and record-keeping. And, in the third section, I discuss the legal prospects for a reversal of *Carter v Canada* in future court rulings, permitting the recriminalization of MAID.

The Neglected Legal Risk to Canadian Health-Care Professionals Participating in MAID

As noted in my discussion of *Carter v Canada* in Chapter 1, in general there is a presumption against the extraterritorial application of criminal law. Recall, for instance, that, if a Canadian vacations in Portugal and while there purchases and consumes cocaine (an act that has been decriminalized in Portugal), then he will not be charged on his return to Canada for violation of Canadian narcotics laws. Similarly, if a Canadian vacations in Holland and employs a prostitute while there, on his return to Canada he will not be charged for violating Canadian laws against prostitution. However, this presumption does not always obtain. If a Canadian visits a foreign country and while there participates in a so-called honour killing, an act often tolerated by officials there but counted as first-degree murder in Canada, then he can be charged with murder on his return to Canada should the facts become known. And, if the murder victim in that foreign country was herself a Canadian citizen (including a dual citizen), then a murder charge will certainly ensue. For grave crimes, in particular murder, extraterritorial prosecution can and does occur. This was why Lee Carter and Hollis Johnson were granted the status of plaintiffs in *Carter v Canada:* They had a legitimate concern that they could face homicide charges in Canada for having facilitated Kay Carter's assisted death procedure in Switzerland – an act legal in Switzerland but not in Canada. By recognizing their status as plaintiffs, both the Supreme Court of British Columbia and the Supreme Court of Canada implicitly validated their concern about potential prosecution in Canada.

With all that in mind, consider the following hypothetical scenario. A dual American-Canadian citizen, resident in Canada, meets the legal criteria for MAID and receives it here. This dual citizen's immediate family mostly resides in Texas. They were vehemently opposed to the procedure and are enraged with the Canadian physician who gave the lethal injection over their objections. Some months later that physician attends a medical conference in Dallas. While there, he is arrested and charged with murder by Texas since the dual citizen's family succeeded in petitioning Texas officials to prosecute the doctor. Texas regards the physician's action as homicide, and the Texas attorney general (perhaps with an eye on the publicity that the case might garner) considers his office duty bound to prosecute the murder of an American citizen. The fact that the murder was committed in Canada is no barrier: murder is often regarded as a prime exception to the presumption against the extraterritorial application of criminal law.

How likely is this scenario? It is difficult to say. I chose the United States as an example because the massive number of dual American-Canadian citizens resident in Canada renders it inevitable that such a citizen will seek and obtain assisted death here (it has probably already happened). I chose Texas because it is a religiously and politically conservative state in which the opposition to assisted suicide and euthanasia is widespread and deeply held. Utah or Mississippi might have worked equally well as an example, Vermont or New York less so. And of course Canadian health-care practitioners would have nothing to fear in the few US states that themselves have legalized one or another form of assisted death. My point is simply that there is no clear legal barrier to the occurrence of the Texas scenario. Nor is there any easy way for the Canadian government to secure practitioners against it, even by diplomatic channels. Recall that, though there is such a thing as a federal crime in the United States, for the most part criminal laws there, including laws against murder, fall under state jurisdiction. (This is in marked contrast to Canada, where criminal law is under federal jurisdiction.) In the United States, an act that is criminal in one state might not be in another. Penalties also vary from state to state – hence, Texas has the death penalty, but Vermont does not. The Canadian government does not have formal diplomatic treaties with individual US states.

The possibility that Canadian health-care personnel could face prosecution for murder in foreign jurisdictions on account of euthanizing dual citizens has not been discussed in the popular media coverage of *Carter v Canada* and Bill C-14 or by legal scholars. This might be because of a simple oversight or a (questionable) assumption that the sort of scenario just contemplated is too improbable to be worthy of discussion. Regardless, this remains a serious issue for Canadian physicians and nurse practitioners who carry out MAID on dual citizens. We need to bear in mind that, even though Canadian law no longer treats voluntary active euthanasia as a crime, for better or worse nearly every other nation on Earth disagrees and still regards such acts as murder. Just as the Canadian government would prosecute someone for the "honour" killing of a dual Canadian citizen that took place in a foreign country (where it is not regarded as murder by the legal system of that country), so too officials in that nation might prosecute someone for the assisted death of a dual citizen that took place in Canada (where it is not regarded as murder by the Canadian legal system). I am not equating here the moral status of MAID and "honour" killing; there are degrees of evil. Although I believe that the former is impermissible, the latter is certainly a worse kind of act. My point is simply that norms vary from one country to the next, and we should not be shocked by the prospect that countries with different norms might subject Canadian physicians and nurse practitioners to prosecution in those countries for deliberately causing the deaths of their citizens.

At the least, there is something to be said for making Canadian health-care personnel aware of the possible risks here; provincial medical associations, for instance, might include a brief discussion of this in their professional guidelines for MAID.

Information Sharing and Record-Keeping

The reader might recall that section 4 (3.1) of Bill C-14 leaves unspecified the standards on information sharing and record-keeping:

The Minister of Health, in cooperation with representatives of the provincial governments responsible for health, may establish guidelines on the information to be included on death certificates in cases where medical assistance in dying has been provided, which may include the way in which to clearly identify medical assistance in dying as the manner of death, as well as the illness, disease or disability that prompted the request for medical assistance in dying.

This does not state explicitly that the death certificate will have to include mention of assisted death as the proximate cause of the patient's demise, but that is clearly the assumption.

My hope is that this remains a given; going forward it is vital that accurate records be made and preserved long term to allow researchers to track the prevalence of MAID. Tracking is necessary for a variety of reasons, including enabling governments to identify relevant patterns and trends. If it is noticed, for instance, that a much higher percentage of terminal pancreatic cancer patients in (say) Prince Edward Island are applying for assisted death than patients with the same terminal illness in (say) Newfoundland and Labrador, then this might enable researchers to identify inequities in the quality of palliative care services between the two provinces.

Left unmentioned in the bill but likewise important is accurate record-keeping of the total number of requests for assisted death, even those that are denied, and thankfully Health Canada has indeed been keeping data on unsuccessful requests. These records need to be inputted promptly and made available not only to government archivists and academic researchers but also to physicians and nurse practitioners. When a physician or nurse practitioner receives a request for assisted death (especially if the request is from a patient with whom there is no prior professional relationship), a question needs to be asked: "Am I the first health-care professional whom this patient has consulted about assisted death, or has the patient already sought the procedure out and been turned down?" The risk to guard against is a sort of "physician/nurse shopping" in which a suicidal patient simply goes from one health-care provider to another until one is found willing to accede to the procedure. One hopes that the safeguards already put in place in the bill will help to forestall such occurrences – still, in cases in which, for instance, the patient's legal competence is questioned, knowing whether that patient has a prior record of requesting assisted death will be of use in making that assessment.

Might *Carter v Canada* Be Reversed?

If future federal governments retain Bill C-14, and refrain from invoking the notwithstanding clause to overturn *Carter v Canada*, then this does not automatically mean that the nation is permanently shackled to this ruling. *Carter*, by overturning *Rodriguez*, reminds us that the Supreme Court can overturn its own prior rulings, even in cases whose relevant facts, at least outwardly, are closely analogous.[1] How might this come about? And which aspects of the ruling are most vulnerable to future revision?

Decriminalized MAID for those experiencing complete physical incapacitation is likely here to stay. Although the Supreme Court's reasoning on this point is questionable (i.e., the claim that people in this situation might be driven to premature suicide, such that criminalization violates the right to life), it is unlikely that future courts will revisit this particular point; reversals of prior opinions do occur, but it is difficult to imagine a future court ruling that a previous court simply made erroneous inferences from the Charter right to life.

Marginally more likely is a scenario in which a future court imposes much narrower restrictions on MAID in response to new empirical data. The justices in *Carter v Canada* (both Justice Smith's ruling in British Columbia and the federal ruling) displayed considerable confidence that empirical data from the Netherlands, Oregon, and other relevant jurisdictions showed that concerns about coercion and the extension of assisted death to the legally incompetent are misplaced. For the sake of argument, granting their assessments of these other jurisdictions, future Canadian experience might not be as fortunate. I do not expect that Canadian physicians, nurse practitioners, and pharmacists are any more prone to abusive or negligent practices than those in Oregon; rather, if in the future serious concerns arise regarding subtle (or less than subtle) coercion of patients, or killing of those incapable of providing legal consent, they are liable to arise from two new factors. First, in the next twenty years, a far higher percentage of the Canadian population will be elderly and subject to major health problems, placing great financial burdens on the public health-care system. Second, new methods of euthanasia will become available. I mentioned in Chapter 1 the practice of euthanizing patients not by lethal injection but by putting them under general anaesthetic and removing their vital organs for transplant. There is a shortage of organ donors in Canada, and the need will only increase in coming decades. Should these two factors coalesce at some point in the future, one can envision a scenario in which terminally ill patients are made aware (whether by health-care providers or activists or bureaucrats) that they are costing the state a great deal of money and that, if they just checked out early, they would thereby fulfill a civic duty to spare the state that expense and fulfill a humanitarian duty to save the lives of multiple younger people of greater value to society. Should anything resembling that disturbing future come to pass, Canadian courts might decide that such patients are experiencing coercion, and they might decide further that the only feasible way to stop it is to recriminalize MAID or at least make it more narrowly available.

It is also possible that public opinion on MAID will shift in the coming years, with opposition overtaking support. Such a shift could become part of a future legal case for overturning *Carter,* insofar as changes in public values are now seen to be among the legitimate grounds for overturning past rulings by the Supreme Court of Canada. The reader will recall the reference by Justice Smith to shifting public opinion in arguing that she had the authority to overturn *Rodriguez.*[2] Although it is a bit unsettling to realize the extent to which our highest courts have subjected themselves to the legal relevance of opinion polls, that they have done so provides additional hope to opponents of MAID. Public opinion might shift back against assisted death.

Conclusion

Let us briefly recap what I have presented in this book. In the introduction, I provided a synopsis of the topic, some clarification of key terms, and a short overview of the book's contents. Chapter 1 consisted of a review of the major court rulings leading up to the legalization of MAID and included some evaluative remarks about the legal merits of those rulings. In Chapter 2, I reviewed major developments since *Carter v Canada,* notably the passage of Bill C-14. Chapter 3 presented an overview of some important background ideas involving accounts of human well-being (hedonism versus desire satisfaction theory versus objective list theory versus perfectionism) and ethical theory (consequentialism, Kantian deontology, natural law theory, and virtue ethics). In Chapter 4, I summarized some of the main arguments for and against the permissibility of MAID, some of which flowed from an explicitly affirmed background ethical theory, whereas others were compatible with multiple theories. I argued that MAID is impermissible and should have remained legally prohibited. I drew out an implication in Chapter 5: namely, that the federal government has an obligation to invoke the notwithstanding clause to override *Carter v Canada* or, failing that, that the provinces have an obligation to obstruct assisted suicide and euthanasia by other means. In Chapter 6, I took up the neglected question of the morality of public funding for MAID and formulated a disjunctive argument against funding it. In Chapter 7, I presented a brief argument for respecting the freedom of conscience of health-care professionals, and in Chapter 8, I covered three additional legal and policy issues.

My hope is that the reader will have gained from this book a thorough understanding of what MAID in Canada consists of, the legal history leading up to its legalization, and some of the major moral arguments surrounding it. My further hope, of course, is that the reader will agree with my negative assessment of MAID and the need for a legislative remedy. However, I recognize that many readers will disagree sharply on these points, and I will be content with the more modest aim of having conveyed adequately some reasons that one might rationally oppose the practice. On matters of such deep and profound moral significance, improved mutual understanding in a diverse and pluralistic democracy such as Canada is itself a worthwhile goal.

Yet I do not wish to end on an entirely conciliatory note. If the moral assessment of MAID defended here is accurate, then Canadian society has entered into a frankly disturbing situation in which the deliberate killing of innocent people is not only sanctioned but also *publicly funded,* implicating all of us in its commission. Unless the reader is highly confident in the permissibility of assisted death, the present state of affairs should be regarded with great anxiety.

Glossary

assisted suicide: This occurs when one person intentionally kills himself with the aid of another person, where that aid can be indirect (e.g., providing advice on how to commit suicide) or more direct (e.g., giving the individual a lethal prescription that he later takes). In either case, the final act itself is carried out by the individual, not by the assisting party.

basic moral principle (BMP): This is the common factor underlying moral permissibility – that is, the BMP is what constitutes any morally permissible action as morally permissible.

Bill C-14: This piece of federal legislation enacts the key provisions of *Carter v Canada*, the Supreme Court of Canada ruling that decriminalizes forms of both assisted suicide and voluntary active euthanasia. It received royal assent on June 17, 2016.

Bill C-7: This piece of federal legislation amends portions of Bill C-14 in order to expand the eligibility criteria for MAID beyond those for whom death is reasonably foreseeable. It was put before Parliament in February 2020 in response to a Quebec Superior Court ruling from September 2019. This bill passed on March 17, 2021.

Carter v Canada*:* This is the Supreme Court of Canada ruling that effectively decriminalized forms of both assisted suicide and voluntary active euthanasia in February 2015. (It is also the name of a related Supreme Court of British Columbia ruling, which preceded it in 2012.)

consequentialism: This is a philosophical theory about what constitutes morally permissible actions as morally permissible. According to consequentialism, an action is permissible if and only if (and because) its consequences would be at least as good as the consequences of any alternative action that the agent might perform instead. This theory divides into different versions depending on which specific theory of value it is combined with in order to clarify the sorts of consequences in view.

desire satisfaction theory (DST): This philosophical theory pertains to the nature of human happiness/well-being, according to which it consists solely of getting what one wants. It divides into two main versions: namely, *actualist DST* (according to which one's life is going well just to the extent that one's actual desires are fulfilled) and *hypothetical DST* (according to which one's life is going well just to the extent that the desires that one would have if one were fully rational and well-informed are fulfilled).

doctrine of double effect (DDE): The DDE plays an important part in natural law theory by clarifying the difference between direct and indirect violations of basic human goods (where the former are understood as always impermissible). According to the DDE, an indirect violation is distinguished from a direct violation by reference to the following four criteria: First, the action itself is not *intrinsically evil,* evil in and of itself, irrespective of the broader context and consequences; second, the action is necessary for the fulfillment of the goal (i.e., there is no feasible way of achieving the good aim without incurring the unfortunate side effects); third, the unfortunate side effects of the action are genuinely *side effects* (i.e., not intended by the agent, whether in themselves or as means to the end); and fourth, the unfortunate side effects are proportionate to the good achieved.

ethical theory: This is the subdiscipline of ethics devoted to discovering and explicating the basic moral principle (BMP).

euthanasia: The original Greek literally means "good death." In the context of medical ethics today, it refers to either the practice of allowing a patient to die by natural causes through the withdrawal of treatment or the practice of taking active steps deliberately to end the patient's life. These usages are disambiguated by the distinction between *passive* euthanasia and *active* euthanasia. Those two categories are each further divided into *voluntary*, *non-voluntary*, and *involuntary* varieties, according to how they link up with the expressed wishes of the patient or the patient's surrogates.

hedonism: This philosophical theory pertains to the nature of human happiness/well-being, according to which it consists solely of the acquisition of enjoyment and the avoidance of suffering. It divides into two main versions: namely, *sensory hedonism* (which specifies that the relevant enjoyments are solely of the sensory variety) and *attitudinal hedonism* (which specifies that any sort of enjoyment counts toward happiness/well-being, whether sensory or some other kind).

hedonistic act utilitarianism (HAU): A version of consequentialism, HAU is a philosophical theory about what constitutes morally permissible actions as morally permissible. According to HAU, an action is permissible if and only if (and because) it would produce at least as high a net balance of pleasure (or less pain) as would any other alternative action that the agent might perform instead.

inscrutability proviso: In any case in which reasonable doubt persists concerning the moral permissibility of deliberately killing a person, one ought to refrain from deliberate killing in that case, and the law should refrain from permitting deliberate killing in that sort of case.

Kantian deontology: This philosophical theory involves what constitutes morally permissible actions as morally permissible. According to Kantian deontology, an action is permissible if and only if (and because) the action, to the extent that it bears on the treatment of persons, treats persons (including oneself) as ends in themselves and not merely as means.

MAID: An acronym for medical assistance in dying, this is a blanket term covering both assisted suicide and voluntary active euthanasia.

metaphysical naturalism: This refers to the idea that the only kind of reality is physical reality, such that there is no God, no immaterial human soul, et cetera.

natural law theory (NLT): This philosophical theory addresses what constitutes morally permissible actions as morally permissible. According to NLT, an action is permissible if and only if (and because) in performing the action one does not directly violate any of the basic human goods. NLT is supplemented by reference to the doctrine of double effect (by way of clarifying the distinction between direct and indirect violations of basic human goods).

negative right: The possession of this kind of right obligates others to refrain from doing something to you. In other words, a negative right establishes a moral claim to non-interference.

objective list theory: This philosophical theory pertains to the nature of human happiness/well-being, according to which it consists of attaining a set of objectively significant goods (e.g., health, fulfilling work, loving relationships, etc.).

perfectionism: This philosophical theory is about the nature of human happiness/well-being, according to which it consists of actualizing one's capacities as a human being (especially one's highest, *distinctively human* capacities).

physicalism: This is a synonym for metaphysical naturalism (see above).

positive right: The possession of this kind of right obligates others to do something or provide something for you. In other words, this kind of right establishes a moral claim to assistance.

virtue ethics: This philosophical theory involves what constitutes morally permissible actions as morally permissible. According to virtue ethics, an action is permissible if and only if (and because) it is something that a virtuous and well-informed agent, acting in character, would not avoid doing in the circumstances under consideration.

Notes

Introduction

1 For more on some of these international developments, see, for instance, Keown (2014, 2018), and Martin (2016, ch. 12; 2017).

2 *Carter v Canada*, 2015 SCC 5 at 390.

3 Contrast the relevant wording of what had been section 241(b) of the *Criminal Code of Canada:* "Every one who aids or abets a person to commit suicide, whether suicide ensues or not, is guilty of an indictable offence and liable to imprisonment for a term not exceeding fourteen years." And now section 14 of the Criminal Code: "No person is entitled to consent to have death inflicted on him, and such consent does not affect the criminal responsibility of any person by whom death may be inflicted on the person by whom consent is given." *Criminal Code,* RSC 1985, c. C-46, s 241(b) and s 14.

4 Bill C-14, *An Act to Amend the Criminal Code and to Make Related Amendments to Other Acts (Medical Assistance in Dying),* 1st session, 42nd Parliament, 2016, s 3, 241.2 (2.d).

5 However, further expansion to the legally competent mentally ill would be in line with the ultra-permissive legal regimes in place in Belgium and the Netherlands. A wide range of mental illnesses qualifies one for assisted death (both voluntary active euthanasia and assisted suicide) in these countries, including depression, anxiety disorders, phobias, personality disorders, anorexia, and (at least in Belgium) Asperger's and drug addiction. See, for example, Schuklenk and Van de Vathorst (2015) for details on the Dutch situation and Thienpont et al. (2015) for Belgium. Similarly, in Switzerland, assisted suicide (but not euthanasia) is available for any legally competent person suffering from a mental illness deemed to be long lasting,

severe, and (for that person) incurable. On Switzerland's law, see, for instance, Player (2018), who also provides a brief overview of the Dutch and Belgian contexts. And consult Keown (2018) for a more extensive discussion of the legal situations in these countries. (As this book was about to go to press in early April 2021, I was able to add the following brief update regarding Bill C-7: it received royal assent on March 17, 2021. In its final form, it extended eligibility beyond the terminally ill, as expected. Surprisingly, it also committed to extending eligibility to those suffering solely from mental illnesses, though that aspect of the bill would not come into effect for another two years. The bill does not extend eligibility to minors or permit advance directives, though the government committed to launching a parliamentary committee to study the prospects for those further extensions.)

6   There have also been several commissioned reports directly relevant to these three potential expansions, published in 2018 by the Council of Canadian Academies. They can be found via the council's website, www.cca-reports.ca.

7   Perhaps the closest analogue currently available is the fine anthology edited by Stingl (2010), though of course it appeared too early to take into account the subsequent momentous legal developments.

8   For some (partly divergent) Eastern Orthodox perspectives on the relationship between religion and moral debate in a modern democracy, see Engelhardt (2000); Goss and Vitz (2014); and Iltis (2009, 2011, 2014).

9   Note that some object to the notion of "non-voluntary" euthanasia. For instance, Hendin (1998, p. 276), a psychiatrist specializing in the study of suicide, writes that

> "nonvoluntary euthanasia" is a problematic term. Is one not justified in assuming a desire to live unless there is evidence to the contrary? Could one murder a demented stranger and plead as an extenuating circumstance that we did not know if the victim wanted to keep on living? Nonvoluntary euthanasia is particularly disturbing when applied to partially competent patients whose consent is not sought but who often can be quite clear about whether they want to live or die.

In contrast, Downie (2004, p. 8) argues that

> the distinction between involuntary and non-voluntary is too important to lose. Involuntary euthanasia breaches a competent individual's autonomy, while non-voluntary euthanasia might not. Non-voluntary euthanasia might not be in the individual's best interests, but, although important, that is another matter entirely. It is important to keep involuntariness and non-voluntariness separate, so that the different attributes of the cases (a certain breach of autonomy vs a possible breach of autonomy and a possible failure to act in someone's best interests) can be taken into account in the analysis.

10 That is a bit of a simplification; in some streams of literature on VPE (e.g., those from natural law theorists), many authors restrict the term "euthanasia" to cases in which the physician *intends* the death of the patient. For these authors, any intention to end

the life of the patient is morally wrong, whether that intention is realized passively (by unplugging the patient and letting nature take its course) or actively (by giving the patient a lethal injection); even in the act of unplugging the patient from the respirator, the physician should not intend death. With such an understanding of the terminology, from their perspective, voluntary passive euthanasia would be wrong. Manning (1998, p. 2) explains that

> recent papal documents and some Catholic ethicists prefer to avoid the term *passive euthanasia*. Forgoing or withdrawing medical treatment that offers no hope of benefit to the total well-being of the patient, or that imposes burdens disproportionate to the potential benefits, *allows the patient to die*. This is perfectly acceptable in Catholic teaching because its primary intention is not to cause death, but to either avoid a prolonged course of dying or to avoid a serious threat to the physical, psychological, spiritual, or economic well-being of the individual. Death may be predictable, even inevitable as a result of the action, but it is not directly intended. While the Church would call this allowing the patient to die, some would call it passive euthanasia. The same action – removing a respirator, for example – could be morally permitted or not, depending on the moral intention of those removing the respirator.

For additional examples of this usage, see Finnis (1995, p. 25); Gomez-Lobo (2002, pp. 99–100); Oderberg (2000a, pp. 72–73); and Somerville (2001, p. 26). However, in what follows, for simplicity's sake I will adopt the more common understanding of VPE, according to which no intention of death need be implied.

11 See Downie (2004, pp. 15–28) and Schuklenk et al. (2011, pp. 21–25) for clear discussions of some of the complexities here under Canadian law.

12 Physician-assisted death (PAD), used in some of the relevant court rulings, is no longer appropriate for the Canadian context, insofar as Bill C-14 provides not only physicians but also nurse practitioners with legal indemnity for participation in assisted death. Pharmacists also receive attention in the legislation and a somewhat more limited indemnity, in keeping with their more indirect role in the process.

13 For instance, in the wake of the passage of Bill C-14, Thomas Cardinal Collins (2016), the Roman Catholic archbishop of Toronto, issued a press release that included the following:

> We need to speak forthrightly. When people feel compelled to use language in a way that does not reveal what is actually happening, but instead conceals it, it is a sign that something is radically wrong (and they know it). The now officially accepted terminology ... such as "Medical Assistance in Dying" does not describe medical assistance in dying; it describes killing. Let us say what we mean, and mean what we say.

14 Ideally, the book's title would have included mention of euthanasia, but the demands of concision prompted the use only of assisted suicide. I hope that this will not give the impression that I regard the two as equivalent, whether morally or in other respects.

Chapter 1: An Overview of *Carter v Canada*

1 For those unfamiliar with this terminology, you possess a *negative right* when others are obligated to refrain from doing something to you. A negative right thus establishes a moral claim to non-interference. For example, you possess the right not to be tortured, such that all others are obligated to refrain from torturing you. In contrast, you possess a *positive right* when others are obligated to do or provide something for you. For instance, you have the right to a basic education, such that others are obligated to pay for your basic schooling. (Note that a positive right entails a correlative negative right: if others are obligated to pay for your schooling, then they are likewise obligated not to prevent you from going to school.) It is important not to confuse negative and positive rights. In Canada, for example, if you are a legally competent unmarried adult, then you have the right to marry any equivalently qualified non-blood relative. This is clearly a negative right, obliging others not to prevent you from marrying. If it were a positive right, then someone (the provincial government?) would be obligated to provide you with a spouse.

2 The relevant section of the Criminal Code reads thus: "Every one who (a) counsels a person to commit suicide, or (b) aids or abets a person to commit suicide, whether suicide ensues or not, is guilty of an indictable offence and liable to imprisonment for a term not exceeding fourteen years." *Criminal Code*, RSC 1985, c. C-46, s 241(b).

3 The relevant sections of the Charter read thus: "Everyone has the right to life, liberty and security of the person and the right not to be deprived thereof except in accordance with the principles of fundamental justice" (s 7); "everyone has the right not to be subjected to any cruel and unusual treatment or punishment" (s 12); and "every individual is equal before and under the law and has the right to the equal protection and equal benefit of the law without discrimination and, in particular, without discrimination based on race, national or ethnic origin, colour, religion, sex, age or mental or physical disability" (s 15). *Canadian Charter of Rights and Freedoms*, ss 7, 12 and 15, Part 1 of the *Constitution Act, 1982*, being Schedule B to the *Canada Act 1982* (UK), 1982, c 11.

4 My discussion focuses on the Supreme Court of Canada ruling; for a concise summary of the earlier BC Court of Appeal decision against Rodriguez, see Baum (2015, pp. 159–167).

5 *Rodriguez v British Columbia*, 1993, 3 SCR 519 at 588–589.

6 See again the precise wording of s 7, noted above.

7 *Rodriguez v British Columbia*, 1993, 3 SCR 519 at 595. Note that Sopinka was explicit that "sanctity of life" here did not refer to any particular theological understanding of life; rather, it was a phrase employed by the court to indicate "that human life is seen to have a deep intrinsic value of its own" (p. 585).

8 Ibid., at 608.

9 Ibid., at 611–612.

10 Infringements on rights can be justified by reference to s 1 of the Charter: "The *Canadian Charter of Rights and Freedoms* guarantees the rights and freedoms set out in it subject only to such reasonable limits prescribed by law as can be demonstrably justified in a free and democratic society." *Canadian Charter of Rights and*

Freedoms, s 1, Part 1 of the *Constitution Act,* 1982, being Schedule B to the *Canada Act 1982* (UK), 1982, c 11.

11 Ibid., at 623.
12 Ibid., at 630.
13 Ibid., at 666–667.
14 See Chan and Somerville (2016, pp. 151–155) for a concise overview of these failed legislative efforts. Only one (Bill C-384) actually made it to a floor vote in the House of Commons, in April 2010. It was voted down 228–59, indicating a high level of support among Canadian MPs for what was then the legal status quo.
15 Some readers might have been surprised to see a provincial court functionally invalidating a prior ruling by the Supreme Court of Canada, but there are certain circumstances in which this can take place, and the claim of the Supreme Court of British Columbia was that these circumstances were met in its ruling in *Carter v Canada.*
16 This fact is confirmed to some degree by comparable events in the British legal system vis-à-vis Switzerland. Martin (2016, p. 321) summarizes that

> nobody in Britain has been prosecuted for assisting a suicide by accompanying a patient to a Swiss death clinic, although the penalty for assisting a suicide is up to fourteen years in prison. Examples include the parents of Dan James, a twenty-three-year-old English athlete who was paralyzed from the chest down after an accident on a rugby pitch in March 2007. He tried to kill himself several times over the next eighteen months and finally persuaded his distraught parents to help him go to Switzerland after he threatened to move out of their home and into subsidized housing so he could starve himself to death. A family friend chartered a plane to fly them to Dignitas [an organization providing assisted death in Switzerland], where he died in September 2008 after swallowing a barbiturate dissolved in water. His parents, Mark and Julie James, were arrested and questioned after their return to England with their son's body, but not charged, a decision that was reached only after several tense weeks.

Martin goes on to note that the director of public prosecutions in Britain issued guidelines in 2009 that sought to clarify just how vulnerable to prosecution Britons in this sort of circumstance might be.

17 *Carter v Canada,* 2012 BCSC 1587 at 13.
18 The former forbids counselling someone to commit suicide and reads as follows: "Every one who (a) counsels a person to commit suicide, or (b) aids or abets a person to commit suicide, whether suicide ensues or not, is guilty of an indictable offence and liable to imprisonment for a term not exceeding fourteen years." The latter is relevant to active euthanasia as opposed to assisted suicide and reads as follows: "No person is entitled to consent to have death inflicted on him, and such consent does not affect the criminal responsibility of any person by whom death may be inflicted on the person by whom consent is given." *Criminal Code,* RSC 1985, c. C-46, s 241(a) and 14.
19 *Carter v Canada,* 2012 BCSC 1587 at 74.
20 Ibid., at 74.
21 Ibid., at 80.

22 Keown (2014) would subsequently author a detailed critique of Justice Smith's even-
    tual ruling in the case.
23 Ibid., at 76–77.
24 Ibid., at 83.
25 Ibid., at 84–85.
26 Ibid., at 251.
27 Ibid., at 265–266.
28 Ibid., at 325–326.
29 Ibid., at 328.
30 I will not attempt to summarize the complex case law discussed in this section of the
    ruling, though one key precedent employed by Justice Smith was *Alberta v Hutterian
    Brethren of Wilson Colony,* 2009 SCC 37.
31 Ibid., at 347.
32 Ibid., at 365–366.
33 Ibid., at 384.
34 *Carter v Canada,* 2013 BCCA 435 at para 30–32.
35 Ibid., at para 39. I include this quotation here since it is the only mention in the four
    court rulings of the notion of "public complicity" in assisted suicide; I will examine
    this topic in Chapter 6 when I look at certain moral issues that arise specifically from
    public funding for assisted death, an issue that has received little discussion in the
    ethics literature.
36 Ibid., at para 119.
37 She provides a useful precedent here (para 317) from *New Brunswick (Minister of
    Health and Community Services) v G.(J.),* 1999 3 SCR 46, a ruling of the Supreme
    Court of Canada in which Chief Justice Lamer wrote as follows:

    First, the rights protected by s 7 – life, liberty, and security of the person – are very
    significant and cannot ordinarily be overridden by competing social interests.
    Second, rarely will a violation of the principles of fundamental justice, specifically
    the right to a fair hearing, be upheld as a reasonable limit demonstrably justified in a
    free and democratic society. [At para. 99]

38 Ibid., at para 321.
39 *Carter v Canada,* 2015 SCC 5 at 372–373.
40 *Rodriguez v British Columbia,* 1993, 3 SCR 519 at 614. Emphasis added.
41 *Carter v Canada,* 2015 SCC 5 at 367–368.
42 Ibid., at 384–385. Emphasis added.
43 Ibid., at 390.
44 Ibid., at 369.
45 One might think initially that the requirement of consent would exclude assisted
    death for the mentally ill; however, sufferers from a wide range of mental illness fre-
    quently retain legal competence in the midst of their illnesses, such as anorexia,
    anxiety disorders, compulsive disorders, and depression – even those afflicted with
    schizophrenia can sign a legally valid will or write up a legally valid contract if they
    do so during a period in which the illness is demonstrably under control.
46 See, for instance, Kim and Lemmens (2016) and Yarascavitch (2017).

47 For example, Kirby (2017), Schuklenk and Van de Vathorst (2015), and Tanner (2018) all argue in favour of extending access to MAID to Canadians who suffer solely from psychiatric conditions. See also Warnock and Macdonald (2008, ch. 3), who make a similar case within the UK context, and Player (2018) and Steinbock (2017) for an analogous argument within the American context. (Recall that MAID is the acronym for medical assistance in dying and understood as encompassing both assisted suicide and voluntary active euthanasia.)

48 As advocated by Bollen, Ten Hoopen, Ysebaert, Van Mook, and Van Heurn (2016); Shapiro (2018); and Wilkinson and Savulescu (2012). That discussion is now shifting beyond the academic literature and into Canadian media; see, for instance, the report by Kirkey (2019).

Chapter 2: Developments in Law and Policy since the Ruling

1 For the justice minister's initial reaction, see, for instance, the reporting by Ivison (2015).

2 For reporting on the announcement of the panel, see, for instance, Kirkey (2015b).

3 See Bryden (2016).

4 See Fekete (2016). Given how much attention was given to freedom of conscience issues for Canadian physicians, it is odd that the court said nothing about the ability of superior court justices to recuse themselves from participating in such hearings on the ground of conscience or religion.

5 For some examples, see Carter and Rodgerson (2018, pp. 790–793).

6 See, for instance, MacLeod (2016a).

7 Bill C-14, *An Act to Amend the Criminal Code and to Make Related Amendments to Other Acts (Medical Assistance in Dying)*, 1st session, 42nd Parliament, 2016, s 3 (5.1).

8 This will exclude the practice of so-called death tourism in which non-Canadians travel to Canada to receive assisted death. The reader will recall that the permission of this practice by Switzerland was a proximate cause of the involvement of plaintiffs Hollis and Carter in *Carter v Canada*.

9 Ibid., s 3 (241.2(2)).

10 One area of incompleteness in the law is its failure to specify what should happen if the second medical professional disagrees with the first. For instance, Gallagher (2017, pp. 49–50) writes that

> as a safeguard, another physician or nurse practitioner must agree that the patient meets the eligibility criteria for MAID ... This safeguard is in place to protect vulnerable people and to ensure that all possible solutions to the intolerable suffering have been explored. But what happens if the two practitioners disagree? There is no process for resolving disagreements. Does this mean that someone could seek out as many physicians as it takes to get two to agree?

11 Ibid., s 3 (241.2(3(g))).

12 Ibid., s 3 (241.3). It is odd that the bill does not expand further on this point or more precisely specify differing penalties according to which safeguards are breached. A

physician who, without adequate justification, knowingly breaches the ten-day waiting period will apparently be subject to the same penalties as a physician who pres-
sures a patient into assisted death in collusion with relatives who stand to gain
financially from it.

13 According to the preamble of Bill C-14, "it is desirable to have a consistent approach
to medical assistance in dying across Canada, while recognizing the provinces' jurisdiction over various matters related to medical assistance in dying, including the
delivery of health care services and the regulation of health care professionals, as
well as insurance contracts and coroners and medical examiners."

14 Bill C-14, s 4 (3.1), states that

> the Minister of Health, in cooperation with representatives of the provincial govern-
> ments responsible for health, may establish guidelines on the information to be
> included on death certificates in cases where medical assistance in dying has been
> provided, which may include the way in which to clearly identify medical assistance
> in dying as the manner of death, as well as the illness, disease or disability that
> prompted the request for medical assistance in dying.

15 See, for instance, the reporting by MacLeod (2016b). For further details on the spe-
cifics of this case, see Carter and Rodgerson (2018, pp. 798–799).

16 See, for instance, the reporting by Curtis (2019) and see Ha and Grant (2019) for
further details.

17 Their opposing views on the matter were communicated in stark fashion during the
televised French-language leaders' debate on October 2 and reiterated post-debate.
See Reynolds (2019) for a summary of party leaders' positions at that point in the
campaign.

18 As reported, for instance, by Séguin (2014). For a detailed account of the process
leading up to the passage of the bill, see Martin (2016, ch. 9).

19 See Hamilton and Plante (2016).

20 For coverage, see, for instance, Hopper (2016) and Blackwell (2016).

21 A link to the report was available through various provincial health ministry web-
sites, including that of Alberta Health, which was accessed in the summer of 2016,
http://www.health.alberta.ca/health-info/medical-assistance-dying.html.

22 As reported, for instance, by Loriggio (2018). For a detailed assessment of that ruling
(through both legal and theological lenses), see McGowan (2018).

23 See Grant (2019a).

24 For instance, Alberta has since announced that it will not in fact require physicians
with conscientious objections to make referrals; patients whose physicians refuse
to make referrals can contact the Ministry of Health directly for assistance in
obtaining assisted deaths. The guidelines were listed by Alberta Health and
accessed in the summer of 2016 at http://www.health.alberta.ca/health-info/med-
ical-assistance-dying.html. Note that, when it comes to provincial professional
associations (as opposed to provincial governments), the CPSO is the only one
requiring that all members be willing to make effective referrals for MAID, according to Canadian Physicians for Life (an NGO that supports physicians' rights of
conscience). On the latter point, see the reporting by Kay (2019).

Chapter 3: Background to the Moral Debate over MAID

1 For accessible and balanced entry points to the general topic, consult Cholbi (2011) and Stingl (2010). For moral arguments against the permissibility of MAID, see, for instance, Breck (1998, ch. 5); Breck and Breck (2005, ch. 7); Devine (1990, ch. 6); Engelhardt (2000, ch. 6); Gomez-Lobo (2002, ch. 8); Gorsuch (2006); Kass (2002); Keown (2018); Manning (1998); Meilaender (2013, ch. 6); Oderberg (2000a, ch. 2); Paterson (2008); and Somerville (2001). For moral arguments in favour of its permissibility (in at least some cases), see, for instance, Battin (2005); Downie (2004); Glover (1977, chs. 13–15); Singer (1993, ch. 7); Sumner (2011); Warnock and Macdonald (2008); and Young (2007).

2 For a helpful introduction to this dispute, with special regard to how it has played out in bioethics, see Arras (2010).

3 Readers looking for a more thorough (but still accessible) introduction to these theories and their pros and cons should consult Fletcher (2016).

4 See, for instance, Crisp (2006); Feldman (2002); Lemos (2007); Sobel (2002); and Weijers and Schouten (2013).

5 Hypothetical DST is sometimes called ideal desire satisfaction theory.

6 For further discussion of DST, see, for instance, Carson (2000); Heathwood (2005, 2006); Noggle (1999); and Murphy (1999).

7 For more on OLT, consult, for instance, Arneson (1999); Fletcher (2013); Moore (2000); and Rice (2013).

8 That is not to say that there cannot be trivial fulfillments of higher capacities, the importance of which might be outranked by the ability to fulfill lower capacities. Most of us would prefer to give up crossword puzzles than to give up our tastebuds. (My thanks to Helen Watt for that vivid example.)

9 Physicalism (also known as "metaphysical naturalism" or sometimes "materialism") is roughly the idea that the only kind of reality is physical reality, such that there is no God, no immaterial human soul, et cetera.

10 For more on perfectionism, see, for instance, Dorsey (2010) and Hurka (1993).

11 Of course, one could rewrite or expand these stated actions in such a way as to render them morally problematic. (E.g., eating a healthy vegan sandwich during a lunch break at a chemical weapons lab, walking to a local corner store to purchase a fascist newspaper, pondering the purchase of a bicycle for the purpose of a speedy robbery getaway, etc.) Let us assume, though, that no such broader problematic conditions are operative.

12 The "if and only if (and because)" wording might initially seem to be a bit unwieldy, but it is standard philosophical fare when attempting to provide a formal definition.

13 For more thorough (but still accessible) introductions to these and other ethical theories, consult Timmons (2014, ch. 1); Mizzoni (2010); and Pojman (2002). Note that to save space my overview is even more truncated than that provided for accounts of well-being, and it skips over several significant theories. For instance, I leave out Ross's ethics of prima facie duty, the various versions of social contract theory, care ethics, situation ethics, ethical egoism, divine command theory, et cet-

era. However, most of the core arguments for and against the permissibility of MAID, to the extent that they tie back into an identifiable ethical theory, tie back into one or another of the four theories canvassed below.

14 This wording mostly adheres to the formulation of consequentialism suggested by Timmons (2014, p. 7), except that I substitute "permissible" for "right." Calling an act right in ordinary English can be ambiguous between calling it permissible (i.e., not immoral) and calling it obligatory (i.e., an act such that it would be immoral to refrain from performing it). Timmons is careful to clarify his meaning, but for my purposes here I prefer to stick more closely to ordinary usage. In stating the remaining BMPs, I will mostly adhere to the formulations employed by Timmons, though I will note some additional minor changes in wording as they come up.

15 I leave aside here a variant sometimes known as satisficing consequentialism.

16 The reader might wonder, then, why the wording of this BMP is not something more like this: "An action is permissible if and only if (and because) its consequences would be *better than* the consequences of any alternative action that the agent might instead perform." The reason is that there are situations in which there is no better alternative yet in which an action must still be performed. Consider the well-known case of the "drowning twins." Say Bob and Bub are identical twins, not merely biologically but also in various morally relevant respects (e.g., both are equally virtuous in character, equally productive cancer researchers, parents to the same number of children, donors in equal amounts to equally worthy charities, etc.). You see Bob and Bub drowning side by side in the lake, and you have time to save only one of them. The actual BMP for consequentialism dictates that saving Bob is morally permissible, and so is saving Bub – the consequences of your saving act would be at least as good (for all those affected by it long term) as any alternative action. So the consequences of saving Bob are at least as good as the consequences of saving Bub and vice versa. It is therefore fine to save either one, and since you cannot save both you just have to choose. In contrast, the BMP just suggested (an action is permissible if and only if [and because] its consequences would be *better than* the consequences of any alternative action that the agent might perform instead) would entail that it would be wrong to save either Bob or Bub; after all, neither action is better than the other in terms of its consequences. Rather, the two actions are precisely equal. Yet to allow them both to drown is clearly wrong, so the formulation under consideration in the main text above is preferable.

17 I have changed the wording somewhat from that given in Timmons (2014, p. 8), in particular switching his "would likely produce" to "would produce." There is a debate within utilitarianism about whether to formulate the theory in probabilistic terms, but in my view the more plausible formulation is not probabilistic.

18 Giebel (2015, p. 373) provides another helpful illustration:

> Suppose I hear my eccentric neighbor emit a loud, high-pitched sound and I ask what he is doing. His response, indicating the type of act he is performing, will depend on his intention. For instance, he may be reacting to a bee sting, calling his pet dolphin, breaking a church's stained-glass window, signalling an assassin, or contacting an alien race. The first two possibilities are generally permissible, the third and fourth are not, and the fifth may be permissible or impermissible depending

upon the circumstances and my neighbor's further intentions. (If he responds to my question by saying, "I am emitting a loud, high-pitched sound," I probably shall not take this to be an adequate account of the type of act he is performing.)

19 Cases of promise breaking seem to be particularly problematic for HAU; such a point might be less applicable to versions of consequentialism that pair it with other accounts of intrinsic value. Consider, for instance, perfectionist consequentialism, which Timmons (2014, p. 9) formulates as follows: "An action is right [permissible] if and only if (and because) it would likely bring about a greater net balance of perfectionist goods than would any alternative action one might perform instead." A perfectionist consequentialism might be able to sidestep the worry about promise breaking, insofar as one might claim that fulfilling a capacity for friendship is a good in perfectionism and that failing to keep a promise even to a dead friend is objectively bad for the agent (insofar as it involves a failure to fulfill his capacity for being a good friend), even if no one else knows about it and even if the agent himself is not consciously bothered by the failure.

20 Again, perfectionist consequentialism seems to be less vulnerable to this point, insofar as it would be difficult to identify the fulfillment of any worthwhile human capacity achieved by carrying out torture – unless perhaps one included the capacity for pleasure as a high-ranking member of one's list of important human capacities. But that might just show that a perfectionist consequentialist would do well to rank the capacity for sensory and attitudinal pleasures comparatively low on the list of capacities to be fulfilled (below, e.g., the capacity to exercise beneficent character traits).

21 Although the example is framed in terms of a hedonistic theory of well-being, the problem here does not arise specifically from it. Perfectionist consequentialism, for instance, has the same seemingly untoward implication. For example, taking into account the fulfillment of my distinctively human capacities and those of my aunt, should it turn out that I would benefit more from a stimulating visit to an art museum than my aunt would benefit from my visit, I am again obligated not to visit my aunt.

22 For further discussion of consequentialism and HAU, see, for instance, Crisp (2014); Hardin (1988); Sinnott-Armstrong (1992); Smart (1973); and Williams (1973). I have not discussed a prominent variant of the theory known as rule consequentialism or rule utilitarianism. I am inclined to think that this variant is reducible either to standard consequentialism or to a version of deontology, though I cannot take up this point here.

23 I am thus leaving aside the so-called universal law formulation.

24 This is again a minor change in wording from Timmons (2014, p. 16), with the addition of "to the extent that it bears upon the treatment of persons." I think that this addition is needed to capture the idea that acts can be permissible that simply have no relevance to the treatment of persons.

25 For more on Kantian deontology (and some variant versions of deontology), see, for instance, Donagan (1977) and O'Neill (2013). And, since the topic has come up, consult Matthews (2008) for a good entry point into the ethical debate on torture.

26 Natural law theorists generally see life itself as an intrinsic good and not merely as a necessary precondition for the realization of other goods. This issue is of obvious

relevance to the debate over MAID. Gomez-Lobo (2002, pp. 11–12), for example, puts the point like this:

> Why do some people regard their lives as bad? Why do some people long to die? What makes life bad surely is one or more of the following: chronic illness, acute physical pain, extreme poverty ... Without reference to items such as these one would be at a loss to understand how a person could regard her life as bad. If by fiat one could do away with illness, pain, poverty, and so forth, would it be sensible to say that life itself is bad for that person? Surely not, because, strictly speaking, it is not life that is bad (unless perhaps "life" is understood in a different, not strictly bio-logical sense). The illness, pain, poverty and so forth are the bad things. Life as such is different from those evils, and one cannot conclude that in its own right it is an evil. Perhaps, however, life is a purely neutral thing that derives all of its value or disvalue from other goods ... [But] surely life is not external or instrumental to the good life. The good life is not a product or a consequence of life. It is life fully real-ized. Life, then – as the key ingredient of the good life (though not the only one) – is worth having for its own sake. Life is not neutral, nor is death. Death is totally incompatible with the ultimate goal of human beings.

Gomez-Lobo assumes here, for the sake of argument, that death is the annihila-tion of the person (i.e., there is no afterlife). For further defences of the intrinsic value of life by natural law theorists, see Oderberg (2000a, pp. 66–68; 2000b, pp. 138–143) and Watt (2015).

27 Or at least extended to provide an account of animal *welfare* – some advocates of natural law theory are reluctant to attribute full-blown rights to animals (errone-ously, in my view).

28 The doctrine is also commonly referred to as the principle of double effect or double effect reasoning.

29 Some natural law theorists would object to the language of a "violation" here, given the pejorative connotation. "Permissible violation" arguably does sound odd, but I am not sure that other labels work much better here – perhaps "permissible breach of a human good" or "permissible infringement of a human good" are more appropriate.

30 Here the distinction between a foreseen result and an intended result is important. Although this distinction (and its alleged moral significance) has given rise to an enormous amount of debate, the basic idea is easily grasped. Gomez-Lobo (2002, p. 54), adapting an example from Beauchamp and Childress (1994, p. 209), writes:

> There is a bathroom in your home that has two switches. If you want the light on, you flip the switch on the left; if you want the fan on, you flip the switch on the right. You have two causes (the two acts of flipping) and two effects. If you intend both effects, you simply flip both switches. In the basement, on the other hand, there is a small bathroom in which a single switch turns on both the light and a fan that makes a terrible noise. One cause has two effects. If your intention is to be able to see, you will flip the switch and attain the intended effect of having the light on, but your action will have an unintended side effect: You will have the fan on, making an obnoxious sound. If you could disengage the turning on of the light from the turning

on of the fan, you would do so (as you obviously can in the bathroom upstairs); if you can't, however, you simply have to put up with the foreseeable yet unintended consequence of your choice to turn on the light. This does not exclude the possibility that there may be occasions in which you do want the fan on as well. You then intend both effects. To raise the question: "Why did you do it?" is to try to identify the further goal or intended consequence in the action of an agent. When the action is a cause of double effect, it is perfectly natural to ask: "Did you also intend to proceed this second effect, or was it only something you had to tolerate?" Needless to say, the answer cannot always be determined from the outside, even by an attentive observer, because it is an internal decision of the agent. Sometimes almost heroic integrity is required to answer such a question truthfully, even to oneself.

31 In contrast, attacking an innocent bystander, even to protect your family, would be an intrinsically evil act (or so the advocate of natural law theory wishes to argue). Thus, in a different hypothetical scenario in which the intruder threatens to kill your family unless you go next door and beat your neighbour to death with a hockey stick, natural law theory would rule that beating impermissible, as a breach of the first criterion of the DDE.

32 Note that, as with all of these theories, I am skipping over some complexities and internal disagreements. One point of difference between versions of natural law theory is that some would maintain that, in certain circumstances, a deliberate breach of a basic human good is permissible. In these versions, striking the guilty intruder might be analyzed not as a case of an indirect breach of the good of human health (a breach rendered indirect and hence permissible by meeting the strictures of the DDE) but as a deliberate breach permissible because it is, in the circumstances, a just act. The contrast is perhaps clearest in the case of capital punishment. In the most plausible analysis of what capital punishment consists of, it involves the *deliberate* killing of the guilty; the death of the perpetrator is not a foreseen but unintended consequence, but directly aimed at. Death itself is the intended punishment. Today some natural law theorists are opposed to the death penalty and would reject it partly on the ground that it cannot be justified by reference to the DDE as an indirect breach of a basic human good. In contrast, other natural law theorists would say that the DDE need not even be invoked here since capital punishment is a justifiable deliberate breach of a basic human good – justifiable, perhaps, because the life of a guilty murderer, though still a good in some sense, has lost its status as a good that imposes on others an obligation to intend its preservation.

33 For more detailed explications of the DDE, see, for instance, Devine (1990, pp. 106–133); FitzPatrick (2012); Garcia (2007); Giebel (2015); Oderberg (2000b, pp. 86–126); and Pruss (2013).

34 Or so I would argue – historically, some natural law theorists have maintained that the theory permits torture under certain circumstances.

35 Deontologists and natural law theorists often reply that, though such scenarios might tempt us to abandon our fixed principles (never deliberately kill the innocent, never torture, etc.), whether for the sake of expediency or for dread of even worse consequences, part of what it means to be a moral person is to adhere to certain

principles even in the face of great temptation to violate them – *especially* in the face of such temptation.

36 For more on natural law theory, see, for instance, Besong (2018); Budziszewski (2011); Finnis (1980); and Gomez-Lobo (2002).

37 Here I have made another minor change to the wording of the formulation provided by Timmons (2014, p. 25), adding the "well-informed" criterion.

38 For more on virtue ethics, see, for instance, Anscombe (1958); Hursthouse (1999); MacIntyre (1981); and McAleer (2007, 2010).

39 Garcia (2010), for instance, lays out what might be seen as a hybrid of natural law theory and virtue ethics.

40 Why is that? Because natural law theory provided a way of explaining and clarifying the biblical moral system to pagan audiences in a way that they could understand. Briefly, the Bible seems to provide something like a BMP when it records Jesus assenting to the central Old Testament ethical dictum to "'love the Lord your God with all your heart and with all your soul and with all your strength and with all your mind, and love your neighbour as yourself'" (Luke 10: 27). Jesus then goes on to clarify this by use of the parable of the good Samaritan, showing that by "neighbour" is meant anyone and everyone, not just the members of one's own circle or ethnic group. We might derive from this a *biblical BMP:* an action is permissible if and only if (and because) its performance is compatible with the love of God, others, and oneself. In fleshing this out (for pagan audiences who did not share the commonly understood assumptions concerning well-being found within Judaism), early Christian thinkers often linked this to an account of well-being and to ideas of natural law drawn from Aristotelian and Stoic thought. For example, what does it mean to love someone? A necessary condition for loving someone is desiring her good *for her own sake.* (Desiring a person's good is not enough by itself since in theory you might wish the person well in order that she be able to benefit you in the future.) And what is involved in desiring someone's good, in wishing that person well? Early Christian thinkers explained it to their pagan audiences in terms of desiring that someone obtain the highest possible goods and/or fulfill her highest potential. This included fulfilling her capacities for the core goods enumerated by Aristotle and others (e.g., health and friendship and personal virtue) but especially union with God. So the biblical BMP, when expanded to include clarifications about the nature of love and the nature of human well-being, tended to look something like the BMP for natural law theory laid out above. However, as noted, I expect that the biblical BMP could also be developed in such a way as to lend itself to deontology or virtue ethics or perhaps perfectionist consequentialism.

Chapter 4: Moral Arguments for and against MAID

1 Recall, however, the complication associated with intention. At the least, voluntary cessation of treatment in cases of incurable terminal illness is usually regarded as morally uncontroversial where that cessation is not accompanied by the *intention* that the patient die.

2 See, for instance, Glover (1977, pp. 150–169, 190–202); Singer (1993, pp. 181–192); Sumner (2011, ch. 5); and Young (2007, ch. 11). Warnock and Macdonald (2008, p. 64), writing here specifically of dementia patients who have not issued an advance directive with respect to their wishes regarding MAID, write that

> contemplating the wretched lives of patients with dementia who do not have the luck to need artificial nutrition and hydration [Warnock and Macdonald write of demen- tia sufferers in need of artificial nutrition and hydration as "lucky" in this context because they can be allowed to die of dehydration], who are conscious and capable of swallowing, and whose numbers are increasing every year, we may feel despair. They are allowed to die, many of them, by a slow and horrible death, far from the "good death" or the "death with dignity" that euthanasia would afford them. Many of their relatives, if there are any, must long for them to die. But many of them have no relatives, or none that visit them. Even if palliative care for the dying were far more widely available than it is, they would not qualify for it; for they are not, or not neces- sarily, terminally ill, or suffering acutely. What is to be done? That is a question to which, as far as we can see, society can at present supply no answer. But it must be faced, as we become an increasingly aged population.

One gets a fairly clear impression of the answer that Warnock and Macdonald would supply, and in fact they state it more explicitly later (pp. 134–136).

3 The fact that the Alzheimer Society of Canada recently reversed its long-standing opposition to advance directives for MAID might be a bellwether for what is to come; see the report by Grant (2019b). So is the announcement by Quebec Minister of Health Danielle McCann that the province has established a group of experts to write a report for the government on the possibility of expanding access to MAID to Alzheimer's patients, as reported by Plante (2019).

4 See, for instance, Warnock and Macdonald (2008, pp. 51–54) and Young (2007, ch. 9).

5 See again Kirby (2017); Schuklenk and Van de Vathorst (2015); and Tanner (2018). See also Player (2018) and Steinbock (2017) for arguments in favour of the same basic position (extending MAID to legally competent psychiatric patients), but from an American perspective, and see Warnock and Macdonald (2008, ch. 3), who make a similar case from within the UK context.

6 For a thorough set of moral and legal arguments in its favour, see Guichon, Mohamed, Clarke, and Mitchell (2017).

7 Battin (2005, p. 18), for instance, classifies the arguments from relief of suffering and from autonomy as the two principal arguments for the permissibility of MAID. Sumner (2011, p. 90) concurs: "The arguments from well-being and autonomy provide the basic justificatory framework for assisted suicide and voluntary euthanasia." Williams (1997, p. 125) likewise writes that "fear of suffering and of the loss of autonomy are the main reason[s] why people might desire euthanasia for themselves. The two principal reasons why others support these wishes, even from their loved ones, are respect for them as persons and beneficence or compassion." Finally, consider Meilaender (2013, pp. 62–63):

> Why might we be tempted to ask for or offer euthanasia? One of the reasons has already been suggested in the discussion of suicide: our commitment to autonomy or

self-determination. I am tempted to believe that my life is my own to do with as I please – and tempted to believe that another's life is her own to do with as she pleases. A second reason, equally powerful and tempting, is our desire to bring relief to those who suffer greatly. The argument for euthanasia rests chiefly on these two points, taken either singly or together.

8 Recalling the case of the drowning twins, note that "maximize" here should not be taken to mean "produce better results than any other alternative" but "produce results at least as good as any other available alternative."

9 The impact on participating health-care practitioners, however, should not be treated lightly. Hendin (1998, pp. 160–161), a psychiatrist specializing in the study of suicide, writes that

> physicians who perform euthanasia are often troubled by it even years afterward. Some speak of a need for absolution ... The average doctor's discomfort with ending a patient's life is not so surprising. Even when justified by the exigencies of war, most soldiers pay a price for participating in killing. Just as a minority of soldiers deal with the horror of war by embracing the power to end someone's life, a minority of doctors fervently embrace assisted suicide and euthanasia ... That a small number of doctors do a great number of the cases is one of the unexamined aspects of the Dutch euthanasia story; one admits to close to a hundred, while another is proud to have done many times that number.

Even in Canada, some limited discussion of this issue has emerged. Kirkey (2017), for instance, reports that

> some doctors who have helped the gravely ill end their lives are no longer willing to participate in assisted death because of emotional distress or fear of prosecution if their decisions are second-guessed, according to their colleagues. In Ontario, one of the few provinces to track the information, 24 doctors have permanently been removed from a voluntary referral list of physicians willing to help people die. Another 30 have put their names on temporary hold. While they do not have to give a reason, a small number have advised the province that they now want "a reflection period to decide whether medical assistance in dying is a service they want to provide," according to a health ministry spokesman. The Canadian Medical Association says reports of doctors backing away from the act are not just anecdotal. "I can't tell you how many, but I can tell you that it's enough that it's been noted at a systemic level," said Dr. Jeff Blackmer, the CMA's vice-president of medical professionalism. For some doctors, the act is simply too distressing, he said.

Conversely, some physicians seem to be utterly untroubled by performing MAID, as evident in Khoshnood et al.'s (2018) qualitative study of sixteen Canadian physicians active in MAID, whose chief complaints during in-depth interviews were about inadequate pay for their time, increased workload, and strained relationships with doctors opposed to MAID. Note, too, that witnessing an assisted death can be traumatic for family members; comparatively little research has been done on that aspect of MAID, but see Wagner, Keller, Knaevelsrud, and Maercker (2011) for a relevant study in Switzerland.

10 At one point, Glover seems to indicate a preference for a version of consequentialism allied with desire satisfaction theory instead of one allied with hedonism, but this would be a misreading. In the end, he favours HAU but with a recognition of the important role that desire satisfaction plays in providing for attitudinal pleasure (1977, pp. 62–66). His formulation of HAU is further complicated by an attempt to integrate a role for autonomy into the theory; again, though, his view in the end appears to be that autonomy is morally significant not as an independent factor but because of its role in desire satisfaction and resultant attitudinal pleasure (pp. 74–82).

11 Those with qualms about assisted death might find that quotation a bit disconcerting; when someone fails to see any value in her life, is not the proper reaction rather to help her see its value? McKay (2007, p. 196) makes a relevant comment: "For we who share Judeo-Christian intuitions about man and his place in the world also think that even those who are alone and unloved, whose families are clearly waiting for them to die and are annoyed that they have not; we think that even these lives are important and valuable."

12 Cholbi (2011, p. 82), for instance, asks

> do suicidal people fully and accurately take into account their future wants and desires when considering whether to end their lives? We human beings are prone to short-term thinking in any case, but the frequency with which suicidal thoughts are associated with mental illnesses such as depression raises additional red flags, for one of the defining symptoms of depression is a tendency to have not only a negative image of oneself, but also an irrationally pessimistic (or even nihilistic) view of the future. Thus, depressed individuals may often lack a clear enough sense of their desires, current or future, to be in a position to rationally determine whether suicide advances their interests or well-being.

13 This is the consequentialism adopted by Singer (1993, pp. 12–15), who later employs it to support a similar argument in favour of the permissibility of assisted suicide and euthanasia.

14 Warnock and Macdonald (2008, p. 97) write that

> more recently the development of palliative care as a speciality has facilitated the refinement of pain management in both choice and delivery of effective medication. It is now very possible in most cases for pain, even when severe, to be well controlled by the sustained administration of analgesia which just controls the person's symptoms (while still enabling the patient to remain alert and cognitively functional) … Yet despite advances in palliative medicine, there remains a small proportion of patients in the last days and hours of their lives whose symptoms persist uncontrolled or unendurable despite the best efforts of experts in symptom control.

Note that Macdonald writes as a clinical oncologist with much palliative care experience. Manning (1998, p. 41), a medical doctor and Roman Catholic priest, concurs at least partly:

> Most experts agree that in the vast majority of cases, pain and suffering can be minimized with proper application of medical technology; the fear that one will be forced to endure a lingering and painful death over which one has no control is not generally well founded. On the other hand, experts will also readily admit that in many cases, the care of the terminally ill is not optimal, and that there may be unnecessary pain and suffering at the end of life.

15 Sumner (2011, p. 49) writes that

> a minority of patients at some stage of the dying process will experience pain (or other refractory physical symptoms) that cannot be adequately managed by administration of even the most sophisticated analgesics. Timothy Quill estimates this minority to be somewhere in the 2–5 percent range; for these patients "the dose of opioids and sedatives must sometimes be increased to the point where the patients lose conscious awareness of their suffering." Like analgesics, doses of sedatives can be titrated to achieve or maintain differing levels of diminished awareness, ranging from drowsiness to deep sleep. Where complete unconsciousness is the intended effect, it can be either intermittent – where the patient is brought back to wakefulness from time to time – or continuous. [The reference is to Quill (1998).]

Consider also Yuill (2015, pp. 44–45):

> No one, of course, would suggest that the problem of pain at the end of life has entirely faded into the past. But the answer to the pain issue is improved pain control. Pain control continues to improve with technological advances being made ... Moreover, if dealing with pain is the real motivation behind the campaign of legalized assisted suicide, so-called "terminal sedation," also known as palliative sedation, whereby patients in pain are put into a deep sleep until they die naturally, might be posed as an excellent compromise, preventing the need for assisted suicide.

Somerville (2001, p. 162) takes a similar stance:

> Although we might find the idea of total sedation disturbing, we should consider whether it is preferable to euthanasia for terminally ill people experiencing severe, otherwise unrelievable, pain and suffering. Both interventions render patients unaware – they are either unconscious or dead – and, in this sense, the results do not differ. The harmful impact of euthanasia on societal values and symbols is avoided, however, if total sedation is used instead.

Of course, such sedation is a realistic option only in cases in which the patient is suffering in the final stages of a terminal illness. With that aspect of Bill C-14 having been overturned, MAID will now be legal in situations in which death is not "reasonably foreseeable" – as such, this point will be inapplicable. However, in cases of non-terminal illness, the potential efficacy of other forms of medical intervention will likely weaken the case for death as the only other option for the relief of suffering.

16 You possess a *negative right* when others are obligated to refrain from doing something to you. In contrast, you possess a *positive right* when others are obligated to do or provide something for you.

17 For further reflection on this, see Somerville (2001, ch. 6).

18 For more on the disputed notion of dignity in the context of bioethics, see, for instance, Daly (2013); Gentzler (2003); Kass (2002); and Lee (2001).

19 Dworkin (1993, p. 217) employs similarly strong language, writing that "making someone die in a way that others approve, but he believes to be a horrifying contradiction of his life, is a devastating, odious form of tyranny" (quoted in Begley, 2008, p. 441).

20 Note that, in speaking of the choice as irrational, I mean that the *object* of the choice is irrational – that is, the person aims at something that, from the perspective of an objective assessment of his interests, he should not aim at. I am assuming throughout that the agent himself nevertheless has the capacity for rational choice and counts as legally competent.

21 It is worth recalling that Battin, in her expert submission to the Supreme Court of British Columbia, recognized this explicitly:

> Physician assistance in bringing about death is to be provided only when the patient voluntarily seeks it (autonomy) and only where it serves to avoid pain or suffering or the prospect of them (mercy). Because these principles do not operate independently, it cannot be claimed that permitting physician-assisted dying would require assisting lovesick teenagers who are not suffering from a serious medical condition to die; likewise it cannot be claimed that permitting physician-assisted dying on the basis of the principle of mercy would require involuntary euthanasia for someone who is in pain but nevertheless desires to stay alive. Both principles must be in play; but when they are in play, they jointly provide a powerful basis for permitting and respecting physician aid in dying. Those who oppose physician aid in dying must show that the principles of liberty and freedom from suffering that are basic to an open, liberal and democratic society should be overridden.

Quoted in *Carter v Canada*, 2012 BCSC 1587 at 74.

22 This might also be framed in terms of rights: "A terminally ill patient, suffering grievously, has the right to choose among any efficacious means of alleviating that suffering, provided that no one else is thereby badly harmed." One would then have to specify whether a negative right or a positive right is being invoked (i.e., whether others have an obligation *not to interfere* with the person who receives MAID or whether something stronger is involved: namely, an obligation by others *to assist* the person in obtaining MAID).

23 Someone who wanted to defend the current Canadian legal situation in the wake of the "reasonably foreseeable death" provision of Bill C-14 being struck down might reformulate premise 1 here to refer to "a seriously ill patient, suffering grievously" rather than "a terminally ill patient, suffering grievously."

24 I am tempted to formulate premise 1 more simply than I have presented it above, replacing it with the following: "It is impermissible deliberately to kill a person." I find very appealing the idea that human life should never be taken intentionally.

This more robust formulation of the principle, however, would have two obvious drawbacks. First, it would be out of step with the majority of the published literature opposing MAID, most of which refrains from adopting that more robust premise. That in turn would be out of step with the main goal of this chapter, to introduce the reader to the most common arguments for and against MAID. Second, it would be vulnerable to the obvious objection that there seem to be situations in which it is morally justifiable to kill in self-defence. So in what follows I will employ the formulation used in the main text above. I will just say something briefly about the second drawback. There might be ways in which the doctrine of double effect can be employed to preserve the moral acceptability of killing in self-defence while also preserving the idea that *deliberate* killing is always wrong. Consider, for instance, the police officer who faces down a murderer and the only feasible way of stopping the threat is to shoot him. Even here we might envision the officer taking the shot while hoping that it merely incapacitates her adversary without also killing him. If the intention is to halt a threat, with death being a foreseen risk but not an intended outcome, then the shooting might not be counted an instance of deliberate killing. Obviously, much more needs to be said to render such an analysis plausible (even for those already sympathetic to the DDE); moreover, cases of killing in a just war typically would be more difficult to analyze in this fashion. And capital punishment, of course, would be ruled out altogether.

25 Consider the following much-discussed scenario. Five upstanding, productive citizens (say a cancer researcher, a social worker, a climate scientist, an elementary school teacher, and a solar panel engineer), all of whom have spouses and multiple dependent children, are facing imminent death but could be saved with organ transplants. No organ donors are available. Then a helpful medical technician points to an elderly, unhappy, homeless man with no family or friends who apparently is not contributing to society but whose blood type is known to match that of the five upstanding citizens and whose organs are in remarkably good shape. He could be captured and killed and his organs harvested without anyone ever learning how the organs were obtained. Is it permissible to kill the homeless man against his will and appropriate his organs to save those five citizens? The advocate of HAU seemingly must say yes: it is not only permissible but also obligatory to commit murder in this case.

26 Here Cholbi is citing Velleman (1999, p. 625).

27 I will follow here most Kantian ethicists in making the assumption (for the sake of argument) that there is no afterlife.

28 Breck (1998, p. 223), an Eastern Orthodox priest and not himself a natural law theorist (as that theory is typically understood), goes further here, claiming that withdrawal of treatment in certain cases can be morally *required:*

> Human life, created by God and bearing the divine image, is sacred by its very nature and must always be respected and protected as such ... In cases of terminal illness (where the dying process is irreversible and death is imminent), it is nevertheless permissible to withhold or withdraw life-support that represents nothing more than a burden to the patient. Particularly in cases of brain-death, it is immoral – and not merely "useless" – to maintain the patient on life-support systems.

29 Watt (2015, p. 223) again writes that

> permanently unconscious adults, like anencephalic babies, are sometimes assumed to have no interests. However, if the human moral subject is in fact still present in the PVS [persistent vegetative state] patient (we are living bodies, and this is the same living body he or she always was), there will be, it seems, *some* objective interests and even promotable interests that the subject will retain ... A PVS patient may not be raped, for example, or used (as one writer has seriously suggested [Ber 2000, pp. 165, 167]) as a surrogate mother, even with her prior consent. Nor is respect for the PVS patient the same as respect for a corpse: necrophilia is a horrible act of disrespect for a now-deceased person, but sex with a living PVS patient is actual rape, just like any other non-consensual sex. Human persons are not disembodied souls, and it is the living, bodily person herself who is violated when her body is violated.

30 See the report by Hutchins (2015).

31 Colwell (1996, pp. 11–12) draws out a closely related point:

> Whatever one believes about post-mortem existence, this last question is profoundly difficult to answer. [The question of this section of Colwell's paper is "Will Killing Him Relieve Him of His Misery?"] It cannot be glibly answered in the affirmative, as so many proponents of VAE [voluntary active euthanasia] seem to imply. Broadly speaking, one of two presuppositions will underlie our thinking about the person who died. Either he will survive beyond the point of physical death in some conscious state, or his conscious life will be permanently extinguished and he will be no more ... If we hold the first presupposition, our question becomes even more acute. Are we confident that the conscious state he will enter will be an improvement upon the one from which he now yearns to find an escape? Waiting for death has at least the virtue of allowing a person more time to ponder his destiny and "make his peace," where that seems right.

For further discussion of this kind of argument, see Gamble (2018).

32 I wish to note that, in opting to frame the preceding argument using agnosticism rather than theism, I am not conceding the illegitimacy of employing distinctly religious arguments in the public sphere. I simply wish to sidestep long-standing disputes about their legitimacy. However, many religious thinkers, including members of my own Eastern Orthodox community, argue proactively for the value and even necessity of including the distinctive voices of diverse faith traditions in public moral debates. For example, Iltis (2009, pp. 227–228) writes that

> attempts to create a neutral shared space within which public bioethics discussions may be conducted fail. The space created by such efforts is neither neutral nor should we expect those whose beliefs are cast out or marginalized to occupy the space alongside those who dismiss their positions ... Secular moral reasoning is not neutral, just as no tradition-bound form of moral analysis – religious or otherwise – is neutral. The assumptions that inform individuals' secular rational moral analyses are no more tradition-free, objective, or neutral than the insights that inform religious positions.

A bit later (p. 230) she continues:

> All discourse requires a foundation – a series of assumptions – that generate[s] content. Moral content does not come from nowhere, and to privilege some sources (e.g., secular reason shaped by particular philosophical traditions) over others (e.g., Orthodox Jewish insights) is to ignore the fact that all these positions rely on fundamental assumptions that cannot be definitively defended as the valid starting point for deliberation and none of which can be proven to be the right starting point ... One is forced to ask whether a truly neutral public discourse would not admit all moral perspectives and their bioethics, both secular and religious, to the public forum and its reflections on health care policy and uses of biotechnology. The issue of whether human life has ultimate meaning and is governed by the requirements of a personal God should be a matter of significance for all persons. The discussion of such issues should at least be admitted into the public forum for all to explore and assess.

33 One common way of developing this objection is by reference to the related claim that certain sorts of lives simply are "not worth living." For a detailed discussion of the nature of that claim (and some of the conceptual ambiguities often bound up with its use), see Fumagalli (2018).
34 Posner (1995, pp. 243–253), for instance, employs a comparable line of reasoning. His version, however, is formulated more broadly, insofar as it focuses not just on those who face imminent total physical incapacitation but also on a range of groups who have reason to fear future loss of self-control, of varying degrees of severity. See also Downie (2004, pp. 5–6): "People may be committing suicide earlier than they would if assisted suicide were legal because they fear getting to that point where they would need, but would not have access to, assisted suicide."
35 The idea here, the reader will recall, was that the individual might be driven to commit suicide earlier than she would wish to otherwise.
36 For critical discussions of Begley's version, see Butts and Rich (2008) and Sellman (2008).
37 Meilaender (2013, p. 58), for instance, writes that "Christians have held that suicide is morally wrong because they have seen in it a contradiction of our nature as creatures, an unwillingness to receive life moment by moment from the hand of God without ever regarding it as simply 'our' possession." The idea of life as a gift is often raised in this context, but that notion is not really necessary to make the present point. Sometimes the notions of gift and stewardship are run together, presumably via the assumption that, if one receives an especially precious gift, then one can thereby acquire certain responsibilities toward it. Manning (1998, pp. 35–36), for instance, writes that

> Catholic doctrine teaches that our human choices are limited by divine sovereignty. Though we are responsible for making informed health care decisions, there are limits to human freedom. Life is a gift from God, and only God has control of its giving and taking. The principle of divine sovereignty asserts that God alone has absolute sovereignty over creation. Our stewardship over creation is limited: we share in

God's dominion only as creatures ... The Bible has taught that human dominion over life, including our own, is limited. Aquinas asserted that we have the *use* of our lives, not their *possession*.

Warnock and Macdonald (2008, p. 69), however, think that the notion of gift is less plausible here than the notion of stewardship:

> For, after all, most gifts are thought, once given, to belong to and be the responsibility of the person who received the gift. The donor loses all right over what he gave, though he may sometimes attach conditions to it, as is the case with trusts set up for specific purposes. Perhaps the religious argument would be more plausible, even for believers, if the emphasis were more on the suggestion that life is held in trust for God's purposes than that it is a gift.

38 Recall that metaphysical naturalism (sometimes called "physicalism" or "materialism") is roughly the idea that the only kind of reality is physical reality, such that there is no God, no immaterial human soul, et cetera.

39 See again Kirby (2017); Schuklenk and Van de Vathorst (2015); and Tanner (2018). Their work is for an academic audience, but advocacy for the legalization of MAID for the legally competent mentally has also appeared in the popular press. See Bayliss (2016) for an early post-*Carter* example. More recently, in a major newspaper, Jocelyn Downie, a professor of law at Dalhousie University, was quoted by Bryden (2020) as saying that the continued exclusion from MAID of those suffering solely from mental illness "undercuts efforts of many people for many years to try to get people to acknowledge that mental illness is as serious as physical illness."

40 For concise discussions, see Carter (2016) and Siegel, Sisti, and Caplan (2014). Here the Belgians are following the lead of the Dutch. Pereira (2011, p. 41) writes that

> until 2001, the Netherlands allowed only adults access to euthanasia or PAS. However, the 2001 law allowed for children aged 12–16 years to be euthanized if consent is provided by their parents, even though this age group is generally not considered capable of making such decisions. The law even allows physicians to proceed with euthanasia if there is disagreement between the parents. By 2005, the Groningen Protocol, which allows euthanasia of newborns and younger children who are expected to have "no hope of a good quality of life," was implemented.

41 For readers who wish to delve into the empirical questions concerning the feasibility of implementing "safeguards" against non-voluntary forms of euthanasia, and against subtle coercion and other forms of abuse, et cetera, there is certainly a substantial literature available. For arguments in favour of the basic workability of such protections, see, for instance, Cholbi (2011, pp. 148–157); Downie (2004, ch. 11); Schuklenk et al. (2011, pp. 51–65); Sumner (2011, pp. 174–189); Warnock and Macdonald (2008, ch. 7); and Young (2007, ch. 10). For arguments to the effect that the Netherlands and other jurisdictions supply empirical grounds to be wary of legalization, see, for instance, Boer (2007); Cohen-Almagor (2015); Gorsuch (2006, ch. 7); Hendin (1998); Keown (1995, 2014, 2018); Manning (1998, ch. 7); and Pereira (2011).

42 Gomez-Lobo (2002, p. 111) likewise takes slippery slope arguments to play at best a
    secondary role in pressing the case against MAID, though for a somewhat different
    reason:

> I take arguments such as this one quite seriously, especially in light of the possibility
> that this may be happening already in the Netherlands. However, arguments of this
> nature only help to bring home the negative consequences of the progressive devalu-
> ation of life. They play a supporting role, not a central one in rationally deciding the
> issue. If, by some miraculous arrangement, foolproof safeguards were put in place,
> and Dutch physicians never practiced nonvoluntary or involuntary euthanasia, it
> still would be wrong of them to kill a patient at his or her request. Voluntary eutha-
> nasia remains an attack on the grounding human good.

43 For example, among the many ideas that warrant attention but that I cannot
    address here are the following: 1) A more complete account of the theologically
    grounded defence of premise 1 of the third argument (the inviolability of life argu-
    ment) would have to take into consideration the historically novel positions of
    certain Christian theologians who actually *support* MAID. See, for instance,
    Badham (1998) and Bartmann (2003). Such a stance, whatever its independent
    plausibility, is out of step with the historical consensus within Christianity, one
    still upheld today by the Roman Catholic Church and Eastern Orthodox Church
    and many Protestant denominations (as well as Orthodox Judaism). 2) In the eth-
    ics literature, there has been considerable debate about the notion that voluntary
    passive euthanasia is genuinely distinct morally from voluntary active euthanasia
    and assisted suicide; much of this debate revolves around disagreements over the
    distinction between killing and letting die and, more importantly (in my opinion),
    the distinction between intention and foresight – the latter distinction being cru-
    cial for the doctrine of double effect. For in-depth arguments to the effect that, at
    least in many cases, VPE and VAE are not morally distinct, consult Sumner (2011,
    chs. 2–4) and Young (2007, ch. 6). For a contrasting view, see, for instance,
    Oderberg (2000a, pp. 71–80) and more broadly the pro-DDE literature cited in the
    previous chapter. I have not delved into these discussions in much detail here, for
    two reasons. First, they are probably the most complex and technical areas of the
    ethics literature on MAID, and frankly I had a difficult time determining how they
    might best be covered in what is intended to be a concise and accessible introduc-
    tion. Second, at least in Canada, that set of issues has not played much of a role in
    the legal history of MAID, unlike the rest of the arguments discussed here, most of
    which show up (if in truncated and/or implicit form) in the court rulings can-
    vassed in Chapter 1. The alleged equivalence of VPE and VAE was taken up, in fact,
    by the Supreme Court; in particular, the reader will recall Justice Sopinka's reply to
    the equivalency claim in his majority ruling in *Rodriguez*. There Sopinka empha-
    sized the foundational role played by the intention versus foresight distinction in
    our system of criminal law. That later rulings did not substantively challenge this
    aspect of *Rodriguez* is significant and buttresses his claim. The fact that the distinc-
    tion serves as a pillar of our jurisprudence also gives us a reason to treat with sus-
    picion philosophical arguments attempting to undermine it – not itself a *decisive*

reason, of course, but a reason nonetheless. 3) One whole side of the debate that I have not addressed is the position that MAID, though morally permissible in some cases, nevertheless ought not to be legalized. One might morally approve of MAID while opposing its legalization because of fears about the impact of MAID on the medical profession, or a belief that society should never send a message through legislation that some lives are not worth living, or because of slippery slope worries about where legalization might lead, et cetera. See Yuill (2015) for a detailed development of this type of position. 4) I have not addressed the position that, though assisted suicide might be permissible, *physician-assisted* suicide is not, given the nature of the medical profession and the distinctive obligations of a medical doctor. Many have argued that, even if MAID is to be legalized, physicians should have no role in performing the procedure. For a recent case to that effect, from a Canadian perspective, see Chan and Somerville (2016, pp. 171–172).

Chapter 6: The Ethics of Public Funding for MAID

1 Gutmann and Thompson (1996) suggest this as a compromise in the debate over public funding of abortion (still an area of active contention in the United States), such that abortions would be publicly funded but only by taxpayers who self-identify as pro-choice.

2 See the review of Canadian polling data in Schuklenk et al. (2011, pp. 17–20); see also the 2016 Angus Reid survey of 1,517 Canadians, which found that 24 percent of respondents failed to approve of MAID even for the terminally ill. However, that survey also found that only 10 percent supported an outright legal ban on MAID in any situation. See Kirkey (2016) for a report on the Angus Reid results.

3 There are some conflicting Dutch polling data available on this issue; for instance, a poll discussed in Kouwenhoven et al. (2013) found that only 28 percent of the Dutch public and only 33 percent of health-care professionals approved of assisted death for psychiatric patients.

4 See again the report by Kirkey (2016).

5 For the full study details, see Rousseau, Turner, Chochinov, Enns, and Sareen (2017).

6 To access the complete data tables, go to https://www.ipsos-mori.com/research publications/researcharchive/3592/Public-Attitudes-to-Assisted-Dying.aspx. For the resulting story, see the *Economist* (2015).

7 See again the *Economist* (2015). See also Onwuteaka-Philipsen et al. (2012) on the Netherlands and Chambaere, Vander Stichele, Mortier, Cohen, and Deliens (2015) on Belgium. Note, though, that worries persist about under-reporting, such that these numbers might be underestimates. For a discussion of under-reporting and data collection problems in these and other jurisdictions, see Keown (2014).

8 See the report by the Canadian Press (2019).

9 As noted earlier, relatively little has been written on the ethics of public funding for MAID. But see Iltis (2011) for an approach different from the one that I have adopted here, though one that also reaches a conclusion opposed to public funding.

Chapter 7: Freedom of Conscience for Health-Care Providers

1 Evidence has begun to emerge that at least some physicians in some regions are feeling pressured to participate directly in MAID against their conscientious objections. The following is a portion of the testimony of an oncologist who works at a Toronto hospital, before a standing committee of the Ontario legislature, and related in a law journal article by Murphy (2017, pp. 343–344):

> At my institution, physicians are being bullied into accepting the role of the most responsible physician for MAID patients. This forces these physicians to be legally responsible for the MAID act, even when that goes against their conscience or religious beliefs. It gets worse: At one of our staff meetings, a psychiatrist stood up and announced that any physician who didn't actively support MAID should not be working at our hospital ... There's a horrendous stress level at our hospital. Physicians are afraid to speak up. Physicians are afraid that they will lose their jobs if they say anything. Even just speaking to my colleagues about this, we use alternative email addresses and we speak in code. We feel sometimes like we're in some sort of dystopian novel.

2 Nurse practitioners, of course, are governed by their own independent professional associations. Just as variations exist between different provinces regarding obligations on physicians to provide referrals and/or information about MAID to patients requesting it, so too such variations exist for nurse practitioners – as do associated freedom of conscience considerations. For a discussion of these interprovincial variations and the complications that they raise for the nursing profession in Canada, see Banner, Schiller, and Freeman (2019). The situation for pharmacists in Canada is arguably even more complex regarding freedom of conscience in this context; although pharmacists are not the first point of contact for patients contemplating MAID and thus do not face the typical referral dilemma, those with a conscientious objection to the practice can still be faced with the difficulty of deciding what to do on receiving a prescription request clearly intended for use in MAID.

3 Despite the aforementioned concern about regulatory practicalities, in a later paper Savulescu and Schuklenk (2017, p. 164) write further on the idea of expanding eligibility to perform MAID beyond physicians and nurse practitioners:

> Finally, if conscientious objection continues to be tolerated in medicine and results in treatment denial, alternative ways of guaranteeing reasonable and fair access to these goods ought to be provided. One way of doing this is to de-monopolize the provision of the relevant service. If the quality of such a service could match that provided by medical professionals, and sufficient supply could be ensured, then this would be a viable alternative. This would require new training, selection, regulatory and oversight procedures, which would be cumbersome and expensive. But there is no reason why only doctors could competently provide, for example, contraception, abortion or assisted dying services.

Although these authors oppose allowing physicians to invoke conscientious objection in this context, they do concede (p. 168) that, if MAID were in fact evil, then making a referral for it would likewise be evil (i.e., they grant that referrals do nothing to safeguard the consciences of those with conscientious objections).

4 As reported in Loriggio (2018).

Chapter 8: Additional Legal and Policy Issues

1 A note for readers with a legal background: In using the terms "overturn" and "over-rule" in describing *Carter* in relation to *Rodriguez*, both here and in previous portions of the book, I have been speaking a bit loosely, employing these terms in their everyday English sense rather than in their technical legal sense. In that latter sense, when one court "overturns" the ruling of another, it is on account of the finding of a legal error. Arguably, that does not describe what happened here, insofar as the key factors in the change from *Rodriguez* to *Carter* were shifts in case law and new social conditions/empirical data on MAID from foreign jurisdictions that had legalized it in the interim. Yet, even if one is speaking in terms of that technical legal sense, a case can still be made that *Carter* essentially overturned *Rodriguez* – such at least is the (plausible) claim made by Chan and Somerville (2016, pp. 155–156, 161–164). It is not uncommon even for legal scholars to use this terminology in its ordinary, non-technical sense – for instance, Baum (2015, p. 195) also refers to *Carter* as "overruling" *Rodriguez*.

2 See again the portions of her ruling cited in Chapter 1, specifically *Carter v Canada*, 2012 BCSC 1587 at 265–266.

References

Anscombe, E. (1958). Modern moral philosophy. *Philosophy, 33,* 1–19.

Arneson, R. (1999). Human flourishing versus desire satisfaction. *Social Philosophy and Policy, 16,* 113–142.

Arras, J. (2010). Theory and bioethics. In *Stanford encyclopedia of philosophy.* Retrieved from http://plato.stanford.edu/entries/theory-bioethics/.

Aviv, R. (2015). The death treatment: When should people with a non-terminal illness be helped to die? *The New Yorker,* June 22.

Badham, P. (1998). Should Christians accept the validity of voluntary euthanasia? In R. Gill (Ed.), *Euthanasia and the churches* (pp. 41–59). London, UK: Cassell.

Banner, D., Schiller, C., & Freeman, S. (2019). Medical assistance in dying: A political issue for nurses in Canada. *Nursing Philosophy, 20,* 1–7.

Bartmann, P. (2003). Physician assisted suicide and euthanasia: German Protestantism, conscience, and the limits of purely ethical reflection. *Christian Bioethics, 9,* 203–226.

Battin, M. (2005). *Ending life: Ethics and the way we die.* Oxford, UK: Oxford University Press.

Baum, D. (2015). *Life or death: A matter of choice?* Toronto, ON: Dundurn.

Bayliss, G. (2016). It doesn't get better: The mentally ill deserve to die with dignity. *The Walrus,* July–August, 13–15.

Beauchamp, T. L., & Childress, J. F. (1994). *Principles of biomedical ethics* (4th ed.). Oxford, UK: Oxford University Press.

Begley, A. M. (2008). Guilty but good: Defending voluntary active euthanasia from a virtue perspective. *Nursing Ethics, 15,* 434–445.

Ber, R. (2000). Ethical issues in gestational surrogacy. *Theoretical Medicine, 21,* 153–169.

Besong, B. (2018). *An introduction to ethics: A natural law approach.* Eugene, OR: Cascade Books.

Bishop, J. (2016). Arts of dying and the statecraft of killing. *Studies in Christian Ethics, 29,* 261–268.

Blackwell, T. (2016). An odd twist in Alberta's road to assisted death. *National Post,* March 4.

Boer, T. (2007). Recurring themes in the debate about euthanasia and assisted suicide. *Journal of Religious Ethics, 35,* 529–555.

Bollen, J., ten Hoopen, R., Ysebaert, D., van Mook, W., & van Heurn, E. (2016). Legal and ethical aspects of organ donation after euthanasia in Belgium and the Netherlands. *Journal of Medical Ethics, 42,* 486–489.

Breck, J. (1998). *The sacred gift of life: Orthodox Christianity and bioethics.* Crestwood, NY: St. Vladimir's Seminary Press.

Breck, J., & Breck, L. (2005). *Stages on life's way: Orthodox thinking on bioethics.* Crestwood, NY: St. Vladimir's Seminary Press.

Bryden, J. (2016). Liberals in time bind on assisted dying law. *National Post,* January 8.

–. (2020). Assisted dying bill gets mixed reviews. *National Post,* February 27.

Budziszewski, J. (2011). *What we can't not know: A guide* (rev. ed.). San Francisco, CA: Ignatius.

Butts, J., & Rich, K. (2008). Comment by Janie B Butts and Karen L Rich on: "Guilty but good: Defending voluntary active euthanasia from a virtue perspective." *Nursing Ethics, 15,* 449–451.

Canadian Press. (2019). About one percent of deaths in Canada medically assisted, Health Canada says. April 25.

Carson, T. (2000). *Value and the good life.* Notre Dame, IN: University of Notre Dame Press.

Carter, B. (2016). Why palliative care for children is preferable to euthanasia. *American Journal of Hospice & Palliative Medicine, 33,* 5–7.

Carter, R., & Rodgerson, B. (2018). Medical assistance in dying: Journey to self-determination. *Alberta Law Review, 55,* 777–803.

Chambaere, K., Vander Stichele, R., Mortier, F., Cohen, J., & Deliens, L. (2015). Recent trends in euthanasia and other end-of-life practices in Belgium. *New England Journal of Medicine, 372,* 1179–1181.

Chan, B., & Somerville, M. (2016). Converting the "right to life" to the "right to physician-assisted suicide and euthanasia": An analysis of *Carter v Canada (Attorney General),* Supreme Court of Canada. *Medical Law Review, 24,* 143–175.

Cholbi, M. (2011). *Suicide: The philosophical dimensions.* Peterborough, ON: Broadview Press.

Cohen-Almagor, R. (2015). First do no harm: Intentionally shortening lives of patients without their explicit request in Belgium. *Journal of Medical Ethics, 41,* 625–629.

Collins, T. (2016). Euthanasia is a path to nowhere. Press release reported in *Catholic Register,* June 20. Retrieved from http://www.catholicregister.org/item/22545-euthanasia-is-a-path-to-nowhere-says-cardinal-collins-on-bill-c-14-s-passing.

Colwell, G. (1995). Slippery slopes, moral slides, and human nature. *Informal Logic, 17,* 43–66.

−. (1996). To be in pain, or not to be: That is the question. *Lutheran Theological Review, 9*, 5–12.

Crisp, R. (2006). Hedonism reconsidered. *Philosophy and Phenomenological Research, 73*, 619–645.

−. (2014). Taking stock of utilitarianism. *Utilitas, 26*, 231–249.

Curtis, C. (2019). Quebec court nullifies euthanasia laws as too restrictive. *National Post*, September 12.

Daly, T. (2013). Whose dignity? Reflections on a deceptively difficult term in bio-ethical debates. *Ethics and Medicine: An International Journal of Bioethics, 29*, 151–165.

Devine, P. (1990). *The ethics of homicide*. Notre Dame, IN: University of Notre Dame Press.

Donagan, A. (1977). *The theory of morality*. Chicago, IL: University of Chicago Press.

Dorsey, D. (2010). Three arguments for perfectionism. *Noûs, 44*, 59–79.

Downie, J. (2004). *Dying justice: A case for decriminalizing euthanasia and assisted suicide in Canada*. Toronto, ON: University of Toronto Press.

Dworkin, R. (1993). *Life's dominion*. New York, NY: HarperCollins.

The Economist. (2015). Final certainty and attitudes towards assisted dying. *The Economist*, June 27, 16–20.

Engelhardt, H. T. (2000). *The foundations of Christian bioethics*. Lisse, Netherlands: Swets & Zeitlinger.

Fekete, J. (2016). Court grants extension on assisted death law. *National Post*, January 16.

Feldman, F. (2002). The good life: A defense of attitudinal hedonism. *Philosophy and Phenomenological Research, 65*, 604–628.

Finnis, J. (1980). *Natural law and natural rights*. Oxford, UK: Oxford University Press.

−. (1995). A philosophical case against euthanasia. In J. Keown (Ed.), *Euthanasia examined: Ethical, clinical, and legal perspectives* (pp. 23–35). Cambridge, UK: Cambridge University Press.

FitzPatrick, W. (2012). The doctrine of double effect: Intention and permissibility. *Philosophy Compass, 7*, 183–196.

Fletcher, G. (2013). A fresh start for the objective list theory of well-being. *Utilitas, 25*, 206–220.

−. (2016). *The philosophy of well-being: An introduction*. London, UK: Routledge.

Fumagalli, R. (2018). Eliminating "life worth living." *Philosophical Studies, 175*, 769–792.

Gaind, K. S. (2016). How mental illness complicates medically assisted dying. *The Globe and Mail*, May 30.

Gallagher, R. (2017). Medical assistance in dying: Living with dignity until life naturally ends. *BC Medical Journal, 59*, 49–52.

Gamble, N. (2018). Can euthanasia be classified as a medically beneficial treatment? *Ethics & Medicine, 34*, 103–111.

Garcia, J. L. A. (2007). The doubling undone? Double effect in recent medical ethics. *Philosophical Papers, 36*, 245–270.

−. (2010). The virtues of the natural moral law. In H. Zaborowski (Ed.), *Natural moral law in contemporary society* (pp. 99–140). Washington, DC: Catholic University of America Press.

Gentzler, J. (2003). What is a death with dignity? *Journal of Medicine and Philosophy*, *28*, 461–487.

Giebel, H. (2015). On why and how intention matters. *American Catholic Philosophical Quarterly*, *89*, 369–395.

Gill, M. (2014). A moral defense of Oregon's physician-assisted suicide law. In M. Timmons (Ed.), *Disputed moral issues: A reader* (3rd ed.) (pp. 365–378). Oxford, UK: Oxford University Press.

Glover, J. (1977). *Causing death and saving lives*. New York, NY: Penguin.

Gomez-Lobo, A. (2002). *Morality and the human goods: An introduction to natural law ethics*. Washington, DC: Georgetown University Press.

Gorsuch, N. (2006). *The future of assisted suicide and euthanasia*. Princeton, NJ: Princeton University Press.

Goss, B., & Vitz, R. (2014). Natural law among moral strangers. *Christian Bioethics*, *20*, 283–300.

Grant, K. (2019a). Doctors must provide patients with an "effective referral" for services they morally oppose, Ontario top court affirms. *The Globe and Mail*, May 16.

–. (2019b). Alzheimer Society won't fight potential legal changes allowing patients to make advance requests for MAID. *The Globe and Mail*, October 14.

Guichon, J., Mohamed, F., Clarke, K., & Mitchell, I. (2017). Autonomy and beneficence in assisted dying in Canada: The eligibility of mature minors. *Alberta Law Review*, *54*, 775–802.

Gutmann, A., & Thompson, D. (1996). *Democracy and disagreement*. Cambridge, MA: Harvard University Press.

Ha, T. T., & Grant, K. (2019). Quebec court strikes down restriction to medically assisted dying law, calls it unconstitutional. *The Globe and Mail*, September 12.

Hamilton, G., & Plante, C. (2016). Euthanasia cases reported in Quebec. *National Post*, January 16.

Hardin, R. (1988). *Morality within the limits of reason*. Chicago, IL: University of Chicago Press.

Harris, J. (1995). Euthanasia and the value of life. In J. Keown (Ed.), *Euthanasia examined: Ethical, clinical, and legal perspectives* (pp. 6–22). Cambridge, UK: Cambridge University Press.

Heathwood, C. (2005). The problem of defective desires. *Australasian Journal of Philosophy*, *83*, 487–504.

–. (2006). Desire satisfactionism and hedonism. *Philosophical Studies*, *128*, 539–563.

Hendin, H. (1998). *Seduced by death: Doctors, patients, and assisted suicide* (rev. ed.). New York, NY: W. W. Norton.

Hopper, T. (2016). Calgary woman gets ok to die with doctor's aid. *National Post*, March 2.

Hurka, T. (1993). *Perfectionism*. Oxford, UK: Oxford University Press.

Hursthouse, R. (1999). *On virtue ethics*. Oxford, UK: Oxford University Press.

Hutchins, A. (2015). What Canadians really believe: A surprising poll. *Maclean's*, March 26.

Iltis, A. (2009). The failed search for the neutral in the secular: Public bioethics in the face of the culture wars. *Christian Bioethics*, *15*, 220–233.

–. (2011). Bioethics and the culture wars. *Christian Bioethics, 17,* 9–24.

–. (2014). Law, public policy, and the secular state. *European Journal of Science and Theology, 10,* 67–77.

Ivison, J. (2015). The public backs court on decision. *National Post,* February 7.

Kass, L. (2002). *Life, liberty and the defense of dignity.* San Francisco, CA: Encounter Books.

Kay, B. (2019). The euthanasia slippery slope is here. *National Post,* February 13.

Kelsall, D. (2018). Physicians are not solely responsible for ensuring access to medical assistance in dying. *Canadian Medical Association Journal, 190,* E181.

Keown, J. (1995). Euthanasia in the Netherlands: Sliding down the slippery slope? In J. Keown (Ed.), *Euthanasia examined: Ethical, clinical, and legal perspectives* (pp. 261–296). Cambridge, UK: Cambridge University Press.

–. (2014). A right to voluntary euthanasia? Confusion in Canada in *Carter. Notre Dame Journal of Law, Ethics, and Public Policy, 28,* 1–45.

–. (2018). *Euthanasia, ethics and public policy: An argument against legalisation* (2nd rev. ed.). Cambridge, UK: Cambridge University Press.

Khoshnood, N., Hopwood, M.-C., Lokuge, B., Kurahashi, A., Tobin, A., Isenberg, S., & Husain, A. (2018). Exploring Canadian physicians' experiences providing medical assistance in dying: A qualitative study. *Journal of Pain and Symptom Management, 56,* 222–229.

Kim, S., & Lemmens, T. (2016). Should assisted dying for psychiatric disorders be legalized in Canada? *Canadian Medical Association Journal, 188,* E337–E339.

Kirby, J. (2017). Medical assistance in dying for suffering arising from mental health disorders: Could augmented safeguards enhance ethical acceptability? *Journal of Ethics in Mental Health, 10,* 1–18.

Kirkey, S. (2015a). Canadian psychiatrists fear patients with severe depression could qualify for assisted suicide. *National Post,* September 9.

–. (2015b). Panel to review assisted dying. *National Post,* July 18.

–. (2016). Majority rejects assisted suicide for mentally ill, poll finds. *National Post,* April 1.

–. (2017). "Take my name off the list": Some doctors backing out of assisted death. *National Post,* February 27.

–. (2019). "Death by donation": Why some doctors say organs should be removed from some patients before they die. *National Post,* May 22.

Kouwenhoven, P., Raijmakers, N., van Delden, J., Rietjens, J., Schermer, M., van Thiel, G., Trappenburg, M., van de Vathorst, S., van der Vegt, B., Vezzoni, C., Weyers, H., van Tol, D., & van der Heide, A. (2013). Opinions of health care professionals and the public after eight years of euthanasia legislation in the Netherlands: A mixed methods approach. *Palliative Medicine, 27,* 273–280.

Lee, P. (2001). Personhood, dignity, suicide, and euthanasia. *National Catholic Bioethics Quarterly, 1,* 329–344.

LeMasters, P. (2008). *The goodness of God's creation: How to live as an Orthodox Christian – A guide to Orthodox ethics.* Salisbury, MA: Regina Orthodox Press.

Lemos, N. (2007). Hedonism and the good life. *Philosophical Studies, 136,* 417–423.

Loriggio, P. (2018). Conscientious doctors must give referral: Court. *National Post,* February 1.

MacIntyre, A. (1981). *After virtue: A study in moral theory.* Notre Dame, IN: University of Notre Dame Press.

MacLeod, I. (2016a). Bill spells out limits to assisted dying. *National Post,* April 15.

—. (2016b). Woman with degenerative disease challenges Liberals' suicide law. *National Post,* June 28.

Manning, M. (1998). *Euthanasia and physician-assisted suicide: Killing or caring?* Mahwah, NJ: Paulist Press.

Martin, S. (2016). *A good death: Making the most of our final choices.* Toronto, ON: HarperCollins.

Martin, S. (2017). A human rights perspective of assisted suicide: Accounting for disparate jurisprudence. *Medical Law Review, 26,* 98–116.

Matthews, R. (2008). *The absolute violation: Why torture must be prohibited.* Montreal, QC, & Kingston, ON: McGill-Queen's University Press.

McAleer, S. (2007). An Aristotelian account of virtue ethics: An essay in moral taxonomy. *Pacific Philosophical Quarterly, 88,* 308–325.

—. (2010). Four solutions to the alleged incompleteness of virtue ethics. *Journal of Ethics and Social Philosophy, 4,* 1–20.

McGowan, C. A. (2018). Conscience rights and "effective referral" in Ontario. *National Catholic Bioethics Quarterly, 18,* 255–268.

McKay, A. (2007). Publicly accessible intuitions: "Neutral reasons" and bioethics. *Christian Bioethics, 13,* 183–197.

Meilaender, G. (2013). *Bioethics: A primer for Christians* (3rd ed.). Grand Rapids, MI: Eerdmans.

Mizzoni, J. (2010). *Ethics: The basics.* Oxford, UK: Wiley-Blackwell.

Moore, A. (2000). Objective human goods. In R. Crisp & B. Hooker (Eds.), *Well-being and morality: Essays in honour of James Griffin* (pp. 75–89). Oxford, UK: Oxford University Press.

Murphy, M. (1999). The simple desire-fulfillment theory. *Noûs, 33,* 247–272.

Murphy, S. (2017). Legalization of assisted suicide and euthanasia: Foundational issues and implications. *Brigham Young University Journal of Public Law, 31,* 333–394.

Noggle, R. (1999). Integrity, the self, and desire-based accounts of the good. *Philosophical Studies, 96,* 303–331.

Oderberg, D. (2000a). *Applied ethics: A non-consequentialist approach.* Oxford, UK: Blackwell.

—. (2000b). *Moral theory: A non-consequentialist approach.* Oxford, UK: Blackwell.

O'Gara, E. (2015). Physically healthy 24-year-old granted right to die in Belgium. *Newsweek,* June 29.

O'Neill, O. (2013). *Acting on principle: An essay on Kantian ethics* (2nd ed.). Cambridge, UK: Cambridge University Press.

Onwuteaka-Philipsen, B., Brinkman-Stoppelenburg, A., Penning, C., de Jong-Krul, G., van Delden, J., & van der Heide, A. (2012). Trends in end-of-life practices before and after the enactment of the euthanasia law in the Netherlands from 1990 to 2010: A repeated cross-sectional survey. *Lancet, 380,* 908–915.

Palmer, S. (2015). "The choice is cruel": Assisted suicide and Charter rights in Canada. *Cambridge Law Journal, 74,* 191–194.

Paterson, C. (2008). *Assisted suicide and euthanasia: A natural law ethics approach.* Hampshire, UK: Ashgate.

Peck, M. S. (1997). *Denial of the soul: Spiritual and medical perspectives on euthanasia and mortality.* New York, NY: Harmony.

Pereira, J. (2011). Legalizing euthanasia or assisted suicide: The illusion of safeguards and controls. *Current Oncology, 18,* 38–45.

Plaisted, D. (2013). An undignified side of death with dignity legislation. *Kennedy Institute of Ethics Journal, 23,* 201–228.

Plante, C. (2019). Number of Quebecers seeking assisted death has jumped, commission finds. Canadian Press, April 3. Retrieved from https://nationalpost.com/pmn/news-pmn/canada-news-pmn/number-of-quebecers-seeking-assisted-death-has-jumped-commission-finds.

Player, C. (2018). Death with dignity and mental disorder. *Arizona Law Review, 60,* 115–161.

Pojman, L. (2002). *Ethics: Discovering right and wrong* (4th ed.). Belmont, CA: Wadsworth.

Posner, R. (1995). *Aging and old age.* Chicago, IL: University of Chicago Press.

Provincial-Territorial Expert Advisory Group on Physician-Assisted Dying. (2015). Retrieved from https://novascotia.ca/dhw/publications/Provincial-Territorial-Expert-Advisory-Group-on-Physician-Assisted-Dying.pdf.

Pruski, M. (2019). Professional objections and healthcare: More than a case of conscience. *Ethics & Medicine, 35,* 149–160.

Pruss, A. (2010). What is the essential harm in murder? Retrieved from www.alexanderpruss.blogspot.co.uk/2010/09/what-is-essential-harm-in-murder.html.

–. (2013). The accomplishment of plans: A new version of the principle of double effect. *Philosophical Studies, 165,* 49–69.

Quill, T. (1998). Principle of double effect and end-of-life pain management: Additional myths and a limited role. *Journal of Palliative Medicine, 1,* 333–336.

Reynolds, C. (2019). Liberals would improve assisted dying laws. *Daily Press,* October 4.

Rice, C. (2013). Defending the objective list theory of well-being. *Ratio, 26,* 196–211.

Rousseau, S., Turner, S., Chochinov, H., Enns, M., & Sareen, J. (2017). A national survey of Canadian psychiatrists' attitudes toward medical assistance in death. *Canadian Journal of Psychiatry, 62,* 787–794.

Savulescu, J., & Schuklenk, U. (2017). Doctors have no right to refuse medical assistance in dying, abortion or contraception. *Bioethics, 31,* 162–170.

Schuklenk, U., & van de Vathorst, S. (2015). Treatment-resistant major depressive disorder and assisted dying. *Journal of Medical Ethics, 41,* 577–583.

Schuklenk, U., van Delden, J., Downie, J., McLean, S., Upshur, R., & Weinstock, D. (2011). End-of-life decision-making in Canada: The report by the Royal Society of Canada Expert Panel on End-of-Life Decision-Making. *Bioethics, 25,* 1–73.

Séguin, R. (2014). Quebec first province to adopt end-of-life legislation. *The Globe and Mail,* June 5.

Sellman, D. (2008). Comment by Derek Sellman on "Guilty but good: Defending voluntary active euthanasia from a virtue perspective." *Nursing Ethics, 15,* 446–449.

Shadd, P., & Shadd, J. (2019). Institutional non-participation in assisted dying: Changing the conversation. *Bioethics, 33,* 207–214.

Shapiro, M. (2018). Euthanasia by organ donation. *Dalhousie Law Journal, 41,* 153–171.

Siegel, A., Sisti, D., & Caplan, A. (2014). Pediatric euthanasia in Belgium: Disturbing developments. *Journal of the American Medical Association, 311,* 1963–1964.

Singer, P. (1993). *Practical ethics* (2nd ed.). Cambridge, UK: Cambridge University Press.

Sinnott-Armstrong, W. (1992). An argument for consequentialism. *Philosophical Perspectives, 6,* 399–421.

Smart, J. J. C. (1973). An outline of a system of utilitarian ethics. In J. J. C. Smart & B. Williams (Eds.), *Utilitarianism: For and against* (pp. 3–74). Cambridge, UK: Cambridge University Press.

Sobel, D. (2002). Varieties of hedonism. *Journal of Social Philosophy, 33,* 240–256.

Somerville, M. (2001). *Death talk: The case against euthanasia and physician-assisted suicide.* Montreal, QC, & Kingston, ON: McGill-Queen's University Press.

Steinbock, B. (2017). Physician-assisted death and severe, treatment-resistant depression. *Hastings Center Report, 47,* 30–42.

Stingl, M. (Ed.). (2010). *The price of compassion: Assisted suicide and euthanasia.* Peterborough, ON: Broadview Press.

Sumner, L. W. (2011). *Assisted death: A study in ethics and law.* Oxford, UK: Oxford University Press.

Tanner, R. (2018). An ethical-legal analysis of medical assistance in dying for those with mental illness. *Alberta Law Review, 56,* 149–175.

Thienpont, L., Verhofstadt, M., van Loon, T., Distelmans, W., Audenaert, K., & de Deyn, P. (2015). Euthanasia requests, procedures and outcomes for 100 Belgian patients suffering from psychiatric disorders: A retrospective, descriptive study. *BMJ Open, 5,* 1–8.

Timmons, M. (2014). *Disputed moral issues: A reader* (3rd ed.). Oxford, UK: Oxford University Press.

Trigg, R. (2017). Conscientious objection and "effective referral." *Cambridge Quarterly of Healthcare Ethics, 26,* 32–43.

Varelius, J. (2007). Illness, suffering, and voluntary euthanasia. *Bioethics, 21,* 75–83.

Velleman, D. (1999). A right of self-termination? *Ethics, 109,* 606–628.

Wagner, B., Keller, V., Knaevelsrud, C., & Maercker, A. (2011). Social acknowledgement as a predictor of post-traumatic stress and complicated grief after witnessing assisted suicide. *International Journal of Social Psychiatry, 58,* 381–385.

Warnock, M., & Macdonald, E. (2008). *Easeful death: Is there a case for assisted dying?* Oxford, UK: Oxford University Press.

Watt, H. (2015). Life and health: A value in itself for human beings? *HEC Forum, 27,* 207–228.

Weijers, D., & Schouten, V. (2013). An assessment of recent responses to the experience machine objection to hedonism. *Journal of Value Inquiry, 47,* 461–482.

Wilkinson, D., & Savulescu, J. (2012). Should we allow organ donation euthanasia? Alternatives for maximizing the number and quality of organs for transplantation. *Bioethics, 26,* 32–48.

Williams, B. (1973). A critique of utilitarianism. In J. J. C. Smart & B. Williams (Eds.), *Utilitarianism: For and against* (pp. 77–150). Cambridge, UK: Cambridge University Press.

Williams, J. R. (1997). *Christian perspectives on bioethics: Religious values and public policy in a pluralistic society.* Ottawa, ON: Novalis.

Yarascavitch, A. (2017). Assisted dying for mental disorders: Why Canada's legal approach raises serious concerns. *Journal of Ethics in Mental Health, 10,* 1–24.

Young, R. (2007). *Medically assisted death.* Cambridge, UK: Cambridge University Press.

Yuill, K. (2015). *Assisted suicide: The liberal, humanist case against legalization.* New York, NY: Palgrave Macmillan.

Index